beautiful railway bridge of the
SILVERY TAY

reinvestigating the Tay Bridge disaster of 1879

beautiful railway bridge of the
SILVERY TAY

reinvestigating the Tay Bridge disaster of 1879

PETER R. LEWIS

To the victims, everywhere

First published in 2004 by Tempus Publishing
Reprinted 2005

Reprinted in 2008 by
The History Press
The Mill, Brimscombe Port
Stroud, Gloucestershire GL5 2QG
www.thehistorypress.co.uk

Reprinted 2014

© Peter R. Lewis, 2004

The right of Peter R. Lewis to be identified as the Author of this work has been asserted by him in accordance with the Copyrights, Designs and Patents Act 1988.

All rights reserved. No part of this book may be reprinted or reproduced or utilised in any form or by any electronic, mechanical or other means, now known or hereafter invented, including photocopying and recording, or in any information storage or retrieval system, without the permission in writing from the Publishers.

British Library Cataloguing in Publication Data.
A catalogue record for this book is available from the British Library.

ISBN 978 0 7524 3160 4

Typesetting and origination by Tempus Publishing.
Printed and bound in Great Britain.

Contents

Acknowledgements	7
Foreword	9
Preface	11
1 An Introduction	13
2 Bridging the Tay Estuary	27
3 The Bridge in Use	43
4 Disaster Strikes	57
5 Inquiry at Dundee	69
6 Henry Law Investigates	89
7 Disaster Theories	107
8 Finale	123
9 Hindsight	133
10 Aftermath	149
Epilogue	169
Glossary	173
Chronology	177
Dramatis Personae	181
Select Bibliography	185
Index	189

Acknowledgements

I would like to thank Dr D.R.H. Jones of the Engineering Department of Cambridge University, whose enthusiasm for the case study helped stimulate my own interest. He also gave permission to reuse several figures we have used in our course T839 at the Open University, and used again here. John Rapley was an effective devil's advocate of many of my ideas. Addison Bain's reinvestigation of the Hindenburg disaster of 1937 proved inspirational.

I thank my colleagues at the Open University (Department of Engineering Materials) who helped during the research of the Tay disaster, especially Ken Reynolds and Colin Gagg, who gave feedback on metallurgy. Dr George Weidmann, Dr Mike Fitzpatrick, Dr Sarah Hainsworth of Mechanical Engineering (Leicester University) and Victor Bignall of the Systems Discipline gave support, while Roger Dobson, Clive Fetter and Robert Wood provided constructive criticism. Thanks are due to Rehana Malik and Ian Norman for preparing and modifying scans and diagrams, Gordon Imlach, Jim Moffatt and Bob Clark for the Scottish perspective, Richard Hearne (Design and Innovation Discipline) and Stan Hiller (Materials Engineering) for help in printing the many photographs from the Dundee scans. Dr Colin Goodchild, Professors Roy Crawford and Robert Young encouraged me to bring the subject to a wider public. The Open University Library allowed access to the Parliamentary archive on microfiche, and *The Times* on microfilm. Their staff were always helpful and accommodating to my frequent requests (such as for the weighty tomes of the *Illustrated London News*). The Open University, the Engineering and Physical Sciences Research Council (EPSRC) and London Metropolitan University provided financial support for the course Forensic Engineering (T839) where the Tay Bridge was used as a case study, and first sparked my interest.

The Institution of Civil Engineering were helpful in providing high-quality diagrams from their Tay Bridge archive, as were the Scottish National Archive in Edinburgh, the Bodleian Library in Oxford, the National Archive at Kew, the British Library in London and the Library of Congress in Washington. The Royal Academy of Engineering gave financial support for several visits to historic disaster sites in the USA. The members of the History Study Group of the Institution of Structural Engineering provided many stimulating ideas when I lectured there on the subject. The Construction History Society provided a congenial venue for his lecture to their annual meeting in London. The Cambridge section of the Institute of Materials gave a warm reception to the topic during an invited lecture, thanks to an invitation from Drs Fitzpatrick and Hainsworth. The Cosby Historical Society and Professor Andrew Strang were hospitable when I lectured there in 2003, as was the Leicestershire Industrial History Society and David Lyne later that year.

David Kett of the Central Library at Wellgate, Dundee, scanned the unique collection of photographs in their archive, and Dundee Museum courteously gave full access to the collection of Tay disaster artefacts. The library of St Andrews University scanned a set of relevant Valentine pictures for our course, and some have been re-used here. All extended their help during the filming of *The Riddle of the Tay Bridge Disaster* and *The Challenge* by the BBC team (Lisa Stevens and Jayne Topping, producers). Thanks also to Tom Martin, Professor

Macleod of Strathclyde University, Bill Dow, Professor David Swinfen of Dundee University, and Professor Rod Smith of Imperial College for their co-operation during the filming. Dr Denis Smith of Kirkaldy Museum hepled during filming of the tensometer in the Kirkaldy test house in Southwark. Professors Roland Paxton and Ted Turner provided useful historical details. Keith Horne of Ross-on-Wye read and commented on early ideas about the Dee and Tay accidents. Robin Lumley in Australia provided stimulating ideas during development of his own book on the disaster.

John White of Milton Keynes, chair of the White Star Society, was an enthusiastic supporter of my research, and provided some artefacts. Drs John Bellerby and Mike Edwards of the Shrivenham campus of Cranfield University invited me to lecture to their Forensic Engineering and Science MSc students in 2003, and Mike gave great help in the creation of the BBC website on the disaster. Harry Hutchinson, executive editor of *Mechanical Engineering* magazine in the USA, highlighted the disaster in several issues (April, May and June, 2004). Professor Henry Petroski of Duke University provided an insight into the history of bridges, while Dr Harry Reemsnyder advised on metal fatigue. *The Scotsman* and *The Independent* newspapers gave coverage to our ideas as to the causes of the accident. Howard Cattermole, editor of *Interdisciplinary Science Reviews*, kindly published two preliminary articles on the Tay and Dee accidents.

Open University Forensic Engineering students have been a prime stimulus for this book, especially for their assiduous study of the disaster, which has been the basis of assessment. Last, but not least, I would like to thank my four children and my father for their unstinted interest and understanding of my many late hours on the project. My daughter, Fiona, assisted me when photographing the Bouble Viaduct.

The Dundee and St Andrews photographs from the Valentine collections were scanned at 300–600 dpi and saved as TIFF files and archived on CD. The images were searched using Graphic Converter on an AppleMac computer, and enlargements or selections made for significant details. They are printed here with minimal changes, although in a few cases, brightness and/or contrast have been changed to improve visibility of details. The extracts taken from the Tay Bridge Inquiry of 1880 are quoted verbatim, and have not been edited in any way so as to preserve the integrity of the evidence. Since the extracts are mainly of oral evidence in court, there are inevitable ambiguities, awkward, convoluted and ungrammatical language, as well as simple errors. We have pointed out errors wherever possible. However, the evidence of the time remains the best source of uncontaminated material for any re-interpretation of the Tay Bridge disaster. Moreover, because the oral testimony was collected quickly, there is less chance of collusion, memory lapses and other problems associated with eyewitness evidence.

Dr Peter R. Lewis
Dept of Materials Engineering
The Open University
Walton Hall
Milton Keynes
MK7 6AA

(p.r.lewis@open.ac.uk)

Foreword

The Tay Bridge collapse on the stormy night of 28 December 1879 remains unique in British railway history. It was, and still is, the only accident in which all the staff and passengers on a train have perished. At the time, the accident caused the largest number of fatalities of a British railway accident and the bridge was the longest railway bridge in the world.

One can easily imagine the shock generated amongst a public confident of the supremacy of engineering. Many aspects of the Inquiry revealed the then common lack of understanding of loads, stresses, material behaviour, manufacturing and construction techniques. Practical experience counted above all else. Nevertheless, it is remarkable to consider what was achieved in the heroic age of railway building. In some ways, it is fortunate that the age of risk aversion and the safety case had not yet arrived, because if it had, it is unlikely that the empirical advances of practical experience would have happened. We forget, at our peril, the debt we own to the age of real enterprise and 'can do' attitudes, assisted by generous helpings of finance and unencumbered by cost benefit analysis, only a burning ambition to get things done.

Of course, the price was paid in accidents. But as far as the railways were concerned, given the extent of railway travel, the number of accidents was tiny, and, with the exception of railway workers, who had to wait until the second half of the twentieth century for real improvements, the number of passenger fatalities was relatively small. However, the publicity accorded to railway accidents was enormous, and served to expose the railways to public consciousness and criticism. Railway safety is now once again a matter of public concern, but the reality differs from the myth as on any reasonably normalised measure, railway safety in Britain is equal to that of other systems worldwide. More people are killed in road accidents every year than passengers have been killed throughout British railway history.

It is with the greatest of pleasure that I write this forward to Peter Lewis's study of the Tay Bridge disaster. Staff from the Open University have generated some outstanding case studies over the past forty years, and this current work stands comparison with the best. Peter's investigation has been extremely thorough, as evidenced in the text and by his long list of acknowledgements. Many other previous studies of the Tay Bridge disaster have come to different conclusions. This work is perhaps the most extensive re-examination of the available material, and the task has been carried out with the greatest attention to detail.

It comes as no surprise to me that the conclusions differ to those of previous investigators. It also comes as no great surprise that the phenomenon known as fatigue probably played a key role. It is, however, surprising that fatigue still causes major railway accidents. One hundred people were killed when the wheel of a German high-speed train failed by fatigue in 1998, and although only four unfortunate passengers were killed in the Hatfield derailment of 2000, the repercussions were magnified by a lack of understanding of the fatigue of rails, causing gross disruption to the whole of the railway network in Britain and, eventually, to the demise of Railtrack. Evidently, we still have a lot to learn!

Professor Roderick A. Smith
Imperial College, London

Preface

1879 was a bad year for Disraeli's government. The economy was in a bad shape, with depression in manufacturing owing to competition from the USA and Germany, among others. Agriculture was suffering from the cheap grain available from the Prairies, and Disraeli was reluctant to protect farmers for fear of offending the newly enfranchised working classes. Most of the country was now covered with an efficient rail network, enabling imported products to be transported cheaply to the buying public. There had been two imperial adventures: one in South Africa, the other in Afghanistan. A force had been raised at great expense to invade Zululand to extend the Empire. An even larger force was directed to seize Kabul to forestall an imaginary invasion by Russia. However, losses were large, an entire brigade being wiped out at Isandhlwana in January 1879, despite a courageous rear guard action at Rorke's Drift. Although Kabul was captured, the Queen's emissary was butchered, together with many officers, in September of that year.

And then at the tail end of the year, the world's longest bridge collapsed in a storm. The bridge had been approved by the government's own Board of Trade for passenger traffic in February 1878, and had fuelled the growth of the textile industry of Dundee by shortening the route to the south. It had become a spectacle to be seen by visiting dignitaries like Ulysses S. Grant, the former US President, and the Queen herself had travelled over the structure en route to the south, from Balmoral. The engineer-in-chief of the bridge, Thomas Bouch, had been knighted for his work in July 1879, and he was starting work on a new scheme to span the Firth of Forth with a giant suspension bridge. But the fall of the bridge changed everything.

As the facts about the tragedy emerged from that strange period between Christmas Day and New Year, it was clear that it was no ordinary railway accident. For a start, a whole train had been lost when the centre part of the bridge collapsed. There were no survivors at all, some seventy-five passengers and crew being killed as the train fell nearly 100ft into the Tay estuary. The fall occurred in a severe storm raging on Sunday 28 December 1879, and many commentators jumped to the conclusion that the wind had toppled the giant structure. In terms of human misery it was the worst ever rail disaster, even compared with the crash at Oxford when thirty-four lives had been lost on Christmas Eve, 1874, or the Abbots Ripton collision which killed fourteen in a snowstorm in January 1876. The Tay Bridge disaster would haunt Disraeli for many months to come, as the sad truth emerged from the Public Inquiry. The very public agony ended for Disraeli in April 1880, when his government was swept from office by a landslide victory for Gladstone and the Liberal Party. His personal agony ended when he died in 1881.

Although the Inquiry publicly blamed the disaster on Sir Thomas Bouch, for a bad design, and a badly constructed and badly maintained bridge, it was ambiguous about how the bridge had fallen. It has thus remained something of a mystery to this day how such a large structure could be destroyed so quickly. This was one reason why we chose to study the disaster using original material still available in public archives. We have come to very different conclusions to those of some recent commentators. We do not believe that the train derailed and hit the bridge, so causing the collapse, nor do we think the evidence supports the theory that the bridge was simply blown away. On the contrary, the evidence we have seen amply supports the conclusions of the original Court of Inquiry. We can go a little further in the light of modern knowledge, because the excellent photographs ordered by the Inquiry seem to show features which could be explained by metal fatigue. This, then, is our reinvestigation of the fall of the Tay Bridge, an event which shook a complacent government and the engineering world to its very core.

1
An Introduction

The railways of Britain have long held a particular fascination for the public, perhaps because they were first developed here and so led the world into a new age of fast communications. It has left a rich heritage of buildings and engineered structures that have inspired artists, film directors and writers, both at the time of their construction and with the passage of time. Turner's mysterious picture, 'Rain, Steam and Speed', painted around 1844, celebrated the longest brick arch ever built in a bridge on the Great Western Railway as it crossed the Thames at Maidenhead.

Railway accidents were instrumental in shaping the national consciousness, such as the harrowing experience of Charles Dickens in the Staplehurst disaster of 9 June 1865. A boat train was derailed and fell through a small bridge made from cast-iron girders because the rail had been removed by platelayers, and not replaced in time. Dickens was travelling in the only coach to survive intact, and gave comfort to dying and injured passengers. The trauma led him to write a ghost story, *The Signalman*, the following year. It was dramatised in the 1970s by the BBC, starring Denham Eliot in the main role, and follows the original story very closely. It includes a terrifying crash in a tunnel (possibly based on the Clayton tunnel crash of 1861, which killed 23 and injured 176 passengers), presaged by a phantom under the red warning lamp at the entrance to the tunnel. The phantom warns the railwayman of his own demise, which he fails to recognise in time. According to L.T.C. Rolt, the after-effects of the Staplehurst crash contributed to Dickens' early death at the age of fifty-eight in 1870.

At a later time, the railway network became deeply embedded in the British consciousness, with the release of *Nightmail* by the GPO film unit (1936) and the Forth Bridge sequence in Hitchcock's *The Thirty-Nine Steps* (1937). *Brief Encounter* (David Lean, 1945) was set almost entirely in a railway station and, albeit incidentally, gave the steam train a romantic aura. The railway age was initially pioneered by great Victorian railway engineers and entrepreneurs such as Telford, Brunel and the Stephensons, father and son. Engineers such as W.H. Barlow and his son, who built the new Tay Bridge, and John Fowler and Benjamin Baker, the builders of the Forth Railway Bridge, were pioneers of the later efforts to complete the system to cover all of the United Kingdom.

There is, however, another side to those great successes: the many accidents which occurred on the early railway system, both of individuals and groups of passengers killed or injured by unsuspected events with the new technology of the era. As events unfolded, many new and quite unsuspected problems occurred, although some were entirely predictable.

The First Fatality

The very first accident occurred on the opening day of the first passenger rail service on the Manchester–Liverpool line in 1830. The victim was William Huskisson, the local MP and a vocal proponent of the new railway. He was injured by The Rocket while attempting to enter the compartment of a carriage, and died a few hours later. Such an eminent victim attracted great attention to the problem of public safety with the new machines, and further vitriol from their powerful opponents, the canal owners. While the accident might have been misadventure, it also gave the first indication of the problem of large machines moving at speed on a fixed track with poor means of braking.

But when all the glitches had been ironed out from this first railway line, it achieved almost notorious success in fast passenger transportation between Liverpool and Manchester, two pre-eminent cities of the Industrial Revolution. That success fuelled further growth, especially in trade carried along the new line. It was to have great significance for development of an expanding network, often at the hands of entrepreneurs like George Hudson, who exploited public enthusiasm for the technology. It led to railway mania, which was at its height in the subsequent decade, the 1840s. As the system grew to cover much of England, the potential for accidents grew too. Not dissimilar events were occurring in France, never far behind Britain in the development of the new technology.

The Tragedy at Versailles

The first ever major rail disaster occurred when a passenger train travelled from Paris to Versailles in 1842. The train involved had been scheduled to carry visitors to the great palace outside Paris to celebrate the birthday of the king, Louis Philippe, an event which featured a display of the famous fountains in the equally celebrated gardens. The return train (drawn by two locomotives and tightly packed) left Versailles at about 5.30 . on 8 May. When travelling at speed between Bellevue and Meudon, an axle on the front locomotive fractured, and the body of the engine fell onto the track. The second locomotive ran into the remains, and the ensuing pile-up of the carriages caused great loss of life, mainly because the carriages were ignited by hot embers from the wrecked fire boxes of the locomotives.

According to one commentator writing in 1879, fifty-two or fifty-three passengers lost their lives and forty were injured, although the exact number of deaths remained uncertain since so many bodies were totally consumed by the fire. One reason for the large casualty list was the practice of locking carriage doors to prevent passengers leaving the train while in motion. The early carriages were also rather flimsy and were mainly built from wood, so encouraging the subsequent fire. Bodies were burned beyond recognition. One distinguished victim was Admiral D'Urville, who was identified in an investigation by the Academy of Sciences. They employed a sculptor, who was able to recognise his skull from a cast he had recently made.

At the time the cause seemed obvious enough, and a number of investigations probed more deeply into the reason for the fractured shaft. However, none appeared to have discovered the root cause of the axle failure. Modern re-evaluation indicates that the broken shaft probably failed by fatigue from a sharp corner machined into the axle. Sharp corners in highly stressed components concentrate the applied stress, so that it can be many times the applied load. The material cannot withstand the high stress, so a crack forms at the corner and slowly grows with every application of stress. Every time the shaft was driven, the crack grew slowly until it reached a size when the solid iron could no longer support the load, and it suddenly failed catastrophically. Some early Victorian engineers, such as Rankine and Braithwaite, became aware of the problem, but their pioneering observations were not followed up by others. Fred Braithwaite pointed to a wide variety of products, such as cast-iron girders and steam engine beams as well as wrought-iron axles, which had failed suddenly and mysteriously. It was not until later (in the 1860s) that systematic research in Germany explored the problem of railway

(1.1) Etching of the 1847 accident scene published in the *Illustrated London News*, showing the broken outermost girder, carriages in the river and the abutment damage.

wheels and axles in greater detail. The solution was very simple: remove the sharp corners in a shaft by rounding it out. Such failures of shafts and wheels were to create many more accidents before their causes were correctly identified and remedial action taken by designers. But fatigue is a problem with us still, and has caused many disasters of recent times, such as those of the Comet aircraft and the Hatfield crash, when an express derailed at high speed in 2000.

The Fall of the Dee Bridge

Bridge failures could be almost as catastrophic, the first such major accident being on a bridge recently erected by Robert Stephenson on the new Chester–Holyhead section of the railway. This part was the final section of the London–Holyhead railway, crossing the country from south to north-west, and had been conceived nine years before in 1838. It would require many bridges, not least one across the Menai Straits itself. While it would be several years before completion of the massive Britannia Bridge, other bridges on the line were finished for local traffic, including a bridge across the tidal Dee River at Chester. Following Parliamentary approval by an Act of 1845, large cast-iron girders were laid on piers across the river near the city of Chester. It was completed by the end of 1846, and inspected and approved for traffic shortly afterwards.

Less than a year later, disaster struck on 24 May 1847. While a passenger train had almost crossed to the far side, one of the cast-iron girders suddenly fractured near the centre of the third or final span. The locomotive gained the far side but the tender and the carriages crashed about 30ft into the shallow river below *(1.1)*. The locomotive actually reached the far bank of the river, but the tender derailed and struck the abutment, causing some damage to the masonry.

The driver of the locomotive stopped as soon as he realised what had happened but, seeing he could do little at the scene, drove off at speed to raise help. After giving the alarm at the nearby station, Saltney Junction, he changed over to the opposite line and re-crossed the intact side of the bridge to stop oncoming trains. Such action required no little courage, given the earlier collapse! Although only five passengers died, and sixteen were injured, the accident created a furore among the public. They wanted to know why such a new bridge could fail so suddenly.

The subsequent Inquest provided the details of the design of the bridge, its specification and events leading up to the failure. Eyewitness statements described the sequence of events very precisely. Detailed reports were provided by numerous experts, including a thorough account by Captain Simmons of the newly appointed Railway Inspectorate. Robert Stephenson, the designer and builder, came under attack, but was advised to raise the defence that the locomotive had derailed, hit the bridge and caused the girder to fail. So what really happened that day?

Eyewitnesses

It was fortunate that the day was clear and that there were many people close to the bridge when it failed. The fall had actually been seen by several witnesses. Thomas Jones, a publican and milkman, was on the Grosvenor Bridge 700 yards away, and he described what he saw as the train crossed over:

> I saw the train at the ship yard; I put my milk cans down and watched it across the middle of the bridge; when the train got on the furthest arch on the Saltney side, I observed a crack open in the middle of the girder; the engine and tender were about the centre; the crack opened from the bottom; the engine had passed the crack, and the tender was right upon it; the engine and tender went on, and I saw the tender give a rise up; the carriages gave a jump and fell backward; the last carriage went down first according to my judgment; the next [thing] I saw was the large stones fall off the wall on the Saltney side; I heard a crash when they fell; I am certain the girder opened from the bottom; all went smooth before the tender jumped, and went against the corner of the abutment; the bridge was broke before the tender jumped; I think the jump of the tender broke the coupling of the carriages.

Many witnesses were so close that they were on the scene very quickly, as were many other local residents who had heard the crash and rushed to assist. Their assistance to the injured undoubtedly saved many lives, given that the carriages were part submerged in the cold river below the bridge *(1.1)*.

The Painters

The prior and short history of the bridge, and especially its behaviour under load, was described by a number of painters who had been employed on the bridge just before the accident. Indeed, they gave evidence first at the Inquest. William Clegg described the deflection of the girders under load:

> I have painted the girders on the new bridge in April and May last; they had been painted before that; I observed no peculiarity of the joints where the trusses fastened the girder; I was on the bridge when the ballast train passed over it; I observed a deflection of the girder from 1½ inches to 2in on both lines; I observed it also when the passenger trains went over; they went faster than the ballast trains considerably; the extent of the deflection was 3½ inches to 4in; I got my rule and put it under the girder and noticed how much it went down...

The bridge had originally been designed with shorter spans across the river, but the number of piers had been reduced at the direction of others. When in operation and loaded, large deflections had been observed by the painters working on the girders at the time. The failure, based on the evidence of eyewitnesses, showed that the girder fractured near the centre of the last span on the Saltney side.

But what did the experts have to say? The most important evidence was heard from Captain Simmons and Mr Walker, as well as Robert Stephenson and Joseph Locke.

Captain Simmons' Report

The report by the Railway Inspectorate involved detailed examination of the remains, including the fallen broken girders and damaged masonry on the bridge. The final report was actually not published by the government until 30 June 1847, shortly after the end of the Inquest on 18 June, but Simmons and Walker were able to present their preliminary observations directly to the tribunal.

They reported that the structure was composed of three spans on two masonry piers, each span having two pairs of cast-iron girders to bridge the gap. Each girder was in turn composed of three separate castings, bolted together at flanges and reinforced by semi-circular castings across the joint. Further reinforcement was provided by two wrought-iron straps (tension bars), on both sides of the girder.

They were supported on the ends of the composite girder and at the joints, running down diagonally to the first and last joints, and near the base of the centre casting. They were 6in wide and $5/16$in deep in section. The total length of each composite girder was 107.5ft, but 98ft from pier support to support. Each girder had an I-shape, with a narrow upper flange 7in wide and a wide lower flange some 3ft wide. The total height was 3ft 9in. The girders were 12ft apart but tied together by thirteen wrought-iron horizontal tie bars (4in by 1in in section) fixed to recesses moulded into the bases of the girders. The girders supported oak joists laid across on the lower flanges. They were 10in by 10in in section, and supported a track floor of 4in planks, upon which the wrought-iron rails were fixed. A guard rail – an extra set of rails – was laid 3in inside, to act against tipping wheels.

One track of the line was opened in September 1846 and was used by the contractor for trains carrying construction materials. The greatest loading on a single girder came from two locomotives and tenders coupled together (about 60 tons), without apparent damage. Just before opening, one of the new girders was found to be cracked, and replaced. The bridge had been inspected by General Sir William Pasley, Inspector General of Railways on 20 October 1846, and pronounced safe and efficient on 22 October, although at the Inquest, Pasley expressed doubts about the wrought-iron reinforcement. He thought they had little strengthening action on the cast-iron girders, but they had been used on other bridges, apparently safely. On the other hand, the spans on the Dee Bridge were considerably longer than earlier structures.

Captain Simmons went on to describe the events on the day of the accident. Six trains had passed safely over the bridge before the accident but, most significantly, about 18 tons of coarse stone ballast had been laid on the planking of each span just before the fatal train passed over. The stone was intended to improve the fire resistance of the track from sparks and cinders. The total weight of the fatal train was about 60 tons, half being concentrated at the front with the engine and tender. The driver stated that his speed over the bridge was 15 to 20mph, but Simmons thought that it was probably nearer 30mph. The train passed safely over the first two spans, and was about halfway over the final span when he felt the engine sinking below him. He instantly put on full throttle, so reaching the far bank. However, the stoker riding on the tender was thrown off and killed when it derailed and hit the parapet wall, causing some damage. The carriages decoupled and fell back into the river *(1.1)*.

The report went on to describe the nature of the fractures to the composite girder. There were two fractures: one near the centre of the middle casting, the other near the centre of the casting at the Saltney end of the structure. The latter produced separation of a large piece (3ft long at the base and 7ft at the top) by growth of a brittle crack or cracks. The break at the centre was more complex, several separate pieces being formed by crack growth, the largest being 4½ft at the base and 11ft at the top). The fracture was apparently clean, showing no blow holes or other obvious visible defects, although a drawing of the fracture surface was not presented in the report. Simmons said in the report that several pieces of the centre break were not retrieved from the river, a statement presumably based on reassembling the parts, and finding some missing.

Captain Simmons decided to experiment with a locomotive and tender of 30 tons weight (as a precaution) over the surviving girders of the bridge. He performed a static test and then ran the engine over at 15mph, finding a deflection at the centre of from ⅞ to 1⅜in. A repeat experiment with a heavy locomotive and tender of 48 tons weight gave a static deflection of 2.4in but, surprisingly, a slightly lower figure for a moving train. His figures roughly agreed with the foundry test figure. However, he was concerned about the accuracy of measuring a deflection for a moving load, simply because of the difficulty of observing a transient deflection. When a train was moving over the girder, it vibrated to such an extent that he could not see the edge of the beam! Captain Simmons then makes an interesting point, saying that he thought the constantly repeated temporary loads from passing trains 'tends to weaken and injure it (the beam)...'

They also analysed the effect of the wrought-iron reinforcement and concluded that there was no strengthening effect at all, essentially because the tie bars were not independently fixed, so would bend with the beam as it bent. The ends of the wrought-iron tie bars were simply attached to the ends of the cast-iron beams, so if the whole girder sagged, so would the tie bars. The extra cross-sectional area was negligible compared to that of the cast iron. They considered both the wrought and cast iron to be of good quality, although what tests were applied was not stated in their report. There is no evidence that they actually tested samples, and they only examined the failed samples visually. Thus they say that the cast iron was 'technically sound, that is, solid and without hollows...' Blow holes from entrapped gases during casting are a common problem in castings, but could not be found in the fractured parts of the failed girders. They add that, '... the wrought iron which we tried was of very good tough quality.'

They concluded that they thought that the beam was under-designed. They could find no evidence of weakness in the piers, and the sequence of events was clear: the beam broke under the load of the passing train, the first break occurring in the centre of the base, the second break during the fall. The addition of 18 tons of stone to the track just before the accident contributed to the extra load on the beam. Cast iron suffers when loaded repeatedly, and any irregularity would further exacerbate the situation.

So they could find no specific defect in the fractures which could explain the premature fracture of just the one beam. Why did the others on the bridge survive when loaded to just the same extent as the failed beam? There must have been hidden defects or some other problem which they could not identify.

Stephenson's Defence

Because the tender came off the line and hit the abutment at the side of the track, it was possible for Robert Stephenson to invert the argument and suggest that the girder broke as a result of the train derailing. It was a defence which ignored the eyewitness statements, but was supported by several eminent engineers who gave evidence at the Inquest (they included Locke, Vignoles and Gooch). After all, Stephenson was the engineer in charge of the project, and must have approved the design of the beams as well as the choice of materials. If he had known that the structure was defective, he would be negligent, his negligence leading to death and injury quite apart from the material costs of the accident. The charge could be manslaughter. He would defend himself vigorously by claiming that the train came off the track for some unknown reason, and hit the abutment. But he would then have to explain how this impact on the bank of the river could cause the girder over the river to fail.

Inquest

However, the jury visited the site of the accident, and were able to dismiss Stephenson's claims very quickly. Stephenson's derailment theory was unsupported by the eyewitnesses, and is remarkable for having been discussed at all, given the flimsy nature of the case he presented. The tender had derailed *(1.1)* but the witnesses clearly said that it had occurred after the initial break in the centre girder, and not before. The remains of the train were scoured for any support for the theory, but very little could be produced. A single broken wheel, for example, was claimed as strong evidence for derailment of one of the carriages, but eyewitnesses said that the wheel had been broken to rescue the injured. Those passengers who were fit to give evidence concurred: the carriages had not derailed in the accident, a conclusion supported by Mr Clayton, the driver. The jury were able to dismiss much of the scanty evidence said to support the derailment theory, such as the paint scrapes on the tie bars.

In his summing up for the jury, the coroner went out of his way to exclude negligence by Stephenson, let alone the possibility of manslaughter. On the other hand, it seemed clear to him that Stephenson's derailment theory was not a credible explanation for the collapse. If they so wished, then the jury should comment on the design of the bridge.

The jury agreed. They were unequivocal in their own view of the causes of the accident, stating first that all of the victims had died accidentally. Their unanimous opinion was that:

> ... the girder did not break from any lateral blow from the engine, tender, carriage or van, or from any fault or defect in the masonry of the piers or abutments; but from its being made of a strength insufficient to bear the pressure of quick trains passing over it.

Their conclusion implied that:

> ... no girder bridge of so brittle and treacherous a metal as cast iron alone, even though trussed with wrought-iron rods, is safe for quick or passenger trains. And we have in evidence before us that there are upwards of one hundred bridges similar in principle and form to the late one over the river Dee... all are unsafe.

They went on to recommend strong action:

> We therefore call on Her Majesty's government, as the Guardians of public safety, to institute such an inquiry into... these bridges as shall either condemn the principle or establish their safety to such a degree, that passengers may rest fully satisfied there is no danger; although they deflect from 1½ to 5 inches.

Royal Commission on Iron

It was well known at the time that cast iron was a very brittle material. Indeed, the world-famous bridge at Coalbrookdale built in 1779 was so designed that all structural members were in compression. Indeed, the numerous road bridges built to the same design with cast-iron arches was testimony to their integrity. Failures had been caused not so much by brittle fracture of the arches, as by movement of the abutments which took the lateral pressure.

However, curved arches were unsuitable for providing the flat track needed for railways, which is why engineers attempted to use straight girders. The jury's decision was acted upon rapidly by the government. They set up a Royal Commission in August 1847, chaired by Lord Wrottesley, with many distinguished Commissioners. It reported in July 1849 and included the results of numerous and very detailed experiments with cast and wrought iron. Full scale tests confirmed the low strength of cast-iron girders and the decrease in strength with repeated flexing of cast-iron bars:

> The results of these experiments were, that when the depression was equal to one third of the ultimate deflection, the bars were not weakened. This was ascertained by breaking them ... with stationary loads in the centre. When, however, the depressions produced by the machine were made equal to one half of the ultimate deflection, the bars were actually broken by less than nine hundred depressions.

Although not then called 'fatigue', the experiments demonstrated the problem of low cycle fatigue as well as the idea of a fatigue limit. Low cycle fatigue is just fatigue produced by a relatively small number of loading and unloading cycles, and the fatigue limit is the load level below which fatigue failure does not occur. However, they also introduced the erroneous idea that the structure of the metal changed fundamentally, repeated flexure producing '... a peculiar crystalline fracture and loss of tenacity'. By performing experiments on two bridges, they confirmed that the downward deflection at the centre of the supporting beam did indeed increase with the speed of a train passing over.

Stephenson was interrogated in detail about the Dee Bridge and it emerged that he and several other distinguished engineers had used or were planning to use the design in many other bridges. Stephenson insisted that the design was not flawed, strangely, given the accident on the Dee and problems with the castings failing suddenly. Brunel, however, refused to use cast iron at all for structural application in bridges. Nevertheless, the discovery in 2004 of an original cast-iron bridge designed by Brunel in 1838 for the approach to Paddington station, clearly shows that he did use cast iron for some of his first bridges. The design of the bridge uses arches of ironwork and makes little use of bolts, the castings fitting together like the famous structure at Coalbrookdale.

William Fairbairn favoured his own solution of wrought-iron plates riveted together to give large bridge sections, an entirely successful solution because he and Stephenson used it in the Britannia and Conway tube bridges built for the same railway at roughly the same time. The toughness of this material provided a substantial degree of safety to the travelling public. Despite this wise decision, Stephenson still maintained that cast-iron girders could be used safely, and he reinforced his existing bridges by stacking yet more girders on top of existing ones (as in the bridges at Florence on another project). He also made the strange suggestion that flexibility in the girders provided a degree of protection against impact or sudden loads from passing trains!

Analysis of the Failure

In modern eyes, the failure of the Dee Bridge was caused by crack growth from the centre of the girder, probably from the inner sharp corner of the section. Because all the load from the track, recent ballast and the train was supported by the inner flange of the girder, it would have been concentrated at the corner with the vertical web. The section shows that an attempt was made to bolster the corner by designing a cavetto, a method familiar to carpenters, a quarter-round hollow with two sharp corners either side. However, wood is a tough material and can withstand sharp corners: brittle materials like glass and cast iron are sensitive to such geometries. This is why if you need to break plate glass, you score the surface with a sharp scribe and bend across the scratch to break the glass cleanly. The attempt to add an artistic flourish to the casting lowered the strength to a very dangerous level. It is likely that a defect at one of the corners (probably the upper one) started to crack on first loading by a train, the crack growing slowly under each passing train until the fateful day when Stephenson loaded on the ballast. The very next train over promptly broke the girder with catastrophic results.

Consequences for Bridge Building

It was now quite clear that cast-iron girders were doomed as a reliable construction material for bridges bearing moving loads, and all the existing bridges were redesigned to give extra strength. Stephenson attempted to reinforce the Dee Bridge with yet more cast-iron girders, but further brittle fractures occurred, and the attempts were eventually abandoned. The best material to replace the treacherous cast-iron girders was wrought iron, preferably built up into girders by riveting sheets together. The material was tough when loaded and, although more expensive, produced much more secure structures. William Fairbairn had led the way by using the construction method for ships' hulls, as well as the magnificent Britannia Bridge across the Menai Straits. Many of these massive wrought-iron girders are still seen in railway and road bridges, where their longevity is proof of their integrity.

The Crystal Palace

Notwithstanding the problem of using cast-iron beams in tension, its ease of casting to often very complex shapes provided designers with a powerful incentive to use the material in innovative structures. So long as the material was used mainly in compression (as in columns) it could be used safely. Indeed, it had been used in this way for many years in building new warehouses and factories for the expanding economy. Such methods were widely used at Coalbrookdale, for example, where the large-scale manufacture of cast iron had been pioneered. Beams could be used but only with a wide safety margin. Another reason for the low cost of cast-iron columns was a growing market for water and sewage pipes in the early part of the century, stimulated by the need to supply the growing industrial cities with clean water. It was becoming clear that the cholera epidemics, which were such a regular feature of life, were caused by consuming polluted water from wells. Cast-iron pipes could easily be made in large sand moulds, and were fitted with flanges for easy attachment to one another.

The best example of a cast-iron structure is the Crystal Palace *(1.2)*, a building designed by Joseph Paxton, the ex-head gardener of Chatsworth, for the Great Exhibition of 1851. He had already made a large glass house at Chatsworth, inspired by the rib structure of the giant water lily (which he had grown himself). The methods he developed were applied in building the Tropical House at Kew gardens. The Crystal Palace (so named by popular opinion) was made from glass, timber and iron, both cast and wrought. The cast iron provided the columns and horizontal struts, the wrought iron most of the connections making the framework, and within which there were fitted wooden floors and large glazing panes. The integrity of the structure was assessed by a young engineer, W.H. Barlow, and critical components were tested using hydraulic machines. Drainage from the enormous roof was collected by Paxton-patented gutters and channelled down through the hollow columns. Shades and louvres were fitted to the glass panes so that the giant glasshouse did not overheat in bright sunshine. The resulting structure amazed and delighted the public. It was by far the largest man-made structure of any kind at the time (1,851ft long by 408ft wide, rising in three tiers). But, despite the testing of components, public concern after the Dee disaster demanded more realistic tests. Some doubts about the integrity of the structure were raised by Airy, the Astronomer Royal, for example, who also claimed that high winds might wreck the structure. Soldiers were marched across a test floor, and the floors were also deliberately overloaded with ammunition boxes, while cannon balls were rolled across them to simulate dynamic overloading *(1.2)*. Local storms appeared to have no effect on the building.

Nothing amiss was observed, apart from a few leaks in the storms (which did cause some worries for visitors and exhibitors). The structure created vast open and well-lit interior spaces for displaying manufactures from new factories in Britain, and the incredible range of natural and synthetic materials from all over the world.

The structure was innovative for its prefabricated manufacture and modular design. As a result, it was erected in around six months, to meet the deadline for the opening of the Great Exhibition. When over, the structure was quickly dismantled and re-erected in Sydenham, where it survived intact until the 1930s, when it succumbed to a disastrous fire. But it set the style for other innovative structures in future international expositions and exhibitions, conceptually and architecturally.

Crumlin Viaduct

The successful use of cast iron in the Crystal Palace encouraged other designers to exploit the technology in bridges. If assemblies of pipes could be used in buildings, why not in bridges? After all, the system had been shown to support its own load (the deadweight) and imposed loads from the many visitors to the Exhibition. As the Dee accident had shown, it was necessary to be very careful about the way cast-iron structures supported loads. But the main lessons had been learnt, and the first major bridge to be constructed using cast-iron columns was the Crumlin Viaduct in South Wales. It was designed by Thomas Kennard and the foundation stone was laid in 1853, just two years after the Crystal Palace. It was finished in 1857 *(1.3)*.

It was a massive undertaking attempting to cross the valley of the river Ebbw, nearly 500 yards wide and over 200ft deep. The viaduct linked the Abergavenny Railway with the heart of the South Wales coal and iron industry. The supporting piers for the double-tracked railway line were made by assembling clusters of hollow 12in-diameter (walls of 1in-thickness) cast-iron columns fitted with flanges (the pipes). In the largest pier, there were twelve pipes 17ft-long, arranged roughly in plan in an irregular hexagon shape, and bolted to one another by horizontal girders of T-shape made in cast iron. They were then braced together by diagonal wrought-iron rods fixed near to the ends of the girders. The Isabella pier was one of the highest, comprising ten tiers. The form of the construction made assembly fast because when each tier was finished, the workers could stand on the new base and build the next cell above. No

Above: (1.3) The Crumlin Viaduct shortly after completion in 1857. The viaduct supported two tracks of railway linking east and central South Wales (Humber).

Opposite: (1.2) Soldiers testing a trussed floor of the Crystal Palace.

Above: (1.4) The Bouble viaduct built by Eiffel in the 1860s to carry a single-line railway. Cast-iron columnar piers are braced by wrought ironwork, with a maximum height of 190ft above the valley floor.

Below: (1.5) Pier base showing column joints fitted below pipe joint, curved columns for lateral reinforcement, and spiral ladder for maintenance.

scaffolding was therefore needed, the growing pier itself being used to erect higher tiers. Only the central set of columns was vertical, the outer columns being inclined at about 12 to 1 so as to give the pier a pyramidal form, a tower structure inherently more stable than a purely vertical tower. The design philosophy was clearly based on that used in the Crystal Palace, and was much faster (and thus cheaper) to build than a conventional pier built from masonry. Such a pier was also much lighter than one of masonry. The Isabella pier at Crumlin (10 tiers high) weighed about 200 tons, compared with a masonry equivalent of 2,900 tons, so the foundations supported a much lighter structure.

When all the eight piers had been built, work started on lifting the wrought-iron trussed girders onto the pier tops, achieved using block and tackle, but there were many problems in lifting the heavy girders into position, especially with buckling. There were eight such piers, and the spans were 150ft long, each weighing 44 tons. When the structure had been completed and the tracks laid, it was tested by the Board of Trade. They loaded the tracks with six heavy locomotives, each weighing 50 tons, giving a total of 300 tons spread out over a single span. The train of locos was moved slowly at first over each span, and the deflection at the centre of each span measured. It varied from a low of $\frac{7}{8}$in up to 1.25in at the highest speeds. It was approved for general use by the public and officially opened in 1857. It survived until 1964, being demolished (with some difficulty) following closure of the line by Dr Beeching.

Other Pipe Bridges

The success of the concept led to many other such bridges being built over the next twenty years, culminating and dying with the first Tay Bridge. In the immediate aftermath of the success of the Crumlin Bridge, a series of other bridges were built to a similar design, by Kennard, across the world. They included a 2,138ft-long bridge over the river Ebro in Spain, although the piers were much lower in height than at Crumlin. However, another Kennard bridge comprised 16 spans at a maximum height of 89ft over the river Tagus at Villa Nova de Constancia. There were also important projects in Italy: a bridge across the Tiber just outside Rome, and the Velletri Bridge, also just outside the city. It was 600ft long and was supported on two cast-iron column piers 90ft high. At the river Barrakur in India, another Kennard project was a 1,650ft-long bridge, whose claim to fame was that it involved no riveting whatsoever, owing the shortage of skilled labour. All the joints were bolted together. Another UK project mentioned in the *Handbook of the Crumlin Viaduct* is a 650ft viaduct over the river Tees involving only masonry piers, but incorporating a Kennard girder to support the railway. Its designer was Thomas Bouch. But it used masonry rather than iron piers.

In France, the technique of using cast-iron columnar piers was adopted enthusiastically by Gustave Eiffel, who designed numerous bridges in the Massif Centrale. They included many viaducts on the Gannat-Montluçon railway, contructed in the 1860s using cast iron pipes with wrought-iron braces. The viaduct piers were given a parabolic shape, with a wide base tapering to the top in a style not dissimilar to that of the much later Eiffel Tower in Paris. One of the largest of these viaducts is at Bouble, finished in 1869, and crossed the valley of the river Bouble using five cast-iron piers. Over 900ft long, the deck was nearly 190ft above the valley, the piers being supported on masonry platforms. Comprising eight or nine tiers, the bases of every iron pier are splayed out with curved columns *(1.4)*.

All the columns were attached by wrought-iron bars attached, not to the flanges, but some distance below the flange to projections cast into the side wall of the cylinder. Diagonal tie bars also braced the towers, being fixed by rivets to the connection plates. The deck was emplaced by a pioneering method which overcame the problems experienced at Crumlin: it was slid into place from the bank, rather than lifted bit by bit from the valley. One small detail shows his care as a designer: he built a spiral wrought-iron ladder at the centre of each pier so that the braced structure could be inspected easily, a detail he adopted for all of his viaducts. It must have been much easier to paint each pier, especially those difficult to access from ground level, such as those in the middle of rivers. The ladders can be accesed via a walkway slung on the main truss below the rail line *(1.5)*. Such viaducts are still being used by local trains on the single track, striking proof of the intrinsic integrity of the structure.

In many ways, it can be said that Eiffel made his reputation as a result of the construction of this set of spectacular iron bridges in the Auvergne. The viaducts were built very quickly from prefabricated parts, were light in weight and much cheaper than masonry equivalents. It led to many other commissions for viaducts and bridges elsewhere in Europe and overseas. But one of his most important commissions was to build the Statue of Liberty in New York in 1881, and the giant tower in Paris for the World Exhibition of 1889. Although only meant as a temporary structure, it proved so popular that the eponymous tower is a visible reminder of his skill as a practising engineer.

2
Bridging the Tay Estuary

As the rail network expanded in the mid-Victorian period, many rivers and estuaries were bridged, often in spectacular fashion, like Stephenson's Britannia Bridge across the Menai straits, or Brunel's Saltash bridge across the Tamar estuary. In both cases, the design of the structures was highly innovative, the former being essentially a tube of wrought iron through which trains passed. The Saltash structure involved two great arches built above one another in two strides across the estuary. The problems of bridging the Firths of Forth and Tay were much more demanding, and required some considerable degree of innovation for their solution.

Railways connected the main cities of the east of Scotland, mainly operated by the North British Railway (NBR), travelling around the estuaries along the banks. Schemes were soon proposed to shorten journey times, initially by a ferry across the narrow Firth of Forth. The Tay estuary represented a more serious obstacle if travellers wanted to reach Dundee, owing to its much greater width. It too was crossed by a ferry from Newport to the heart of Dundee town. Routes to the north were also provided by the Caledonian Railway – the main competitor to the NBR – via inland routes which provided shorter travel times *(2.1)*.

The Problem of the Firths

North of Edinburgh lie two great estuaries, the Firth of Forth and the Firth of Tay. The Firth of Forth begins at the town of Stirling where it emerges into the North Sea, and runs about 50 miles to the east into the heartland of Scotland. Edinburgh, the capital city of Scotland, is situated on the southern bank at the mouth of the estuary 30 miles east of Stirling *(2.2)*. Eleven miles west of Edinburgh, at Queensferry, the firth narrows down to around a mile in width, but the water is still 40ft – 60ft deep, depending on the tide. The Firth of Tay lies around 25 miles to the north of the Forth: it begins at Perth and runs east for around 25 miles until it too meets the sea *(2.2)*. At this point, near Dundee, the Tay is 1.5 miles wide and is up to 40ft deep.

The two Firths have always been a major barrier to communications to and from Edinburgh, especially when the railways were expanding at a frantic pace in the 1840s and 1850s. A passenger who wanted to go from Edinburgh to Dundee and perhaps on to Aberdeen, had to travel the long way round through Stirling and Perth, adding around 60 miles to the journey.

Alternatively, the passenger had to endure two ferry crossings, across the Forth from Granton to Burntisland, and then across the Tay from Tayport to Broughty Ferry. The fastest

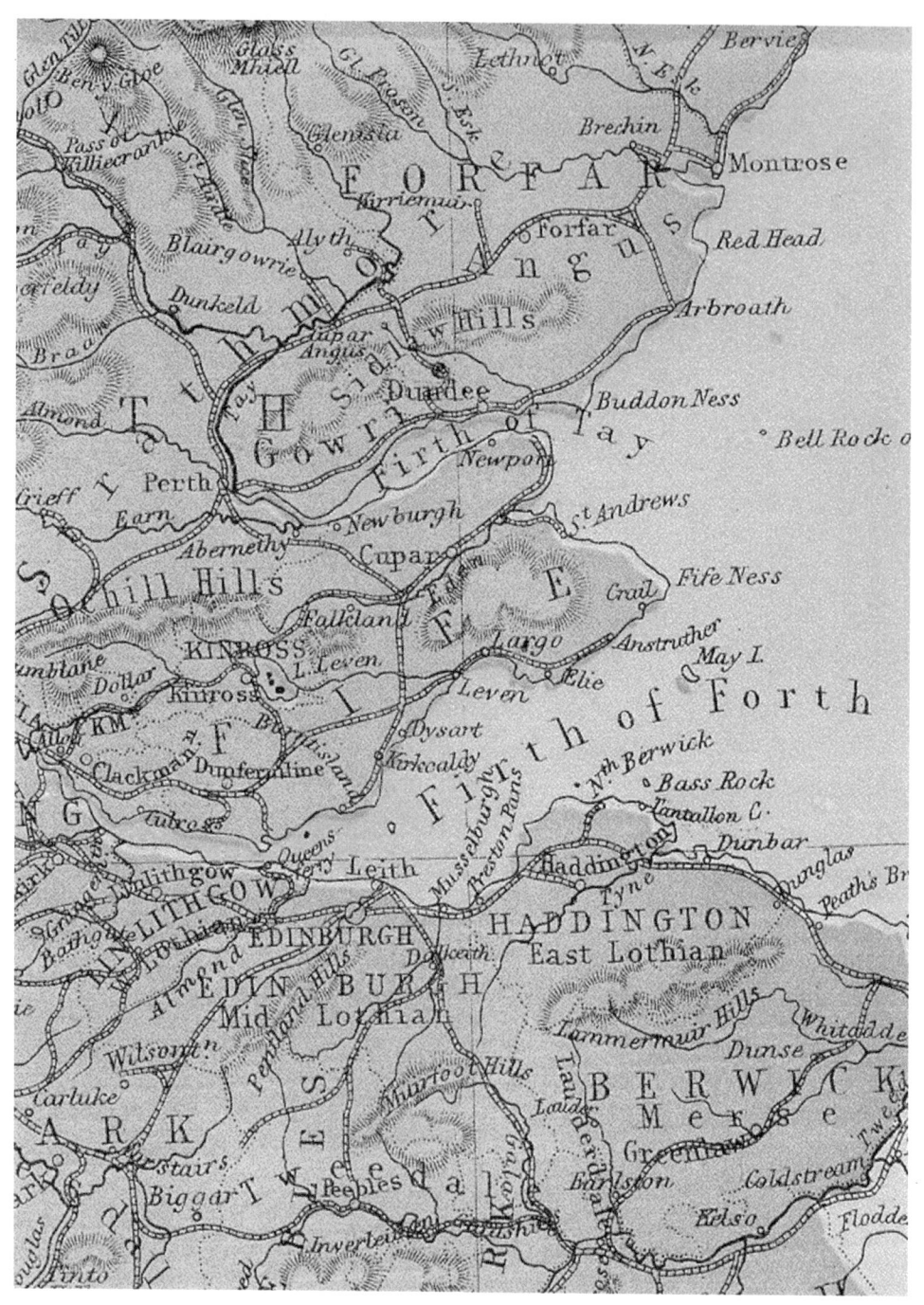

Above: (2.1) The railway network of central Scotland in around 1867, adapted from Virtue & Co.'s map of Scotland (c.1873).

Opposite: (2.2) The Firth of Forth and the Firth of Tay, Scotland (after Bignell).

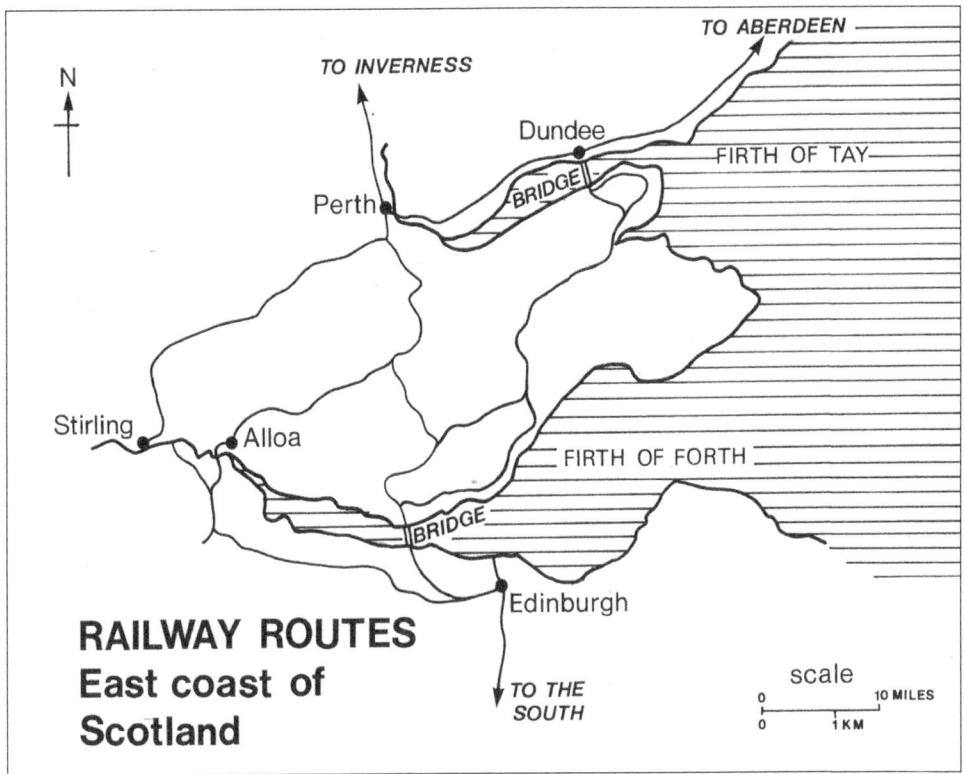

boat train of the day left Waverley station in Edinburgh at 6.25 a.m. and was timed to arrive at Dundee at 9.37 a.m., a journey time of three hours twelve minutes for a distance of only 46 miles (at an average speed of only 14mph!). In bad weather the ferries might not run at all; if they did the hapless passengers would probably arrive cold and sea-sick. Freight traffic posed special problems because goods had to be off-loaded at the ferry terminals.

Genesis of the Project

The route was operated by the Edinburgh & Northern Railway. In 1849 they appointed a civil engineer, Thomas Bouch, to be their manager. Twenty-six years old at the time, he immediately set about improving the ferry service and, by 1851, had built what was the world's first roll-on, roll-off train ferry. It proved a major innovation in cutting travel times, simply because goods could be kept on the trains and did not need to be unpacked for the journey across the water. Although it improved the efficiency of the crossing, it could not solve the basic problem of stormy weather, which could seriously delay crossings. A similar ferry service was introduced to the Tay estuary crossing in the same year. Bouch realised, however, that this was only a stop-gap measure: the real answer to the problem was to build railway bridges over the Forth and Tay. In 1854 the Edinburgh & Northern Railway was taken over by the rapidly expanding North British Railway. Bouch put his proposal for a pair of bridges to the directors of the NBR, but they dismissed it as the 'most insane idea ever to be propounded'. In the long run, of course, the case for the bridges was overwhelming; but the chequered progress of the project gives an insight into the ruthless commercial politics of the railway age. Eventually, on 15 July 1870, a Bill was passed by Parliament which authorised the construction of a bridge over the Tay. Bouch, by then an independent consultant, was appointed engineer to the new bridge.

Belah Viaduct

Bouch left the NBR after designing his very successful Tay and Forth ferries scheme and became an independent consultant on a wide variety of different projects for many different railway companies. Among them was the Belah Viaduct on the South Durham line, built in the very short time of just three months in 1860, similar to that of the Crystal Palace. The bridge lay on the east side of the Pennines near the Stainmore Pass, for a railway (opened in August 1861) which took iron ore from the Cumbria mines to blast furnaces on Teeside, and carried coal in the reverse direction. His experience there and at a similar viaduct on the same line at Deepdale was to be significant for the Tay Bridge project, not least because of the design of the viaduct needed to cross a 200ft-deep valley in a length of about 1,000ft. He chose a design which was already well known from the spectacular Crumlin Viaduct in South Wales, and indeed had only been open for three years.

The Belah Bridge was built in the same way, the cast-iron units of the structure being hollow pipes with flanges which were bolted together and braced by horizontal struts and diagonal wrought-iron bars.

The number of columns in each pier was reduced to eight in a rectangular formation, supporting spans of 60ft. There were sixteen towers supporting the single track although the line was renovated in 1889 and a second track added, no doubt as a result of the concerns raised by the Tay Bridge disaster. It suffered the same fate as the Crumlin Viaduct under the Beeching closures, being demolished in 1964. The piers were inclined from the base so as to increase their lateral stability, by no less than a maximum of 30ft in the case of Crumlin, and 28ft at Belah. Both viaducts offered little wind resistance, owing to their open lattice work construction, and passed their proof tests with flying colours.

The original design drawings in the National Archive at Kew show the way the various bracing elements were attached to one another *(2.3)*. The two middle set of 12in-diameter cast-iron columns were vertical, and supported each side by two inclined sets of columns. The columns were bolted together at their flanges, but the horizontal connecting struts (with a channel section) clasped the columns below the flanged joint.

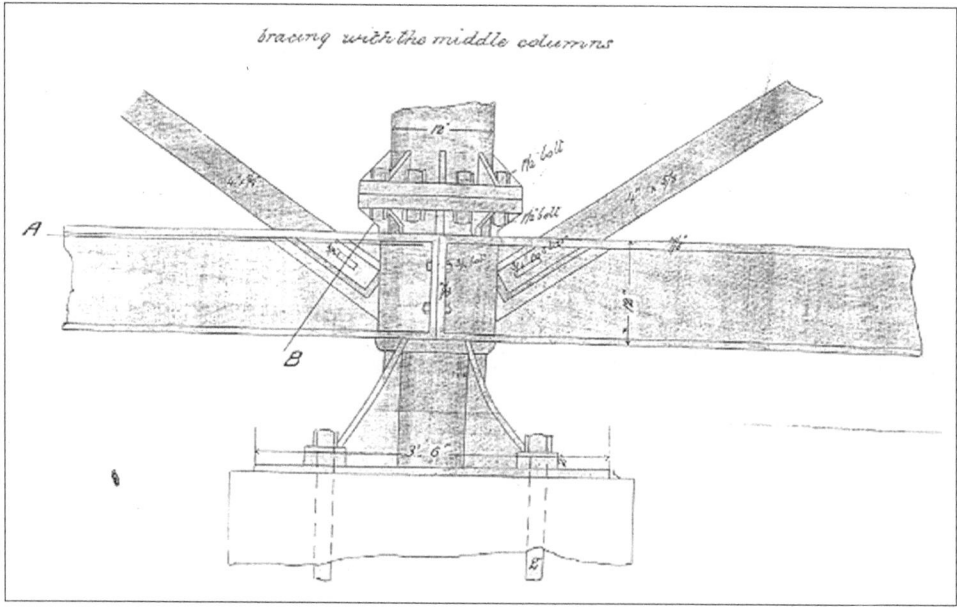

(2.3) Bracing connections on the central vertical columns of the Belah Bridge.

The diagonal braces were attached to the struts and not the columns, and tensioned by knocking in cotters through a slot cut in the wrought-iron bars. Separating the flange joint and the braces was a method also adopted by Eiffel on his similar pipe bridges. By keeping the two types of joint separate, failure of one would not necessarily compromise the integrity of the other.

Building the Bridge

The Tay Bridge project was slow to start and beset by many problems with the contractors. The contract was initially given to Butler & Pitts, with a time limit of three years for completion. Pitts died and the contract was passed, in May 1871, to Charles de Bergue of London. The size of the proposed structure for a single-line railway across the Tay estuary hardly needs to be over-emphasised: it was to be the longest bridge ever built either in Britain or the world, at nearly 2 miles from Wormit on the south shore to near the town centre of Dundee itself. One of the most important appointments made by de Bergue was Albert Grothe (see Dramatis Personae), one of his plant managers, who was charged with managing the contract. Other appointments were made by Bouch himself, including Henry Noble, who had previously worked with Sir Joseph Bazalgette on the London embankment. It would be his job to inspect work as it was finished.

Grothe set up a base in Wormit at the south end of the bridge, including numerous jetties to ship structural elements for the bridge. The original plans as developed by Bouch called for ninety-two piers which supported spans varying from 27ft to 60ft at the shoreline, increasing up to 200ft in the centre, the so-called high girder section. It was this central section in midstream which was highest above the estuary (88ft) so as to allow clearance from high-masted ships passing upriver to the port of Perth. The spans would be made of wrought-iron girders rivetted together to form lattice boxes on which the railway would be laid, except in the high girder section, where the line would run through the girders. The piers would clearly have to be substantial and tall structures to support the ironwork spans, and masonry piers seemed initially to be the best support for the heavy girders for the track. A single-line track was

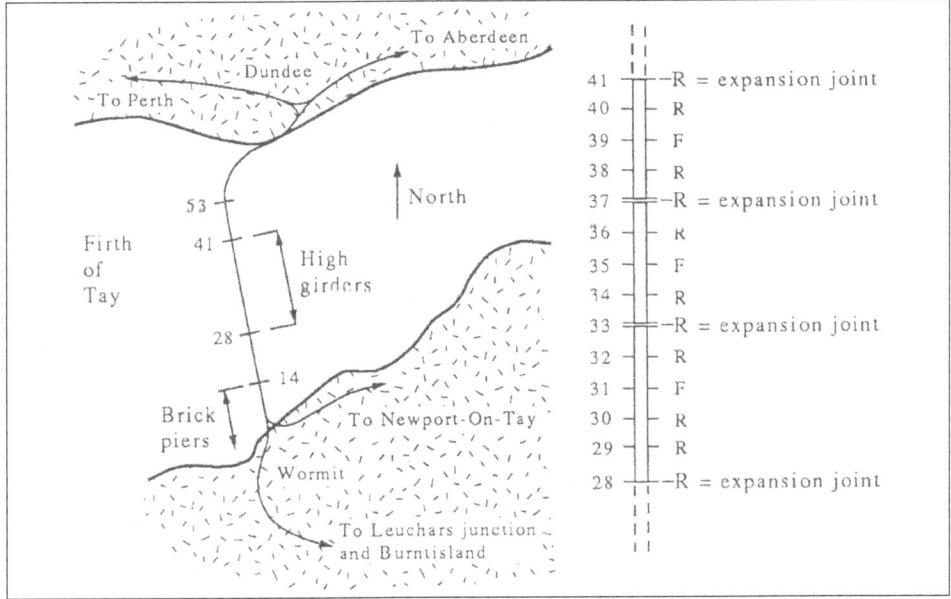

(2.4) Plan of the old Tay Bridge showing pier numbers with details of construction at the right (D.R.H. Jones).

preferred, presumably to reduce the cost of the enterprise. The path of the bridge as finally constructed is shown *(2.4)*, the inset on the right being a blow-up of the high girder section. The large wrought-iron girders supporting the track were laid on the tops of the towers, in most cases resting freely on cast-iron rollers (R). There were three main lengths of girder, fixed at three points to the tops of the towers (F). Where the three girders met, an expansion joint was provided to allow changes in length to be accommodated. This was a necessary precaution because such a great length of ironwork would expand and contract with changes in temperature. If constrained, the metalwork could buckle at high temperature, owing to expansion. Exactly the same problem can occur to fixed rail in hot summer conditions.

Foundations

Work on the first piers to be sunk involved making iron cylinders which could be sunk in the tidal waters at the intended location. They could then be capped and sealed so that the water inside could be pumped out and the foundations prepared by the workmen. It involved excavating sand at the base, and building a brickwork lining, the iron cylinder sinking as sand was removed. The air within the caisson was pressurised to keep the water out. Once solid rock was reached, the hollow core was filled with concrete, and the top erected above the external water level. The girders were placed on the piers via pontoons and rose as the piers were built up, course by course.

But progress was slow, mainly because of poor weather in the winter months. Work on the foundations was hazardous enough without the extra problems of rough water above. The pontoons which carried the iron cylinders and girders out to the piers needed calm, smooth water to be positioned accurately, and deliver their loads. The initial contract stipulated that the bridge be built in three years, so should have been finished by May 1874. Yet only a handful of piers had actually been built: No.14 from the south side of the bank was built by mid-1873 *(2.4)*. Then tragedy struck with the death of de Bergue. Although the firm could apparently continue the contract through his widow and daughter, bad news was received about the state of the foundations on pier No.15. Solid rock could not be found, the bed appearing to be a layer of hard conglomerate resting on sand and clay. The plans for solid masonry piers might have to be abandoned. So what was the problem?

Bouch assumed in his original plans a pressure of 6.25 tons per sq.ft on each pier, a figure he thought was safe for heavy masonry piers rooted on solid rock. However, the figure would apparently need be reduced to 4.5 tons with weaker foundations. His adviser, the mathematician Allan Stewart, thought that Bouch's calculations were inaccurate and that a lower pressure would still be needed. The outcome of the arguments was the proposal by Bouch to erect cast-iron piers similar to those he had used at Belah. They could reduce the pressure to only 2.75 tons per sq.ft, could be built much faster (as experience at Belah had shown) and lower the costs of the contract. They would, however, need painting to resist the corrosive action of sea-borne spray in the estuary. The de Bergue company had to revise its own plans drastically. The amount of cast iron needed would be prodigious, and they decided to establish a foundry at Wormit to produce the columns needed for the piers. The number of columns in each tier would be eight, but this was reduced to six in a hexagon configuration to fit the pier base *(2.5)*.

At the same time, Bouch decided to reduce the number of piers, apparently saving yet more time and money. The high girder section was reduced by one span, so requiring twelve rather than thirteen piers. Span length was now 245ft, with two spans of 227ft.

But the pier bases were very small for the cast and wrought-iron towers to be erected upon them, necessarily reducing the rake angle to virtually zero. This was at variance with the design practice which had been adopted with all other pipe bridges built to that date, both by Bouch himself at Belah, and by Eiffel in France. All such piers had been built with large rake angles so as to provide lateral stability against cross winds as well as loads imposed by passing trains. If

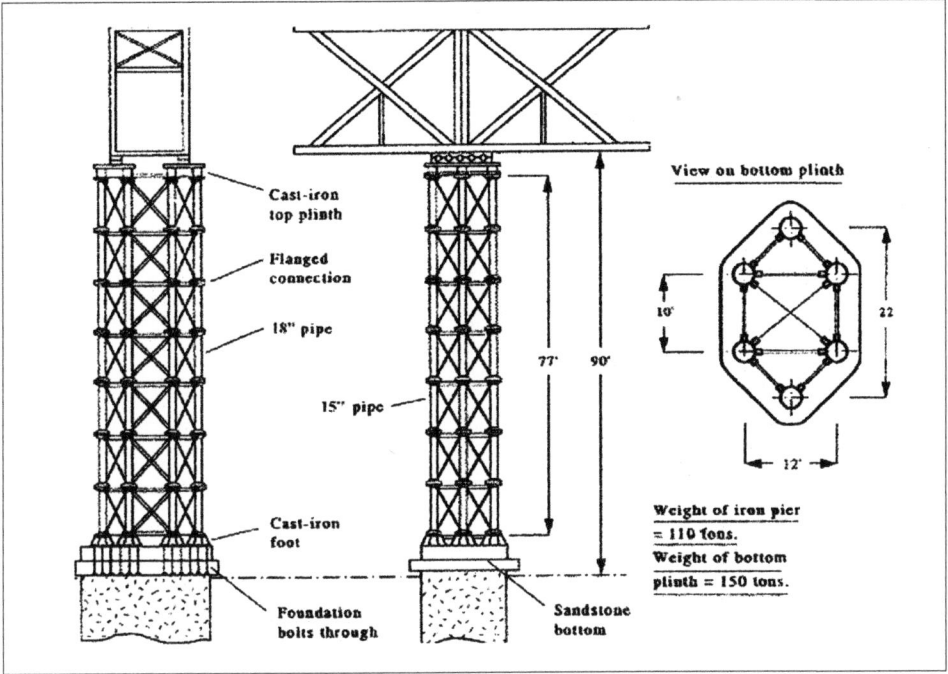

(2.5) Plan and section of a seven-tier tower in a high girder pier (after D.R.H. Jones).

larger bases were to have been used, the caissons would have been at least twice the diameter, or doubled in number, so greatly increasing the cost of the operation. Whether or not Stewart, as scientific adviser to the company, had evaluated the effect of having only vertical towers, remains unknown to this day. At the Official Inquiry after the disaster, he said that he had performed stability calculations based on cross winds at the time of the critical decision, but he could not produce them for inspection by the court.

Centre Spans

The de Bergue company was in considerable financial difficulties, even without the extra pressure for the foundry and extra metalwork needed. Their bid for the Tay Bridge contract had underestimated the cash needed for completion, and they were now effectively insolvent. A new contractor was necessary, and the contract was reassigned yet again, this time to Hopkins Gilkes of Middlesborough. The company had supplied wrought-iron rails to the NBR, as well as material for Bouch's several bridges in the north of England, such as Belah. To maintain the expertise already established, they agreed to take over the de Bergue team.

In August 1873 yet more problems occurred: an explosion at pier No.54 on the Dundee side of the estuary *(2.3)*. Six men died as a result of sudden depressurisation of the cylinders at this pier, and the ultimate cause was never established. Divers retrieved the bodies left below in the flooded caisson. The accident came after many other incidents in which workers were killed or injured, working often at height under difficult conditions. The most severe working conditions were experienced in the central or high girder spans, roughly equidistant from either shore and the most exposed part of the whole structure. If problems occurred here, help would not be close at hand.

The structure of the pier bases allowed for a masonry cap on top of the brickwork, upon which was laid a cast-iron plate to support the tower above. The total weight resting on these central piers would also be greater than on those closer to shore, partly because of the greater

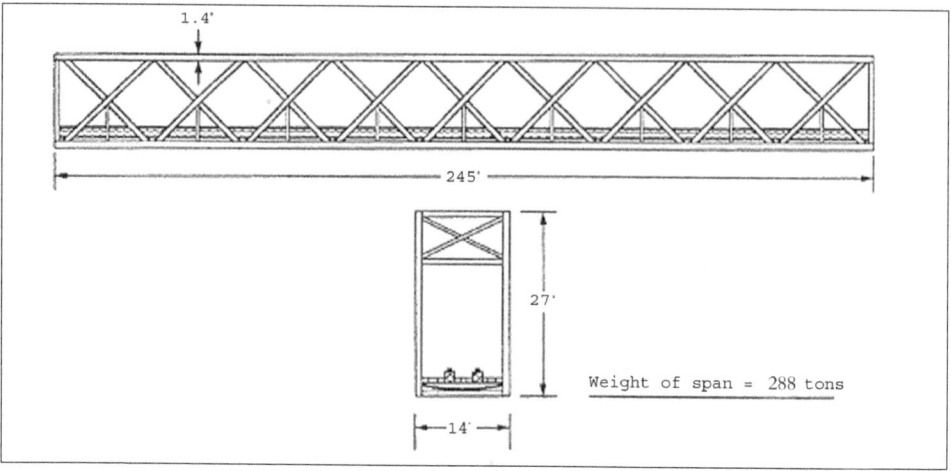

height needed at the centre, and partly because of the greater size of girders spanning the wider gaps between the piers. The data is shown in *(2.5)* and *(2.6)*, with the weight of a span being about 288 tons compared with the weight of a pier at 110 tons. It is easy to see that the towers of the centre section were very top heavy, which could only increase when loaded by a train. The lower towers either side of the centre section were less heavily loaded since the girders of 145 foot were much less substantial because they had to bridge a smaller span.

Bracing the Towers

The girders were supported on cast-iron rollers which in turn rested on a cast-iron plate at the top of each tower. The rollers were needed to allow the 2-mile length of girders to expand and contract as the ambient temperature varied. The central towers were seven tiers high, rising almost vertically above the base. Unlike the earlier structures at Belah and Crumlin, there was little or no sideways support from inclined columns. The columns were bolted into the base by means of cast-iron tapered feet, and stabilised laterally and diagonally in several ways:

1 Horizontal struts between the column bases and tops
2 Diagonal tie bars across each cell
3 Horizontal tie rods between the opposing columns at the core of the plan

These strengthening elements were made from wrought iron, a more expensive material than the cast iron of the columns, but much tougher in resisting pulling forces or tension. By contrast, cast iron is relatively weak and brittle in tension, being many times stronger in compression (which is why they were used primarily as columnar supports). Any owner of an old house with cast-iron gutters will know just how brittle the material can be when over stressed. Guttering is especially liable to break suddenly if dropped, for example, breaking like glass to produce sharp fractures. There are many different types of cast iron available now, but virtually the only kind used then was called grey cast iron (from the colour of its fracture surface). It is very brittle because of its high carbon content, which is normally in the shape of flakes, which lowers its strength. Wrought iron is more familiar as the material of pokers or spades (of some vintage, probably), although steel is much more commonly used nowadays. Both steel and wrought iron will yield if overloaded, rather than breaking suddenly.

The three stabilising elements were connected to the columns by lugs of various design integral with the columns. Each column was cast in a single operation, by pouring molten

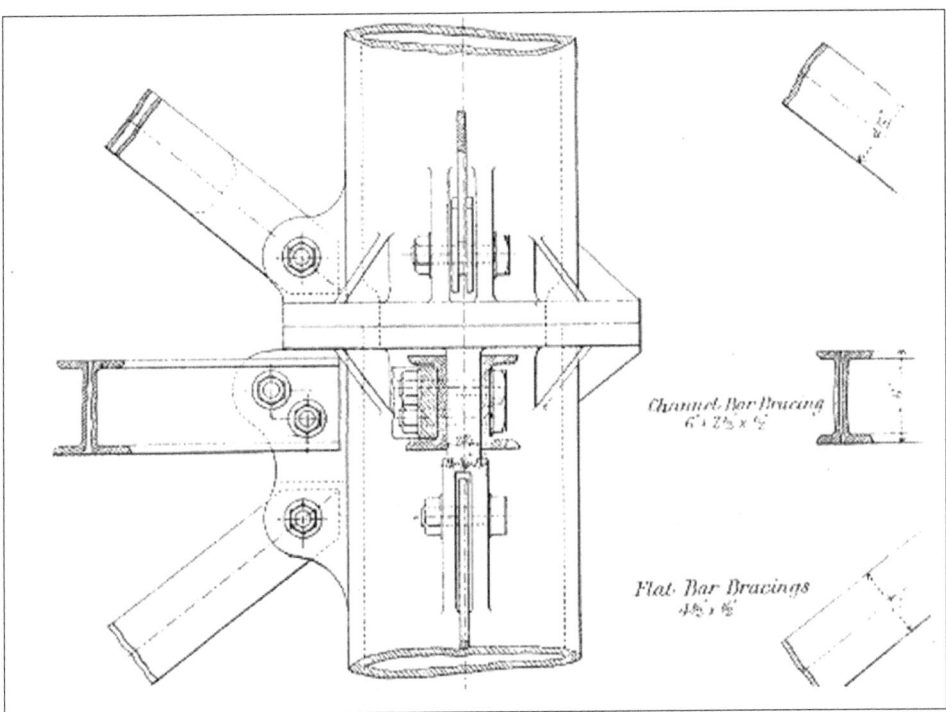

(2.7) Contemporary engineering drawing of a joint in a 15in column.

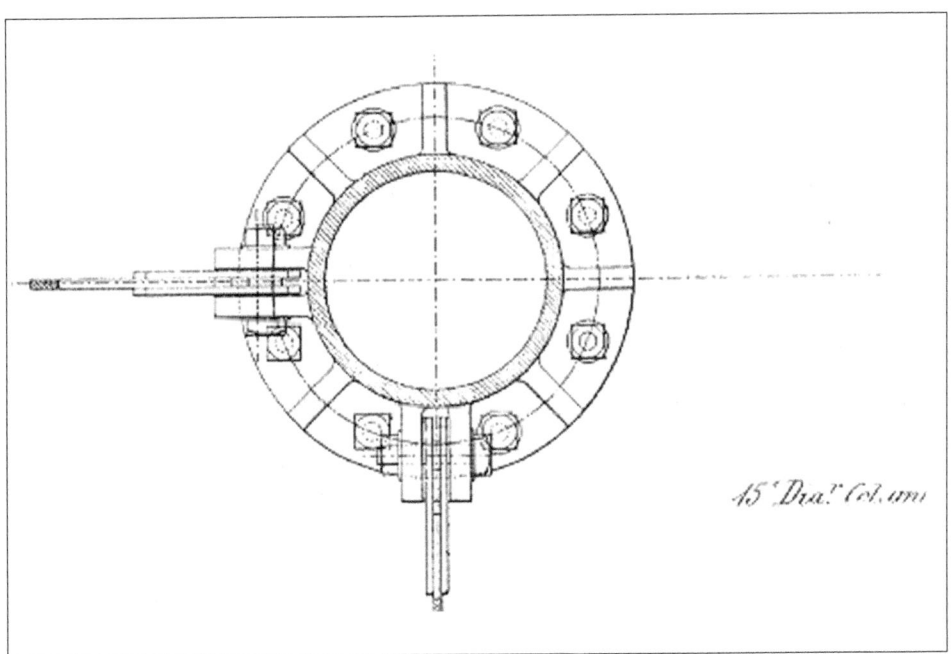

Above: (2.8) Plan of the column ends showing bolt holes in the flanges.

Opposite: (2.6) Section of girder in the centre of Tay Bridge (after D.R.H. Jones).

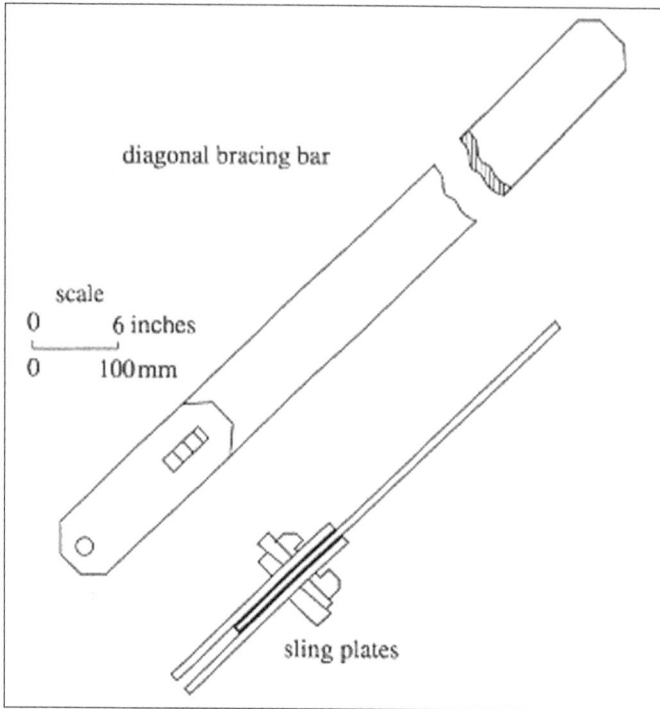

(2.9) Bracing method used in the diagonal tie bars using a gib and two cotters (D.R.H. Jones).

iron into sand moulds, and it probably seemed convenient and economical to include the lugs in each casting. It makes for a more complex operation and some care is needed to ensure that all the metal reaches the furthest extremities of the mould, where the lugs were situated. The design of the connections is shown in *(2.7)*, diagrams prepared at the time.

It shows the joints in a 15in-column, the most common size of column in the bridge. The outermost columns were slightly larger at 18in outside diameter. The centre figure in the diagram shows the joint where two columns met at a flange cast into each column, and by means of which the columns could be bolted together *(2.8)*.

The lugs were of two types, the simpler being that at the lowest end of each column, consisting of two circular plates with a central hole to take a bolt for connection with the diagonal tie bar. The pair of plates (or wings) were separated by a small gap to allow the tie bar to be inserted and bolted into position (plans at top and bottom of *(2.6)*). The upper lug was a more complex affair since it incorporated the upper lug for the diagonal tie bar as well as the lug for the horizontal strut. The latter comprised two U-shaped channels bolted via two holes into this lug. While seeming to be innocent minor details, these lugs were to assume a sinister role in the tragedy to come. The final bracing element, the horizontal diagonal tie rods, were bolted to cast-iron collars fitted to the tops of the columns.

But how was the structure braced? After all, if the struts, tie bars and rods were simply loose, little bracing effect would be achieved. Each tower was a spaceframe in which all parts should be tightly attached to one another, so giving a unitary structure against any external loads. Of course, if every element were precisely dimensioned, a good fit would be achieved, but in practice cast-iron mouldings and fittings will vary slightly in size, so some bracing was essential to hold the structure together. The single bracing method chosen was by means of wedges driven into a joint in the diagonal tie bars, a method similar to that used on earlier iron bridges. The joint is shown in *(2.9)*, the wedges being known as 'cotters' abut directly onto a 'gib' as well as the end of the tie bar. The gib abuts against the two sling plates.

When the cotters are driven home (brute force with a hammer) the inclined surfaces force the tie bar into tension, which braces the cell of the tier involved. There was no quantitative way of telling how tight such joints were, although a hammer was used by the construction workers, presumably tapping the tie bar to ensure that it was tensioned by the sound emitted. While building the towers, cracked lugs would occasionally be found. According to testimony given at the Inquiry later, where lugs had broken during construction, the tie bars were fixed instead to a wrought-iron hoop put around the column and bolted into position. Problems with cracked lugs had been experienced at the Wormit foundry and, if very bad, the columns would be rejected and broken up, and the metal recycled. It was estimated that about 200 such defective columns were rejected at the foundry. Broken lugs could apparently be mended, however, by burning the broken wing back onto the matching fracture surface. According to the later testimony of the foundrymen, very few such broken lugs were burnt-on and used in the bridge. Burning-on was a practice where the matching bits of cast iron would be heated up and molten metal placed in the break so as to reseal the lug. Mr Camphuis was an assistant manager and civil engineer employed on the bridge, and he said in testimony that only ten to twelve such columns had burnt-on lugs, and they were 12in-diameter columns used in the lower parts of the bridge. He personally had tested lugs on columns with a hammer to judge their integrity. It seems to be a foolhardy procedure, requiring skill to ensure that the test did not itself damage the lug.

During construction, the girders of the span would have been placed on the two adjacent pier bases by pontoon (helped by the tides), and the first tier erected under the girders, which themselves were lifted by hydraulic rams. The process would continue until the required height was reached. At each stage, the newly finished tier would be fitted with its reinforcing elements and braced along the diagonals.

Approaching Completion

By the spring of 1876, seventy-six of the eighty-five spans had been finished, with eighteen girders still to be emplaced. To speed the work up in the long and dark winter months, electric arc lamps were installed at Wormit in the autumn of 1876. By 1877 the bridge was looking like a structure nearing completion, with most work concentrating on the high girders at the centre of the estuary. The difficulty of work at the furthest point from land was revealed in February 1877, when a storm hit the estuary and severely damaged this critical part of the structure. The accident apparently occurred on pier Nos 28 to 30, at the start of the high girder section coming from the south end of the bridge. The piers were 245ft apart, the widest in the whole structure, and their wrought-iron girders the heaviest (2.5). The support towers were nearly complete and the girders between the three piers were awaiting final placement. They were resting freely and only held by pins

Fall of Girders

At 4.00 p.m. on 2 February, a storm suddenly arose and the workers headed for cover. Grothe sent a tug to take the men off the isolated piers but the storm prevented the vessel leaving shelter. The forty men sheltered as best they could on the piers, using the wooden staging for cover. The storm was such, however, that much was blown away by the wind. At 8.00 p.m. the tug *Excelsior* made a rescue attempt, but her paddles had been fouled by debris, and they were left to the ravages of the storm. At around 8.15 p.m. the crew of the tug heard three violent sounds, followed by metallic grinding noises followed by a gigantic splash. A gust had blown the two girders from their supports and they came crashing down from a height of 90ft into the estuary below. The wave created by the fall nearly capsized the *Excelsior*. It returned to harbour without reaching the trapped workers. Further attempts to rescue the men were fruitless, but finally the tug was able to approach the stricken piers by the aid of moonlight and by a drop in the wind at around 5.00 a.m. the following morning. The boat was able to tie up at the piers and rescue the men sheltering there. Just one man was missing, presumed dead. One of the girders which fell was left there for recovery later, but the other was lifted and sent to Middlesborough for straightening the distorted beams. It was to be mended and restored to its position near the south end of the high girder section of the bridge.

While the bridge was being inspected during the final stages of completion, many of the gib and cotter joints were found to be loose rather than fully tightened, especially in the tallest towers of the high girder section. Gilkes advised that cutting the tie bars by $\frac{1}{8}$in would solve the problem. The matter was referred to Allan Stewart, scientific adviser to Bouch, who approved this action, and also suggested cutting another $\frac{1}{8}$ at the other end of the tie bar if the first action proved insufficient in allowing full tightening. The question nobody seems to have asked was why some bars were becoming loose at all. If bracing was vital to structural integrity then it was surely important to investigate the causes of loosening. Simply shortening the bars and retightening the ties might alleviate the problem, but might recur if the causes remained unknown.

That Bouch was fully aware of the criticality of the bracing is clear from a letter written to Grothe on 14 August 1877:

> I dare not risk an engine on the bridge until the ties are properly tightened and bear their share of the strain. If any idea were entertained of running an engine on before this is done I would immediately resign the engineering to escape responsibility, and moreover, I would... report the matter to the Procurator Fiscal.

The letter had been written in reply to a request to run ballast trains across to supply material needed for the raising of the embankment at Dundee. Presumably his fears were mollified, because many such goods trains used the bridge after opening during the winter months of 1877/78, according to testimony given by Henry Noble at the Court of Inquiry after the bridge fell. Various inspectors, such as Mr Macbeath, were employed to check the integrity of the joints and lugs in the high girders. He had therefore been working within the high girders when the ballast trains passed over the bridge. When cross-examined, he said that he felt little perceptible movement of the bridge, whether vertical or lateral. Mr Camphuis was also on the high girder section of the bridge when ballast trains passed over, and had felt a general tremor, but nothing in the way of lateral oscillations.

Opening the Bridge

Tightening loose tie bars was not the only job involved in finishing the bridge. Approach railways linking the bridge into the network were needed, as well as work on the new Tay Bridge station in Dundee. But that did not stop the NBR directors from running a celebration train across the bridge on 26 September 1877. It also carried the local MP and the locomotive was driven by the NBR superintendent Dugald Drummond. It travelled slowly, taking fifteen minutes to cross with a mean speed of about 8mph, but the journey was not without mishap. In the high girder section, the roof of one of the carriages hit some scaffolding, which fell into the estuary below.

The connection between the two banks of the estuary was needed for immediate purposes: carrying ballast for the new embankment being built at the Dundee end and cast ironwork for the new Tay Bridge station. It was clearly the most important station on the new line, with four long platforms built in a cutting, and including the entrance to a tunnel taking the line to the docks and to stations further north. It was roofed with glass to counteract the darkness of the cutting. And to these ends the new bridge carried substantial material before it had been tested and approved by the government in the form of the Board of Trade. Approval was necessary for passenger trains, a long established practice from the early days of the railways, and used for example, in the approval of the Dee Bridge.

Testing the Bridge

The bridge was finally ready for approval by the government regulatory agency, the Board of Trade (BoT) in February 1878 *(2.10)*.

All new railway structures had to be inspected and proof tested by the BoT before they could be opened for traffic, the work normally being undertaken by a member of the Railway Inspectorate. They were usually retired Royal Engineers, and had evolved common practice for new bridges and had frequently conducted accident investigations on behalf of the government. Captain Simmons, for example, had investigated the Dee Bridge disaster over thirty years before the Tay Bridge was finished. In this case the inspector was Maj.-Gen. Hutchinson, and his tests on the bridge were to last three days, starting on 25 February 1878.

The greater part of the time was taken up running heavy trains across the structure at varying speeds, with the aim of measuring any excessive movement in the structure. To this end, Hutchinson placed himself on a pier in the high girder section with a theodolite, so that he could observe any lateral motion of the bridge structure when the trains were passing overhead. The greatest load put on the bridge was over 400 tons provided by six trains harnessed together, moving at 40mph across the structure. He reported that he saw 'nothing at all excessive' and commented that 'the ironwork has been well put together both in the columns and the girders'. The chief engineer, Bouch, apparently accompanied Hutchinson during this stage of testing, so both had the chance of observing the towers at close hand. The

(2.10) The new bridge seen from Magdalen Green in Dundee.

(2.11) Enlarged view of high girder section showing the gap at the top of each tower, just below the railway track.

bridge was approved for general use. However, Hutchinson made some qualifications in his report. In the first place he noted that he would wish 'to observe the effects of a high wind when a train of carriages is running over the bridge'. He also commented that there appeared to be some 'slackness' at one or two places in the rails on the bridge and these should be examined and eliminated. He recommended a speed limit of 25mph, and that the bridge be painted white to reduce the effects of expansion and contraction. His comments would in time come to haunt him.

He made no reference in his report to the construction details of the bridge, although some eminent engineers had some doubt about the integrity of the structure. Sir John Fowler (the creator of much of London's underground railway system) refused ever to use the bridge. Perhaps he was concerned by the way in which the high girder section was supported by the twelve towers *(2.11)*.

It shows the seemingly fragile way in which the girders are supported – apparently at only two points. By contrast, the low girders seem to be fully supported (an example is seen at extreme right). It was a critical point which was to be discussed at the Inquiry after the disaster. If the towers in the centre section were top heavy, support against lateral instability or movement would be important for the integrity of the structure, especially against sideways motion of the towers. High winds blowing down the estuary would be one source of sideways forces, for example.

Opening Ceremony

It was after testing had been completed that the bridge was officially opened. The official opening ceremony took place on 31 May 1878, with a train of distinguished passengers travelling up from Waverley station in Edinburgh. When it arrived at Tay Bridge station, it was greeted by Provost Robertson, who welcomed the visitors to the new facility. Bouch could unfortunately not attend, pleading urgent work on his next major project: a suspension bridge across the Forth. He was also hard at work on a new viaduct across the much smaller estuary at Montrose, using a similar structure of cast-iron piers supporting a wrought-iron deck to carry the railway across. It would also lessen the journey time to Aberdeen by removing the detour needed around the flats and marshes of the South Esk River, so making a coastal route for the train services. He did express some revealing thoughts, however, when presented with the freedom of the City of Dundee later on 9 August 1878, when he said that: '... it was a matter of regret that the Tay Bridge was built for a single line, but guided by the experience gained, the bridge across the Forth was to be made for a double line.'

Early Traffic

The official opening of the bridge created enormous demand both for goods and passenger traffic across the new structure. The official timetable started on 1 June 1878, with seven trains each way between Dundee and Edinburgh, the service commencing at 6.25 a.m. from Dundee. The journey took about two hours twenty minutes, about an hour less than the old route through Perth. The passenger traffic was artificially inflated by sightseers, who would take the round trip just for the spectacle of crossing the estuary at over 100ft. The view from the train is as spectacular now as it was then when the bridge first opened. As a direct result, the NBR attracted a very high proportion of the total trade, especially from its main rival, the Caledonian Railway. John Walker, the general manager of the NBR, estimated that his railway was carrying 84 per cent of the Edinburgh traffic, and about 60 per cent of the through traffic to Aberdeen after one year's operation of the new line. And coal transport formed a significant part of the increase in traffic, growing by 40 per cent in only six months.

But, during that first year of operation, and unbeknown to the general public, there were hints of serious structural problems with the bridge.

3
The Bridge in Use

The bridge was officially opened on 31 May 1879, some three months after inspection by the BoT. By this time the foundry at Wormit had closed and the men had moved onto other jobs, which for Bouch meant renewed effort into his project of a suspension bridge for the Forth crossing.

New rolling stock was provided for the services using the new bridge, including two relatively new express locomotives, Nos 224 and 264 (built in 1871) with massive 6ft 6in-drive wheels in a 4-4-0 configuration. There were six 0-4-2 tank engines to run goods traffic over the bridge, especially much-needed coal for the steam engines running the burgeoning jute mills of Dundee town *(3.1)*.

The price of coal dropped as a direct result of the opening of the bridge, and helped stimulate yet further growth of this unique textile industry. Regular passenger services were introduced, both long-distance and local to meet demand for quicker journey times using the new crossing. It was estimated by John Walker that the NBR captured 84 per cent of the Edinburgh-Dundee traffic and 59 per cent of the Edinburgh traffic. Commuter traffic between growing residential areas on the south bank of the Tay and Dundee grew substantially, although ferry services across the estuary still continued.

The working bridge was given the final accolade when Queen Victoria used it when travelling south from Balmoral at the end of June 1879, and Bouch was knighted shortly afterwards in the company of Henry Bessemer, the inventor of a new furnace capable of mass producing steel. In hindsight, it was a portentous meeting.

'Chattering' Tie Bars

It is one thing to build a bridge, quite another to ensure its continuing integrity. That is the role of the maintenance engineer. So who was appointed to this key position? It was Henry Noble, the man originally appointed to inspect masonry works, and who now reappears as a major character in the drama. Although Bouch himself was appointed to the role of 'looking after' the bridge, he quickly brought in Henry Noble for the demanding role of regular inspections of the structure. From his later testimony to the Court of Inquiry, it appears that he was not asked to examine the critical ironwork and concentrate on the foundations to the piers. That could not be farther from the truth, and one which recent commentators have given Noble the benefit of the doubt. Since this bridge was mainly constructed from iron piers, it seems strange that his central role has been so seriously overlooked.

(3.1) A tank engine in the high girders before ballast was laid on the wooden sleepers. The guard rail was provided to stop toppling of the train.

In fact, it is perfectly clear that Noble not only inspected the ironwork, but it was part of his contract to do so. It was he alone who gave testimony to the later Inquiry about the state of the joints in the cast-iron towers, when he was standing isolated on one of the piers in September 1878. Here is his testimony about the sound in the piers he heard as a train was passing overhead, just a few months after the bridge had been opened officially (on the tenth day of the Court of Inquiry, 19 April 1880). He had just been questioned about the work he had done on stabilising the foundations by dumping rocks around their bases:

11,404. Leaving the foundations, let us go up a little bit. Did you discover whether any of the ironwork of the bridge was getting unstable or loose? – In taking those soundings that I have spoken of, I noticed or heard a chattering of the bars.
11,405. You heard then moving or shaking? – Yes.

The questioner, Mr Trayner, chief lawyer to the Inquiry, proceeded to ask if Noble could specify where exactly the sounds originated:

11,406. Was it in the lowest tier of bars nearest the stonework of the piers that you found the bars chattering? – Generally, as far as my remembrance goes, it was something like the third or fourth tier down. I cannot positively say; such a thing might have taken place in the second tier from the top to the bottom.
11,407. Speaking from the best of your recollection, can you say whereabouts in any of those piers or columns, not the supports, you first observed that any of those bars were loose? – I cannot speak from recollection.
11,408. Were those loose bars within the high girders or without the high girders, or both? – They were both.

Noble's memory was hazy to say the least, and he had clearly taken no record of the actions he had taken at the time. Counsel then tried to focus on the cause of the chattering:

11,409. Did you examine the bars in order to see what was the matter with them, or whether they needed any repairs? – Yes.

11,410. Tell me what it was you found to be wrong with the bars on your examination of them? – I do not know whether I can explain it to you. I found that the cotters in coming together had got a little loose – there was not a sufficient width to get a good grip, and they had got a little loose.

He went on to say that he thought the cotters were too small for the hole in the bars (3.2). Apparently, they were not loose enough to be removed by hand, but when tested with a hammer, showed that they were scarcely wide enough to achieve a good grip.

He also thought that they had not been driven tight in the first place. In addition, even when he drove them home with a hammer, they still did not tension the tie bars concerned (3.3).

So, having identified defective joints in the towers, did he report the matter to anyone? No, he did not, and instead decided to remedy the situation by taking matters into his own hands.

Stop the Chattering!

Since the cotters seemed to be too small for the hole in the sling plates and tie bar (or was the hole itself too big?), Noble did what some workers do to stabilise a loose fitting: he hammered a shim into the hole to fill the gap and stop the noisy rattling. And the problem was very extensive, because he estimated that he had fixed about a 100 such joints using this method. He used wrought-iron bar of ½ by ¼inch in section (according to testimony of Henry Law given the next day at the Inquiry) and cut it into lengths. The purchases from a local ironmongers in Dundee started on 21 October 1878 with 5lbs, and continued:

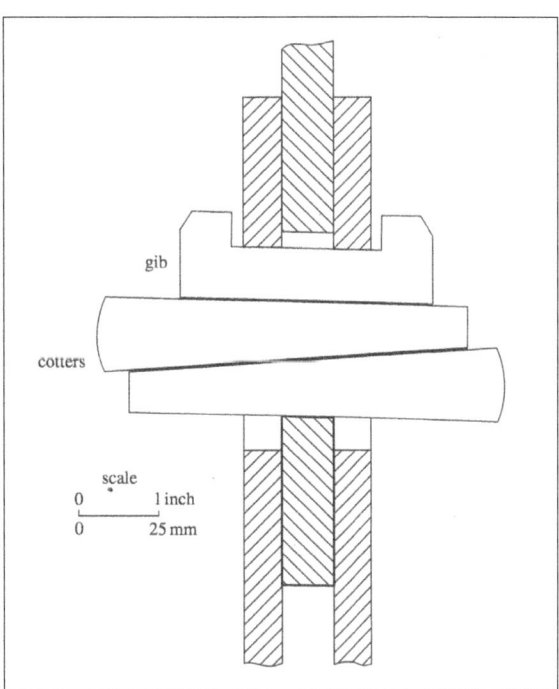

(3.2) Cross-section of a joint in the diagonal tie bars using two cotters and a gib inserted into slots cut into the bar and hangers (D.R.H. Jones).

(3.3) Section of an intact joint seen on pier No.11 (looking east).

First purchase	21 October 1878	5lbs (50 shims)
Second purchase	11 November 1878	21lbs (210 shims)
Third purchase	2 December 1878	10lbs (100 shims)

Wrought-iron bar has a density of about 485lbs per cu.ft, so it is possible to work out roughly how many shims could be made from a given weight of iron. On these figures, 1lb of iron has a volume of 3.56 cu.in, so on a section of ½ by ¼ ins, 1lb should be around 28in long. A 5lb sample should thus be about 12ft long, and this was confirmed by Noble on the witness stand. From this length, they must have only been around 3in long.

Not all the metal purchased went into shims because Noble said that some was left over, and was made into pokers. Henry Law estimated that around 150 were actually used by Noble, although the exact number could never be determined since nearly all the piers of the high girders were lost in the estuary.

Noble's main work was shoring up the pier foundations with ballast, but he also demolished the remains of one of the long girders left in the water after the 1876 accident, using dynamite bought illicitly from a local quarry. From later testimony given by Thomas Bouch, many of Noble's reports were disclosed and, reveal that he did indeed examine and inspect the ironwork of the bridge. For example, he found the cracked column in pier No.10 of the high girders and bound it with four hoops of wrought iron, reporting what he had done to Bouch in one of his many letters to the engineer in charge of the bridge. His denials of his inspection duties for the iron was being economical with the truth, perhaps in an effort to deny his role in the catastrophe.

Painting the Bridge

One important maintenance task was the painting needed to give the bridge some protection against corrosion. The cast-iron columns had been given a thin preliminary coat of black bitumen at the Wormit foundry, but were exposed to the elements both while waiting to be used and when in position on the bridge. They had been painted after construction, but the decision was made to repaint the whole structure in the summer of 1879. Red lead was apparently chosen, a common paint for bridges both then and now (such as the Golden Gate and Forth bridges). The NBR board had wanted to paint the structure white, probably in accordance with Hutchinson's wishes, but agreed to the alternative proposal.

Painters of bridges are well placed to observe a structure at close hand, as had transpired at the Dee Bridge over thirty years before. Indeed, their evidence given to the Inquest in Chester was important in establishing the vertical movement of the cast-iron girders while trains were passing. It was to be no different on the much larger Tay Bridge, as became clear later during the official Inquiry into the disaster. To paint such a big structure as the 2-mile-long bridge required a large crew (about thirty men and boys), and many of them were questioned during the Inquiry in the first few days after the disaster.

Contractor

In fact, the first to be questioned, David Pirie, had only estimated the cost of painting as an independent contractor, but was able to examine a considerable part of the structure. He lost the contract, but gave valuable evidence about the state of the bridge to the Inquiry. He was on the bridge for three days in the spring of 1879. He felt the vibrations of an oncoming train when standing in the northern part of the high girders:

4572. At that point you say you could feel the vibration of the bridge when the train came upon it at the south end? – Yes
4573. Would you describe whether the vibration you felt was a slight vibration or a violent vibration? – It was slight as the train entered the bridge, and it gradually increased until it came with a waving vibration until it passed.
4574. You felt a wavy motion of the bridge before the train came up to you? – Yes.

On further questioning, he gave more information:

4584. Had the train, when it actually came up to the point, any effect in steadying the lattice work, or did it still shake as the train actually went past it? – Yes, as far as my recollection goes, it vibrated extremely.
4585. Was that vibration not only visible to the eye but audible to the ear? – Yes, both.
4586. Would you describe it as a violent vibration? – At times it was more so than others.
4587. How do you account for that – what was it that made it greater at times than at others? – It must have been the speed of the train.

(3.4) Shims similar to those which Noble used to stop the loose cotters rattling in their joints.

So the evidence of Pirie gave the first hint that all was not what it seemed on the bridge when trains passed over. He admitted in cross-examination that he was only about 4ft from the moving train as it passed him, so perhaps he could have mistaken the turbulence from the train for movement of the bridge itself? Only other witnesses could clarify his statements, on this the fifth day of the Inquiry, in February 1880.

Bridge Movement

There followed a sequence of painters who had been employed in actually painting the bridge, so were stationed for considerable lengths of time on the towering piers of the high girders. The next witness was Peter Robinson, who had worked on the bridge for four or five weeks in the summer of 1879, but only at the south end of the high girders. He said in examination:

> 4646. *What effect had the passing of a train on the bridge?* – We felt the bridge shake very much whenever a train passed.
> 4647. *When you felt it shaking were you on the bridge itself or on scaffolding which had been put on the bridge?* – Both.
> 4648. *Did you feel the shaking equally whether you were on the bridge or on the scaffolding?* – I think as near as possible just about equally.
> 4649. *What kind of motion was it which the train in passing produced upon the bridge?* – It just made us jump up and down whenever a train passed on the bridge.

He insisted that it was only an up-and-down movement, but they still needed to tie their tools down for fear of losing them. Peter Donegay was an apprentice painter, aged nineteen, who worked in the high girder section for three months. He also needed to secure his paint pots when trains passed, but had felt a sideways movement in the high girders:

> 4776. *Was there any other motion beside the up-and-down motion that you felt when a train passed?* – No, but when a train was coming onto the large girders at the south end we were at the north end, and we felt it shake before it came onto the large girders; it went backwards and forwards – east and west.
> 4777. *You felt the bridge going eastward and westward from side to side?* – Yes.
> 4778. *As the train was coming up?* – Yes.
> 4779. *Which was the strongest movement, up and down, or from side to side, as the train went past you?* – Up and down.
> 4780. *Was the movement from side to side a strong movement also?* – Yes.
> 4781. *Did that happen every time a train went past?* – Yes.

Here was the first solid evidence for side-to-side movement of the structure when a train was passing over the bridge. Support for this evidence came with the very next witness called, David Dale, a seaman who had also worked on the bridge for three months. He recalled that the movement was very strong and he added some details about his paint pots:

> 4843. *But if you had it (the paint pot) up upon the girders it was not secure I suppose?* – When I was upon the top of the high girders on the top of the plates, if you put the paint pot sometimes very near empty, and sometimes half full, when it was very nigh empty, I have seen it shift about 3 inches with the dirling.

The term 'dirling' is a Scottish word for a 'tingling vibration'. He also remembered that the sideways motion was greatest in the northern part of the high girders, and depended on the speed of the trains. The greater the speed, the greater the movement. As with the other painters, he felt the movement when the train was many piers away as a kind of snaking motion.

Missing Bolts

John Evans was painting the high girders as well, and was able to comment on the state of some of the diagonal tie bars. He had noticed that some of the bolt holes were empty, and as a consequence some tie bars were hanging freely:

4896. Can you give us any idea of how many of these rivets you found without heads? – A very large number.

4897. Which had had heads at some time? – The could be no mistake about that; the remnant was left.

4898. Could you tell by looking at what was in the rivet hole that something had been there originally was not there then? – Yes, had parted.

4899. Do you say that there were a good many of those? – A good many; some of those bars were hanging off altogether, hanging down, displaced altogether, all clear of it.

4900. In consequence of the want of those rivet heads? – In consequence of the want of the rivet heads.

4901. How many bars did you see in that condition? – Well, to the best of my knowledge I think I saw two hanging off in that way, two of those diagonal bars.

Now this transcript is a little confusing because rivets were only used on the girder spans themselves, and not in the cast-iron towers. But it seems from the questions which followed that counsel should have been talking about bolts rather than rivets:

4902. As I understand you, two of the diagonal bars that were there for the purpose of supporting the vertical columns were off? – Yes.

Having clarified the point, Counsel Trayner proceeded to another issue which all the workers on the bridge had mentioned. They had all seen quantities of rivets and screws lying loose on the bases of the piers. They assumed that they had simply been discarded by the fitters who made the final joints, but a more sinister explanation suggested that they had broken free from the joints and dropped onto the bases after the bridge had opened for traffic. When asked about bridge motion when trains were passing, Evans talked about lateral oscillations which could be felt and seen in a pail of water. He faced some very hard questions because of the seriousness of his allegations, especially the damaged diagonal tie bars. Trayner, in re-examination, showed him various photographs of the remains of the bridge taken after the disaster and asked him to identify the parts concerned, a task he found difficult. However, he did say that the tie bars at pier No.3 (each of the piers of the fallen bridge were renamed in sequence from the south by the tribunal) were all slack. In fact, he had named pier No.10 in his testimony, but numbered the piers from the north, so it was pier No.3 he was probably referring to in his evidence. When asked whether he had informed Noble about the problem of loose or free tie bars, he admitted that he had not, an admission he shared with most of the other painters.

John Nelson was the next witness to be called and, after mentioning loose bolts used for the track sleepers, recalled having seen a cracked column in the high girder section. It had been banded to protect its integrity, so presumably was the same one mentioned by Noble in his own testimony later on in the proceedings. He gave yet more credence for the wave motion produced by a fast train:

5159. There was a distinct wave motion several girders before it reached you? – Yes.

5160. Was the girder which was just left behind by the train the one that for the moment shook most in your experience? – When the train had gone past the girder that it had been standing upon the girder shook most.

5161. What was it that you were alarmed at? – Different thoughts came into my head.

5162. What thoughts came into your head? – One thing that I was afraid of was being struck by anything.

5163. But the shaking of the bridge, how did that alarm you? – Just for the fear that might happen what has happened.

Such dramatic answers came only a few weeks after the bridge had fallen, and must have impressed the audience in the court. And it was a view backed up by virtually all the painters working on the bridge in the summer preceding the fall.

John Gray worked on the bridge for up to around five weeks that summer of 1879, but had only spotted one loose bolt on a tower. He had also seen fractured tie bars, having a clear recall of two such bars. At one time he had been painting the tiers on planks suspended by ropes, which started swaying from side to side as a fast train approached. At first alarmed, he became accustomed to the motion.

The Carpenter

The final witness to the state of the bridge in the summer of 1879 was Alexander Stewart. He was a joiner and had been contracted for the wooden casing for the water pipe which crossed the bridge, work which had started in May and extended to the beginning of November, or thereabouts. The pipe was situated by the track in the high girders, so he had been working near the railway for most of his time there. He recalled the vertical and lateral motion produced by a passing train, and the effect they produced:

5383. When the two movements got combined was there a severe movement of the particular place at which you were standing? – Yes, it would make an unaccustomed man feel a little strange.

5384. Not steady on his legs you mean? – Yes, that is the feeling; you felt the under part shaking under you.

5385. And you felt the shaking from side to side? – Yes.

5386. At the place where the movement was greatest, at the joining of the high and low girders, was it enough to produce alarm? – Well, I considered that it was weak there.

5387. What was weak? – That it was alarming.

5388. What was alarming? – The side movement.

5389. What did you think was weak at that place? – Well, I thought from the side movement that the columns must have given way.

Here then is the inference that the movement was caused by some weakness in the towers below the track. When pressed in cross-examination by Mr Balfour, he became accustomed to the movement, but could not measure the extent of sideways motion. On re-examination by Mr Trayner, however, he made some interesting further observations. He had been on the bridge during strong winds, and had not noticed any serious sideways movement. It was only when trains were passing that the motion was felt. Pressed by Colonel Yolland and Mr Trayner, he finally estimated the extent of motion:

5430. Did you form any opinion at the time to what extent the deflection took place? – I would say it was considerable but I could not say exactly in inches what it was.

5431. Did you form any opinion at the time? – Yes.

5432. What was it? – I would say from two to three inches.

5433. You formed an opinion, but you cannot state what it is now? – From two to three inches.

5434. Would that two to three inches be the extreme from the motion eastwards to the motion westwards, or was it half that quantity? - Well, I could not say; it was difficult to measure, but the motion was distinct and large.

5435. And visible? – Yes.

At the conclusion of the sequence of bridge workers, a quantitative estimate of the extent of lateral sway was gained: 2–3in (or it could be 4–6in). It is hardly surprising that such motion could cause alarm when working some 100ft above the estuary. But what is even more alarming is that they became accustomed to the motion, and failed to report it to Noble or Bouch. Coming so early in the inquiry, the evidence of oscillation in such forthright terms was to make a profound influence on the tribunal.

Distinguished Passengers

But if the workers could feel the bridge moving beneath them, what was the experience of passengers on those trains using the bridge? The trains which used the bridge had carried thousands of passengers and, if the bridge had behaved as the workmen had said, there ought to be some among them who could recall any problems in their journeys. There were indeed many troubled people who had complained, but whose views had been ignored by the NBR. Some such passengers were heard by the Inquiry in the early sessions in Dundee courthouse, when impressions were still very fresh in mind.

Provost Robertson

One of those passengers was William Robertson, Provost of Dundee, who was a regular commuter across the new bridge. He lived within sight of the bridge at Newport on the south bank of the Tay, and was able to time the crossing when he travelled. It was a simple matter to use the seconds' hand on his pocket watch to make the observations. He was concerned at the train speeds within the high girders, when he himself had experienced 'mental discomfort'. Both lateral and vertical vibrations occurred within the high girders when trains were running fast, especially when in excess of the speed limit of 25mph. Although the average speed over the whole bridge might be reasonable, north-travelling trains frequently exceeded the limit by a large margin. On one occasion, for example, he measured an average overall of about 25mph from shore to shore, but a peak of about 36mph in the high girders. And it was not an aberration, but reached regularly on the 7.13 a.m. and 8.35 a.m. trains from Newport. The highest speed he had clocked was about 43mph, well in excess of the speed limit.

He was able to elaborate some details of his experiences, suggesting at one point that the reason for the high speeds was that the local train which he used was often held up by the Aberdeen express. As a result, the driver crossed the bridge at speed to make up for lost time. In cross-examination, he was questioned very closely by Mr Balfour about train motion within the high girders:

3287. You said, I think, that what you found uncomfortable was the vibration, both vertically and laterally? – Yes.
3288. Would you kindly describe the vibration, first the vertical and then the lateral? Can you give us any idea of what you consider the limit of distance of the vertical vibration to have been? – I could not very well tell you. I could not indicate any measurement, and I could not very easily describe the impression that the vertical vibration produced upon my mind, but I should say that if it was possible for you to conceive the train lifting bodily from the rails, that is to say leaping from the rails with a sort of bounding movement, that would indicate the impression produced.

It is remarkable that his description tallies very closely with the motions described to the tribunal by the painters. However, such testimony faced an obstacle: how could a passenger distinguish between the vibrations of the train on the track from movement of the bridge? Robertson insisted that he could distinguish between the two motions:

3293. Could you distinguish the lateral movement of the carriages? – Yes, very distinctly.
3294. Can you give us any idea to an inch, how much the bridge might be moving laterally? – No.
3295. Would it be a matter of an inch or inches? – It might be an inch, or it might be two inches.

So, even the amount of lateral movement concurs with the guesstimates of the painters. And in re-examination, he reasserted his evidence about the vertical movement:

3328. had you any doubt at the time that the vertical was the result of the bridge's motion? – None.
3329. The peculiar motion that you have described as a bounding motion was one which would not have happened on a solid basis? – No.
3330. I suppose it resembled the spring or swing that one feels in walking along a suspension bridge? – Yes.

Robertson disclosed that although he had bought a season ticket in November 1879, he relinquished the right to travel north on the bridge, using the ferry instead. He had done that just before Christmas, on 18 November 1879. He had complained about the speed of the trains to the stationmaster at Dundee not just once, but twice, but no action appeared to have been taken.

The very next witness was Thomas Baxter, another commuter from Newport to Dundee, a companion to Robertson on the day he took specific timings of the journey. He confirmed Robertson's story, and gave up travelling by the bridge immediately afterwards. He had felt alarmed by the speed, but had not noticed the vibrations. It was the speed at which the train was going, and the way the girders flashed past which was perturbing. Another passenger, George Hume, had also estimated high speeds of about 35mph, but had never felt vibrations of the kind which had frightened Robertson. However, the following witness, Alexander Hutchison, supported Robertson's evidence in a most interesting way.

As an architect living at Broughty Ferry near Dundee, he worked in both Tayport and Newport, and used the bridge about twice a week in the summer of 1879. He had timed a main line train crossing the 2-mile distance from south to north in four minutes on the Saturday before the bridge fell, giving a mean speed of around 30mph. However, he had also timed local trains which took three and a half minutes, giving a mean of 34mph. The speed had worried him:

3592. You say this speed made you uncomfortable? – Yes.
3593. Mentally or physically? – Mentally.
3594. You apprehended risk or danger? – I did.
3595. From what? – From the movement of the girders.

The feeling was greatest in the high girders, and he went on:

3599. I suppose the vertical motion is quite observable? – It was quite noticeable, much more than the lateral motion.
3600. A distinct bounding movement? – Yes, you felt as if the carriage floor rose up beneath you, just as you feel sometimes in coming to the foot of an incline, you feel a sort of impulse while the train seems to rise.
3601. And you felt the same motion coming through the high girders to such an extent as to make you uneasy? – Yes.

He also faced the same objections put by counsel as before to Robertson, as to how he could distinguish between motion of the train alone and that made by the bridge. But it was his comments on the lateral oscillations were more interesting:

3615. You were in the habit of crossing the bridge occasionally, I suppose, from the time it opened? – About a month after it opened I crossed it first.
3616. Was the oscillation of the bridge more marked in your later experience than at first? – Yes.
3617. (The Commissioner) The oscillation or the vibration? – Both, I should say.
3618. (Mr Trayner) Did you form any opinion as to the cause of that increase in the oscillation and vibration as the bridge got older? – I imagined that it was mainly due to the increased speed of the trains.
3619. What I meant to put to you was this: Did it ever occur to you that the oscillation or vibration, especially the oscillation of the bridge, arose from its getting looser than it had been when it was originally screwed up? Do not take that from me, but did that ever occur to your mind before? – I imagined that it might be due to something of that kind.

Here then, is a preliminary expression of one possible explanation of why the bridge fell, before any detailed evidence from Noble or the painters. It was so important that Mr Balfour returned to the topic in his cross-examination:

3682. Did you ever suggest to any of the officials of the company that the bridge was getting loose? – No, certainly not.
3683. If you had thought it was getting loose, would it not have been a proper thing to give them a hint of it to screw it up? – I should require to have been convinced before I took such a step.
3684. Has not the idea of its getting loose grown up in your mind after the bridge fell? – No.
3685. Do you still think it would have been right if you had seriously thought that the bridge was getting loose to suggest that to those who might tighten it up? – The mere fact of the oscillations being repeated so frequently on the bridge had a tendency to loosen it, that was all I knew.
3686. But you did not think it was loosened to the extent of danger? – I did.

Local Editor

One other distinguished passenger was to give evidence the following day. It was John Leng, editor of the local newspaper, the *Dundee Advertiser*. He lived in Newport and commuted across the bridge twice a day. Although he had not timed the trains, his impression was that some trains going from south to north exceeded the speed limit. There was talk of trains racing the ferry across the estuary. He estimated that the speed was between 30 and 40mph, well above the speed limit set by General Hutchinson when he had approved the bridge in February 1878. And he had felt a motion not experienced on a railway on solid ground:

4441. Was the motion vertical or lateral or both? – Without using scientific terms, I think it might be described as a prancing motion.
4442. It was a motion involving rise and fall? – Yes; a bounding or prancing motion, something like that.
4443. Was it a motion which you have ever experienced in a railway running along a solid basis? – I have felt very similar motions – at least I have an impression that they were very similar motions – in going down a steep incline in a hilly district, such as that of the Caledonian in Dumfriesshire, or the Northwestern of Kendal.

He had also felt a lateral motion but had thought it might be the motion of the carriage rather than that of the bridge itself. He had not felt alarmed by the motion. However, he was aware that other passengers were alarmed, including some ladies, and expressed his opinion to the stationmaster at Dundee, as well as Mr Noble, inspector of the bridge. He had mentioned it twice to Noble:

4468. Kindly tell me upon what subject it is that you spoke to him (Noble), and what was it you said? – In crossing over in a boat late one evening, I believe it was, I mentioned to him that Mr Robertson and myself had been speaking about the velocity of the trains; and I suggested to him whether he should inquire of Sir Thomas Bouch whether or not it would be practicable to have an automatic register at each of the signal cabins which would record the passing of every train from end to end.

Noble apparently mentioned it to Bouch, but nothing more happened because the conversations took place in December 1879, just before the bridge fell.

Official Response

Since complaints about speeding trains had been made, it was only natural that the recipient of those complaints should be examined. It was the stationmaster, James Smith. He had seen Mr Robertson twice, as well as Mr Leng, when they had complained about the trains. He recalled that the last time he saw the men was in December 1879, a few weeks before the bridge fell. He had mentioned the problem to the locomotive drivers, who had all received copies of the NBR Regulations stipulating a 25mph speed limit on the bridge. He had warned them of instant dismissal if the speed limit was breached. After speaking with the gentlemen, he had travelled on several trains, apparently without the drivers' knowledge, and timed their journeys from cabin to cabin on the northward run. He recorded times of five, five and a half, and six minutes, equivalent to 24, 22 and 20mph respectively. But it was put to him, if the average was greatest at 24mph, the trains must have been travelling faster in the high girders if they were only travelling at walking speed (c.2mph) to pick up the baton at the signalman's cabin. They would have been accelerating up the long gentle gradient of about 1 in 350 leading to the summit within the high girders. The stationmaster could not respond to this critical question, and had not measured the maximum speed reached by trains, especially in the high girder section of the bridge. The oscillations and vibrations in that section had never been mentioned by Robertson or Leng, and he had felt none when travelling. He had not mentioned the complaints to any higher authority.

In addition to travelling the northbound trains several times, Mr Smith had also been on the bridge when trains were passing. He had felt a vertical motion, or tremor, several spans away from the approaching train as a wavy motion, but there was never any lateral movement in the bridge. When examined by Mr Balfour's counsel for the NBR, he insisted that trains never exceeded the speed limit. This was a critical point because it directly contradicted the evidence of the several passengers who had given evidence to the tribunal, and Mr Trayner returned to it in re-examination:

3928. You know Mr Robertson, and Mr Robertson you thought had fallen into error? – I did think so.
3929. Was not he likely to be able to check the time of the train if he was standing with his watch in hand? – I think he might have done it.
3930. If he stood with his watch in his hand and watched the time the trains entered the high girders, and watched the time to a second when they left, do you not think that he is very likely to be correct? – It is something almost unprecedented.
3931. Just answer the question. Do you think the Provost, standing with his watch in hand from the time the train entered the high girders till it went out, was likely to be correct in the result of his observation? – I should say that he was quite capable of taking notes.

Mr Smith was clearly under severe pressure on the stand to justify his position. On the point about average and maximum speeds, he was asked the key questions:

3971. Therefore they might have been going 45mph between the high girders, provided they went slower at the beginning or at the end? – (No answer)
3972. Then, if so, the Provost, Mr Robertson, might have been right? – So far as I have checked.

The stationmaster had been grilled very thoroughly on the issue of excessive speeds and, effectively admitted that the passengers were correct in their estimation of maximum speed. But by this time, in December 1879, matters had advanced too far and tragedy was to follow within a few days of the complaints.

Queen Victoria

Queen Victoria herself crossed the bridge at the end of June 1879 when returning from Balmoral to London. The train travelled at half-speed across the bridge, after speeches by local worthies at the Tay Bridge station. Fortunately the weather was calm for the trip across, the train was travelling south rather than north, and nothing untoward happened. It was obvious that no one was in the least bothered by the complaints from northbound passengers, and even less by rumours of strange oscillations from workers on the bridge (if the rumours had crossed the class divide). Things might have been different if the Queen had travelled at 'normal' speeds in the opposite direction, in stormy weather. She had many things on her mind that summer and autumn, with bad news from her favourite Prime Minister, Benjamin Disraeli, about the state of trade, the Irish problem, the condition of the economy (especially farming) and bad news from the edges of her Indian Empire. The situation in Afghanistan was turning sour, and was about to worsen. But she obviously enjoyed the trip across the new bridge, and Bouch was knighted shortly afterwards for his efforts.

Bridge Deterioration

The evidence which emerged during the start of the Inquiry in Dundee about the steadily deteriorating condition of the bridge in the high girder section was devastating. The stories told by the passengers of the strange movements of the high girders cannot have been restricted to the few individuals who complained to the stationmaster. And there was some clear evidence that the condition of the high girders had worsened noticeably during the summer and autumn of 1879. Alexander Stewart expressed the view that the motion had progressively increased while he had been using the bridge, for example. However, the testimony of the passengers might be (and was) questioned, especially concerning the problem of distinguishing carriage movement from that probably emanating from the bridge structure itself.

The evidence from the painters was unequivocal. Their testimony was almost unanimous in describing the effect of a train travelling fast through the high girders. It produced a bounding motion, a combination of vertical and lateral movement of the girders produced by movement of some kind in the cast-iron piers supporting those giant girders. So the passengers were probably right to talk about the bridge moving above and beyond vibration of the carriages as it moved along the track. The motion appeared to be at its most severe in the high girders, and when the speed of the approaching train was highest. No such movement was observed by Bouch and Hutchinson when they observed the effects of very much heavier trains moving at deliberately high speeds through the high girders. The bridge had therefore become unstable in the period from February 1878 to the summer of 1879.

The explanation for the problem lay with loosening of the diagonal tie bars observed by Mr Noble in the autumn of 1878, when he first heard the joints on the tie bars chattering. By hammering 3in lengths of iron bar into the joint, he effectively stopped any sound but locked the joints into a position where no tension was being brought to bear by those diagonals. That left any tie bars which had not loosened to bear any extra loads.

The bridge had opened in the summer of 1878 to much rejoicing and euphoria. An increasing amount of traffic had been diverted onto the bridge from newly built connection lines and captured a large proportion of the east coast, through traffic as well as much local commuter traffic. Goods traffic, too, increased, as cheap Fife coal was delivered to the burgeoning factories of Dundee. There can be no doubt that trains often exceeded the speed limit recommended by General Hutchinson, and this brought extra loads onto the high girder section of the bridge. By the time people began to complain, it was already too late to mount any effective remedial measures before Christmas. Bouch and Noble had one last chance to examine the bridge because Noble had found cracks in two columns in pier Nos 73 and 76 of the low girders. He bound them with four wrought-iron hoops and Bouch inspected them just before Christmas Eve. This was the last time the two were to meet before the catastrophe.

4
Disaster Strikes

The Christmas break from Christmas Day 1879 to the New Year of 1880 is traditionally a holiday period nowadays, although in the Victorian period most workers will have been employed in the factories and other workplaces. However, the railways allowed travel at any time of the year and it was (and it is now) a time to travel and visit relatives. Sunday would have been a good day to travel with all the workplaces closed, and that particular Sunday, 28 December 1879, would have been attractive in Scotland for travelling to celebrate the New Year, a public holiday which has been traditionally celebrated north of the border. Both local and express trains were scheduled to use the Tay Bridge that day, despite the stormy weather that built up later on. There was nothing unusual in storms in the winter months, especially from Atlantic depressions which blew in from the west. In fact, the day started quietly, the sky was clear and the estuary smooth. The ferries crossed the estuary without problem. The skies darkened early this far north, with dusk at around 4.00 p.m., with a full moon expected later.

But a storm was racing in from the west, the wind had freshened, and the barometer had dropped suddenly, heralding a deep depression. A gale was raging by 6.00 p.m., and starting to cause some damage. The stationmaster, James Smith, was called out by the locomotive superintendent, who reported that loaded coal wagons were being pushed along by the wind in the goods yard. *(4.1)*

He arrived at the station at 6.30 p.m. and found that three wagons had been driven 300 to 400 yards along their tracks. He also found that much of the glass roof had been blown in by the wind driving into the mouth of the station, which faced due west. The local Newport train which had just crossed the bridge was shunted back close to the stairs so that passengers for the return trip would not have to cross the open and dangerous platforms. But he made no decision to stop the express due next at the station.

The Penultimate Train

The penultimate train ever to pass over the old Tay Bridge was the local running into Dundee from Tayport. It emerged that the train had experienced some difficulties in crossing the bridge. The train had left Tayport at 5.50 p.m., and comprised five carriages and two brake vans. They reached the Tay Bridge just after 6.00 p.m., the wind was blowing hard from the west and, according to the driver, Alexander Kennedy, crossed normally. He thought that the brakes had been applied just before reaching the curve into the station, and had noticed nothing unusual in the journey. He had been standing on the windward side of the locomotive. But his passengers gave a quite different story of that journey.

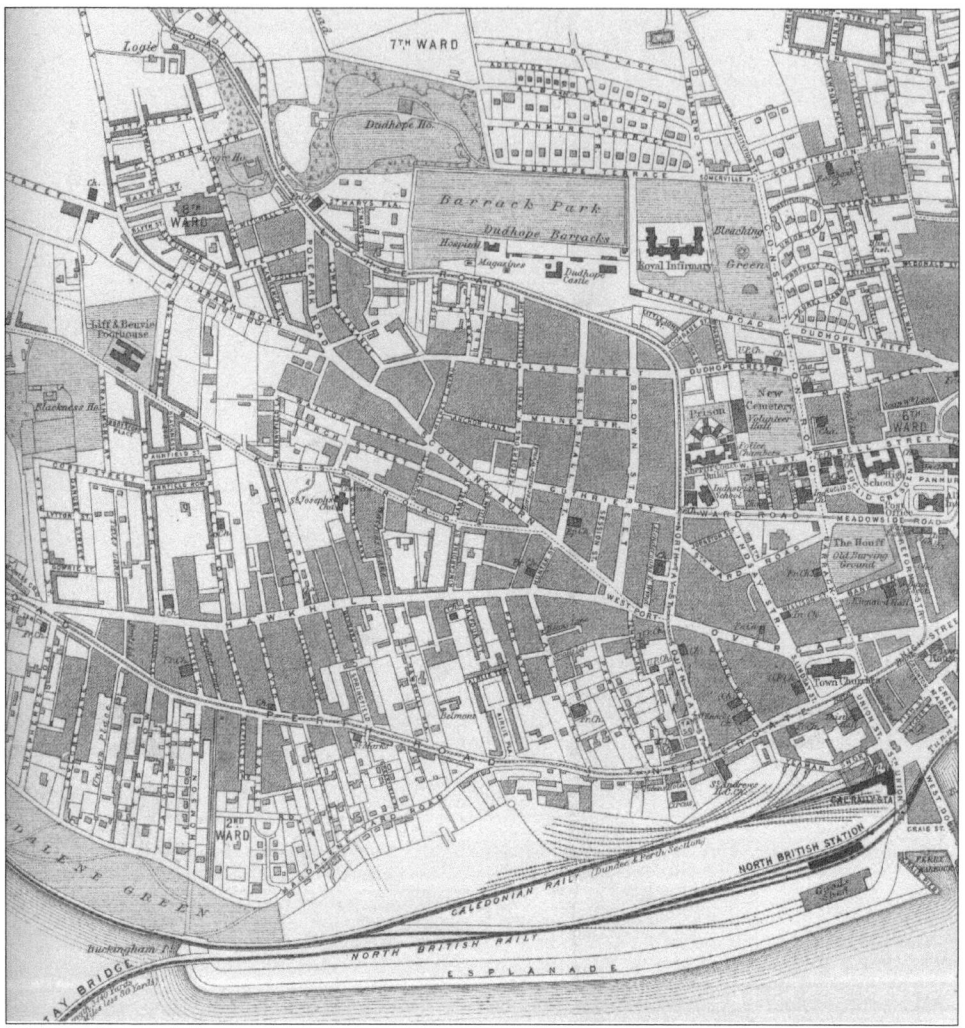

(4.1) Plan of the dockside and railway network near the centre of Dundee (Bartholomew map of c.1882).

The first to be questioned after Kennedy was the guard of the train, Robert Shand. He had first noticed sparks coming from the wheels of a carriage in front, well before they had reached the high girders. The sparks were flying from the east side of the train. He immediately applied the brakes but, instead of stopping the sparks, they started coming from the brake van as well. He had thought a broken axle might have caused the sparks, which is why he had applied the brakes. Then he thought that it was the wind pushing the wheels against the guard rail. However, the sparks ceased as soon as they started to drop into the curve leading to the station. James Black, who worked in the parcels office at Dundee station, was in the same van that night. He confirmed Shand's evidence, and added that the carriages and vans were shaking from side to side, as he thought it, with the wind:

4046. *What was the effect of the gusts of wind upon the carriage? – They seemed to tilt it over in a manner.*
4047. *Whether it was the wind on the bridge affecting the bridge, and the bridge tilting over, or whether it was the wind upon the carriage which tilted it over, you cannot say? – I cannot say.*

More details of the incident were produced in cross-examination. He had seen the carriages tilting over only when looking out of the west window of the van, and he did not feel the tilt on the carriage. But had the wheels of the carriage left the rails?

4080. Can you describe how much of the carriage would be out of the perpendicular? – My opinion at the time was that it had not given way more than the springs would allow, seeing that the pressure of the carriage was thrown over on the east side.
4081. Is that your opinion still? – Yes.
4082. You do not think that the bridge was out in perpendicular? – No.

4099. You are sure that each time you looked out of the west window you could tell that the carriage was rising and falling again, at least to the extent to which the spring would give? – Yes.
4100. Can you tell me whether or not it was just the motion that would have been produced by the bridge itself swaying? – I cannot say.

So the issue of whether or not the wheels of the carriages actually left the rails remained uncertain. If the carriages had tilted only to the extent of the springs, then the wheels were still on the rails when sparking occurred. Sparks could be produced by the wheels tilting against the inner guard rail, or perhaps by the wheel being pressed against the rail on which it was riding, or even by the whole bridge moving laterally. In further cross-examination he could not be sure about the wheels:

4121. When you looked out could you see that the wheels of the carriage were not actually lifted from the rails? – I could not see.

John Buik had been a fellow passenger in the guard's van that night, and corroborated much of the earlier testimony. He had seen flashes of sparks rather than a continuous effect. The guard thought that the carriages were tilting against the guard rail, and applied the brake by screwing the handle down. It appeared to have little effect on the speed of the train. He also showed a red light on the east side of the van, which cannot have been seen by the driver, who was leaning out on the west side of the locomotive. He noticed the van shaking towards the east as well as an up-and-down motion, which started about halfway along the low girders. The driver was recalled to elaborate his testimony and faced detailed questioning about his speed. He said he was going from 23 to 25mph, not more, and indeed the tank engine was not capable of a speed greater than 30mph. He was also questioned about speeds across the bridge prior to that night and insisted that he never exceeded regulation speeds.

With the gale reaching its height, railway officials would presumably warn following trains not to attempt the crossing given the problem experienced by the local service. But it was not to be.

The Last Train over the Bridge

The next train to cross the bridge was the last one ever to use the structure. It was the Edinburgh express. Passengers from Edinburgh would have caught the train at Waverley station at 4.15 p.m., and travelled to Granton on the south shore of the Firth of Forth. The ferry trip lasted about half an hour and passengers and baggage would catch a new train waiting for them at Burntisland on the north shore. The driver of the massive 4-4-0 locomotive was David Mitchell, and the rest of the train consisted of tender, five carriages and a guard's van. While waiting at the station, the wheels of the train were tapped to check for cracks, a common procedure given the problem of fatigue (just two years previously there had been a major disaster near Oxford when a wheel broke and thirty-four passengers were killed in the ensuing derailment). The same inspector also checked the axle boxes, springs and couplings.

The train was fitted with Westinghouse brakes, apart from one second-class carriage. The Oxford disaster had been made much worse by the lack of such brakes. The wheels were to be tapped again at Leuchars junction.

The train left at 5.27 p.m., crossing Fife at a leisurely pace for an express since it stopped at fourteen stations on the way to the bridge. It arrived at Leuchars junction at just before 7.00 p.m., one of the last stops, and one of the passengers alighted for a coach for St Andrews, but re-entered the train when no coach appeared, intending to stay overnight in Dundee. Just before the train departed however, the coach arrived and the lucky passenger left for St Andrews. There were now at least seventy-five passengers and crew aboard the train.

The final stop before the bridge was St Fort station where the tickets of the Dundee passengers were collected. The ticket collector would later recall that several passengers asked him jokingly whether the bridge would be all right on such a night, according to a report in the *Illustrated London News*. One man was travelling with his children, one of them a babe-in-arms, and there were several other children accompanying their parents. The fully laden train arrived next at the signal cabin just south of the bridge to collect the baton. The signalman was Thomas Barclay, twenty-nine years old and living in a cottage just below the box. He was there with John Watt, a foreman surface worker with the railway. The train arrived at the box at 7.09 p.m. and had slowed down to around 3mph for the baton. After the train had left for the bridge, Barclay rang the signal bell at 7.13 p.m. to Dundee to show that the train had passed and was on the bridge. It was acknowledged by one beat, then two and a final bell by the signal box on the north side of the bridge. There had been no instructions to stop trains moving onto the bridge, despite the problems of the previous train through. While waiting for the next train, he raked out the ashes of the stove and prepared a new fire:

207. Then did anything happen to call your attention to something unusual? – This man Watt was standing looking at the cabin door; the door was shut, but Watt was looking, watching the train across the bridge, and after I had done all that I have said, and just when I came up from the fire, he said that there was something wrong with the train, he was sure; that he had seen a great flash of fire and the tail lamps disappear.

208. Was Watt put about at all; did he tell you with any degree of excitement? – No; he was not excited, but I did not believe him.

Barclay thought that the train had simply gone from sight when it descended the final curve into Dundee, so he continued preparing the fire, going out to fetch the coals. The train would reappear as it approached the Tay Bridge station. But the lights did not reappear, and Barclay must have sensed that something was wrong. He checked his signal to the north signal box at Dundee, but got no answer. Other connections with the box also failed to elicit a response, and he then knew that there was a serious problem. He and Watt left the signal box and tried to follow the rail line to the bridge, but the wind was too high and they returned to the box after 20 or 30 yards. Although the wind was whistling, the box was unaffected by the storm, despite being exposed to its full force at the same level as the bridge itself.

Watt was simply in the box as a friend and neighbour, helping to pass the lonely hours. It was curiosity that led him to watch the receding train:

319. And while Barclay was attending to his other duties you saw something that startled you for the time? – Yes.
320. What was it? – I saw fire from the train.
321. Was that while she was still running the permanent way? – Yes.
322. Where was the fire coming from? – It appeared to be coming from the wheels.

Opposite: (4.2) The headline picture of the view from the north side of the last standing pier.

The Illustrated London News

No. 2119.—Vol. LXXVI. SATURDAY, JANUARY 10, 1880. WITH TWO SUPPLEMENTS — SIXPENCE. By Post, 6½d.

THE TAY BRIDGE DISASTER: VIEW OF THE BROKEN BRIDGE FROM THE NORTH END.—SEE PAGE 27.

328. How far would the train be from you when you saw these sparks; how far had she passed the cabin? – Not exceeding 200 yards.

329. That was when you first saw the sparks? – Yes

330. How long did you continue to see the sparks? –- As far as the train went.

The sparks lasted for about three minutes, or around three quarters of a mile along the bridge from the cabin, by which time the train should have entered the high girders, and then the tail lights of the train suddenly disappeared. Just before she disappeared, there was a great flash of fire. He heard nothing except the howling of the wind. He then told Barclay what he had seen. The signal box was buffeted by the gusting of the wind, but was undamaged. The distance to the high girders was 900 yards, so on his reckoning, the train should have been several spans within the high girders when it disappeared. As to the source of the sparks, he recalled that they were coming only from the east side of the train, and he thought that it was the side of the wheel being forced against the rail which caused them:

427. Did you make up your mind at the time whether those sparks were caused by the wheels coming in contact with the rail or with the check rail, or what opinion did you form at the time as to the cause of the sparks? – I formed the opinion that with the wind blowing towards the east side the wheel was hard upon the rail causing the fire.

428. I am speaking of the time when you saw it 200 yards off, did you form any idea of what caused the sparks at that time? – The wind pressing the train onto the east side.

429. Pressing the wheels against the rails on the east side? – I formed that opinion.

On further detailed questioning, Watt was sure that the sparks had not been caused by the brakes being applied since, if they had, sparks would have been produced by both wheels. A broken spring would produce sparks well above the rails. And he thought that the great flash might have been made by the carriages rubbing along the side of the girders. That thought was to be developed by others into a more sophisticated theory of why the bridge fell, by others later in the Inquiry. Events seen at such a large distance away (three quarters of a mile) must also make for some uncertainty in what was seen, a problem to be faced with all the eyewitnesses of the accident.

What was certain was that a very large part of the bridge had fallen, as was observed by the engine shed supervisor who clambered to the edge of the intact part of the bridge *(4.2)*. The view he saw became an image that was to echo around the world.

Witnesses from Magdalen Green

But had any others seen the accident? The obvious other witness was the signalman in the north box. Henry Somerville was questioned next on this first day of the Inquiry. There had been five trains going south over the bridge that Sunday, and five trains going north, excluding the Edinburgh express. All had been clear and only slightly breezy till late afternoon. Then the wind had risen sharply, to such an extent that the chimney on the cabin had been blown off, at around 6.30 p.m. He had little to add other than confirming the bells received from the south cabin. He had looked for the train when communications broke down, and seen the signal light on at around 1,200 yards from his box, on the far side of the high girders, but nothing more. The signal light was probably an open flame paraffin lamp. The box was situated at the end of the downward curve into Dundee, and he had a glancing view of the bridge.

However, there were a number of Dundee residents who were watching the bridge that night, especially those living in the high houses on the north side of Magdalen Green, and they were to give evidence to the Inquiry. Presumably, seeing trains cross over was still a spectacle to the locals, or was there serious concern about a train crossing in the storm?

The first to appear was James Lawson. He had been out walking on the Green looking towards the bridge:

794. Did you see anything that attracted your attention particularly? – Yes, we saw a mass of fire from the bridge.
795. Into the river? – Yes, on the east side of the river.
796. Was it clear at that time, or dark? – The moon was shining; it was occasionally getting between us and the bridge.

851. (Mr Barlow) When you saw that mass of fire coming down, did it fall rapidly, as a stone would fall? – No
852. It fell slowly, did it? – Gently.

The witness realised the bridge had fallen but his viewpoint slightly to the west of the line of the high girders meant that his view of the bridge was foreshortened. George Clark lived on the Green opposite the signal cabin, and was watching the bridge when the Edinburgh train was crossing. He saw it enter the high girders, but then turned round with his back to the window. He heard his brother shout from the next room, 'Look at the fire, the train is over the bridge'. When he turned around, the bridge was dark. His brother was able to provide more detail:

1002. Did you see the train come on the bridge at the south end? – Yes.
1003. Could you follow its light advancing? – Yes; I traced its lights till it entered the high girders.
1004. Follow the train from that moment till you lost sight of it altogether, what happened after you saw the train come on the bridge at the south end? – I followed the train after it came on the bridge till I should imagine it was at the third large girder.
1005. (The Commissioner) You mean the third large pier? – Yes, then it suddenly disappeared; five seconds after that I saw three sudden flashes.
1006. You say you followed it till it came to about the third pier from the south of the high girders? – Yes, then I suddenly lost sight of it.
1007 (Mr Trayner) An interval of five seconds elapsed before you saw anything else? – Yes.
1008. At the end of that five seconds what did you see? – Three sudden flashes from what I should imagine the extreme north end of the large girders.

After the three flashes of light (when he called out to his brother), he noticed that the signal lights at the south cabin were obscured for around ten seconds. He thought that it was obscured by the spray from the falling girders. They had both been approximately three quarters of a mile from the high girders (around the same distance as Watt and Barclay) and the line of the bridge would have been slightly to the east of their position. William Clark had not seen any sparking from the wheels of the train.

Alexander Maxwell lost five chimney pots (or cairns) from his roof at 7.10 p.m., and saw the fall. He was with a group of friends and they turned down the lights to watch the bridge:

953. Tell me what you saw? – The first thing that caught my attention was the signal light, a little to the north of the high girders, it was flickering – I thought that the lamp of the signal was on fire. Then almost at that moment, or shortly afterwards, I saw two lights of the engine coming onto the bridge on the south side, and I followed it on closely to the big girders, where I saw the flashing of the lights; the light would be flashes as it were (sic) passing the spars.

957. When it got to the high girders tell us what you saw? – At that time I thought I saw the lights shaken, but I suppose it would not be the case. Before it came to the big girders I thought I saw the lights shaken, but when it came to the big girders I saw, as it were, flashes passing as it would be the spars of the big girders between me and the train.

958. *You saw it coming on, but it was occasionally observed as it came past a high girder or spar?* – Yes; then it suddenly disappeared about the third or fourth spar from the south side.

959. *At the time of the disappearance did you see any fire or light?* – Not at the time, but a second or two afterwards there was a flash about two girders in advance of the train; then after that there was another light at about another two girders, all coming towards the north; then there was a third flash. Taking it roughly, it would be two girders from the north side.

Because of the importance of his observations, he was asked to repeat his evidence by Rothery, the Chair of the Inquiry. And he elaborated further. The flashes fell into the estuary to the east, and he thought from their colour that they were not friction sparks, but gas igniting by friction sparks. The bridge carried not just water but also a gas pipe for beacons affixed to each of the piers for aiding navigation at night. He thought that the whole sequence – from the loss of the train lights to the final flash – was around fifteen seconds.

Peter Barron also lost a chimney pot that night in his house overlooking the bridge. The house was around 200 yards west of the line of the bridge, and the whole bridge was visible from his vantage point:

2901. *When you came out on Sunday night to look at what had happened to your house, did you see the bridge?* – I went round when I first came out, and one chimney cairn went. I had some glass at the back side of the house, and then I found that it was blown out, and I put a stone locker or two in. I just put them in to keep the glass in. Some splits were coming down round about my ears, and I bolted. Before I went to the house I said I would go and see what the bridge was doing. I knew it was train time. I came straight across Blackness Road, a 20ft-wide road, and there was a gate belonging to Mr Hunter, and two posts, and I took one of them in my arm, and put myself in that position [describing] and kept my eye on the north end of the bridge not further than that [describing], I was in that position for a second or two, and then I saw, as I thought then, and as I think yet, something about the third or fourth girder passing into the river, as it appeared to my eye. I looked immediately behind, and then another fell, and I saw a light, as it were just a mere blink.

2923. *How long a time was there between the two falls?* – Perhaps you might count four or five seconds or more, just the time I rubbed my eyes.

2925. *After the second fall was the gap left as it is now?* – Yes, as it is now, as distinctly as you could see it in daylight; the moon shone brightly.

He went on to say that the light disappeared with the second fall, and he could not say whether it was the light of a lamp or some other flash. He had been holding the post near Blackness Road (shown in *(4.1)* as being higher than Magdalen Green and further north) while these events were unfolding before his eyes:

2956. *Had you got yourself well steadied on the post?* – Yes, for a short time.
2957. *How long did you hold on after?* – A few seconds anyway.
2958. *But how long you cannot say?* – No, perhaps it was half a minute, but I could not tell, I was rather stupefied.
2959. *What did that?* – The horrible sight before me.

2961. *How long did it take to happen?* – Not exceeding, I suppose, thirteen seconds, the whole concern.

(4.3) Contemporary etching of rescue attempts.

(4.4) The disaster scene viewed from the south side of the Tay, with Balgay cemetary on the hill at the left.

Such dramatic testimony clearly impressed the court, especially as it supported the evidence of Maxwell. The collapse of the high girders had been rather slow; lasting a matter of tens of seconds well after the train had entered the section. Although the fall was around a mile from the observers, their accounts tallied reasonably well. Despite the fierce wind at the time, the strong moonlight gave enough illumination to see the tragedy happening in slow motion.

Newport Witness

William Robertson, the Provost of Dundee who complained about the speed of the trains over the bridge, also saw the fall. He lived in Newport on the south bank of the Tay, and was watching the river for personal reasons. His son either caught the train or took the ferry on a Sunday, and he was concerned about his safety. He saw the lights of the Edinburgh train on the bridge, and saw it enter the high girders. After losing sight of the train behind an intervening building which blocked his view, he saw two columns of spray brilliantly illuminated by light – first one flash and then another. They were the girders at the north end of the bridge, from around pier No.7. He thought the flashes came from the gas lights on the bridge being overturned during the fall of the girders because the lights disappeared and the bridge went dark after the fall.

The evidence from eyewitnesses thus pointed clearly to failure having started at the south end, after the train had entered the high girders and had travelled some distance through the section. The collapse was relatively slow, giving the observers time to appreciate what was happening, suggesting that all the piers had failed sequentially and the high girders had fallen fast to create the splash of water.

Recovery Attempts

As the news of the fall spread that Sunday night, attempts were made immediately to send boats out to the scene of the tragedy. It was clear, from the sheer scale of the accident with all the high girders fallen, that the whole train had been taken with the fallen bridge. Could anyone have survived such a terrible fall from nearly 100ft into the cold waters of the estuary? Given the weather conditions, it was not until about 10.00 p.m. that the local ferry, the *Dundee*, attempted to reach the fallen bridge. Conditions in the estuary had abated, and allowed the ferry to drop a rowing boat to explore what remained of the bridge. Although there was much floating timber from the rail line around the stumps of the piers, there was absolutely no sign of life *(4.3)*.

Monday 29 December was clear and bright, enabling intensive efforts to reach the wreckage *(4.4)*.

The steam launch *Fairweather*, with a diver on board, rode up to pier No.3 of the fallen bridge to search for the train. He went down into the water south-east of the pier and almost immediately found the main girder lying on its side around 30ft from the line of the bridge. None of it was broken. He went down twice the next day, further exploring the intact girder near pier Nos 3 and 4:

2194. That was your morning dip on Tuesday; what did you do in the afternoon? – I went down to the north of No.4 pier.

2196. Did you find the girders there? – I found a girder and the first-class carriage.

This was the first sign of the missing train to be found, but on exploration it proved to be empty. He retrieved only cushions from the empty compartments, and the doors had also disappeared with one exception. That intact door was hanging by its hinges, swinging in the current. Visibility was very poor owing to the mud swept up by the tides, and Cox had

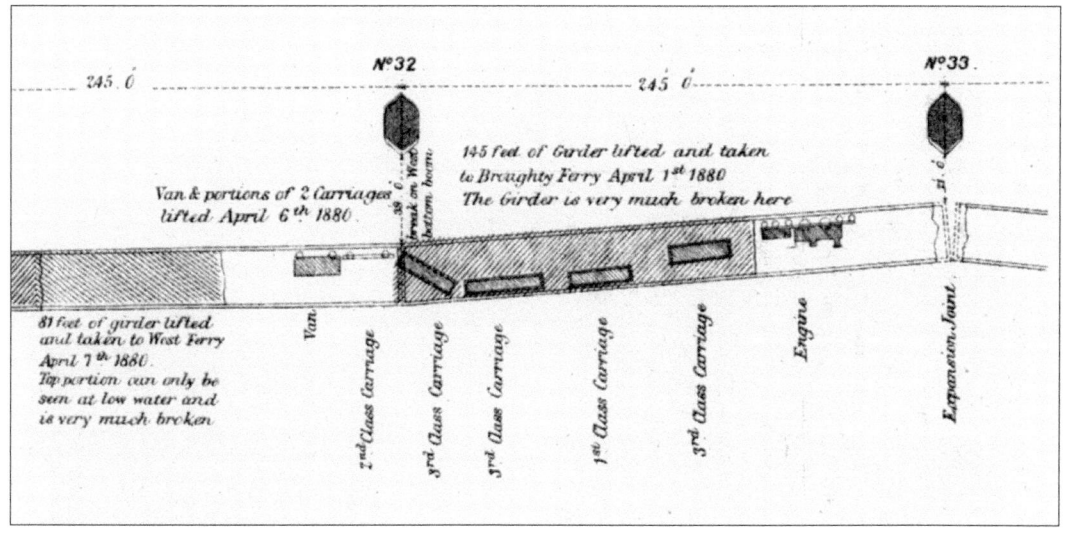

(4.5) Plan of the remains with the train lying within the span between pier Nos 4 and 5.

(4.6) The view looking south showing the side of the high girder exposed at low tide.

(4.7) The locomotive as recovered from the disaster before repairs.

to explore the damaged carriage largely by touch. As the days went by, the divers discovered more and more parts of the train, eventually allowing a plan of the remains to be drawn *(4.5)*. The main damage occurred to the brake van and rear carriage, the rest being relatively intact.

By the early spring the remains of the entire structure had been found and plotted. The largely undamaged high girders lay in a neat waveform shape very close to the bases of the piers. It was clear that the high girders were largely intact, the main damage to them being concentrated near the south end of the section. Since the waters were relatively shallow, they could be seen at low tide *(4.6)*. Lifting the girders proved difficult and, as in the earlier operation to remove the remains of the girder which fell in 1877, explosives were needed to break the structure down into smaller pieces.

The Locomotive

The locomotive No.224 was found at the head of the train and was relatively little damaged after recovery *(4.7)*. The steam had not been shut off, the brakes had apparently not been applied, and the reversing lever was six notches off from the full forward gear, as Dugald Drummond said in testimony much later in the proceedings. The first thing a driver would do in an emergency would be to shut the regulator, but since it was open and the brakes unapplied, the evidence pointed towards a sudden emergency in which the driver had no time to act.

It would be repaired and brought back into service. Owing to its weight (34 tons 12cwt), it created problems in the lifting operation, and fell back twice when the chains broke. Drivers later nicknamed it 'The Diver', having now plunged three times into the river! It eventually went back into service, and survived for many years as a working locomotive. The tender was also very heavy at 24 tons, giving a total load of 58 tons 12cwt. The total static load imposed on the bridge – including all the carriages and brake van – was estimated by Dugald Drummond, the locomotive superintendent, at 130 tons 12cwt. The actual weight may have been greater if allowance had been made for the passengers and their luggage, but of course distributed over the length of the train. That total length was approximately 254ft, so the train would have covered an entire span of the high girders of length 245ft.

5
Inquiry at Dundee

A tribunal was set up extraordinarily quickly to investigate the disaster. It was headed by Henry Rothery, Wreck Commissioner to the government, a lawyer with great experience of marine accidents and with a mathematical training. The reports of his court appeared regularly in *The Times*. He was assisted by Colonel William Yolland, Chief Inspector of Railways, and William Barlow, president of the Institution of Civil Engineers. Yolland had conducted the inquiry into the Oxford disaster of 1876, as well as many other railway accidents. W.H. Barlow had a string of structures to his credit, including bridges and buildings, one being the magnificent station at St Pancras, designed by Gilbert Scott.

They first sat on Saturday 3 January 1880, just a week after the disaster, at the Assize Court in Dundee. In addition to the Procurator Fiscal, two counsel were appointed initially, Mr Trayner for the Board of Trade and Mr J.B. Balfour for the NBR. The two were to play leading roles in the Inquiry and, not surprisingly, clashed frequently, both with one another and with witnesses. Their investigation was to be one of the most exhaustive and searching of any public inquiry, involving not just the local witnesses but some of the most distinguished scientists and engineers of the day. The latter were to appear as expert witnesses, that is, witnesses who could offer their opinions as to probable causes and other contested issues which emerged during the Inquiry. As it turned out, many witnesses of fact appearing before the court were asked for their opinions on causes, such was the shock and disbelief engendered by the disaster.

It was by far the worst accident to occur on the railway network to that date, well exceeding the recent Oxford disaster and the earlier tragedy at the Dee Bridge. A whole train had been lost, half a mile of new bridge had fallen, and the casualties were to number seventy-five, although the initial guesstimates were far larger, before a ticket count had been made, and more exact figures obtained. The initial estimates were several hundred, presumably being based on the numbers normally carried on the Edinburgh express. As *The Times*, pointed out, it was some small comfort that the tragedy had not occurred in a normal working week.

The first actions were actually taken by the solicitors acting for the various parties, especially Thorntons of Dundee, solicitors to the North British Railway. They trawled the local community for eyewitnesses, and obtained statements (or prognostications under the Scottish legal system) upon which the witnesses would be examined. These carefully hand-written documents are now housed in the Scottish National Archive in Edinburgh. Many are frustratingly brief but do give an indication of the nature of the testimony which would be delivered in open court. However, it was the searching nature of the oral examination and cross-examination by Trayner, Balfour and others which was to reveal some of the critical facts which lay behind the construction, design and maintenance of the bridge, some of which has already been revealed in previous chapters. All three Commissioners asked pointed questions of witnesses, using their own expert knowledge.

Another issue which arose on the first day of proceedings was to locate and publish the numerous plans and sectional drawings of the bridge prepared by the NBR during construction, and yet more were to be made by the Inquiry itself. But the first and most important task was a visit to the bridge itself, which was undertaken by steamer at 11.00 a.m. All the officers of the court would want first-hand knowledge of the current state of the remains so as to be able to put accurate and relevant questions to the witnesses who were to appear before them.

Initial Dundee Proceedings

The first witnesses to be called were the several eyewitnesses, signalmen and stationmaster, as well as divers on the wreckage of the bridge and witnesses who were able to give an account of the stormy conditions that night. One important task organised by the court on the third day was to arrange for the remains to be photographed:

> (Mr Trayner to the photographer): The Court desire to have a set of photographs that will show each pier and every side of it. You will also take a view from the west, and a view from the east, and the north and the south, and a photograph inside from the top of each pier, and one each side of it. In your photograph mark each pier with its number counting from the south.

This was a wise move and unprecedented for the time. Previous accident inquiries were only illustrated by line diagrams or drawings, which however useful, could not show the fine detail which might later reveal hitherto unsuspected features. In addition, they would be useful to show to witnesses so as to corroborate testimony or allow key features to be identified. The original set survives to this day at the Dundee City Library with its original captions, presumably made by the photographer William Dobson Valentine, a professional photographer from the family business in Dundee. At a later stage he was asked to take some underwater pictures of the wreckage *in situ*, but failed in his attempt.

The company were later to make a great success in the postcard business, and an archive of their work survives in the University of St Andrews. Unfortunately, the original negatives have not survived, probably because they were recycled both for the silver from the emulsion and the glass plates which could be reused. Nevertheless, the positive contact prints which survive, both from the disaster and prior to the disaster, are remarkable for their quality and detail, as pictures from previous chapters have shown. As far as is known, the positive prints from the Dundee archive are albumen prints, but it is possible that the newly invented dry plate process was used for the Inquiry pictures. The original positives are 12 x 8 inches in size and are generally in excellent condition, although do vary somewhat in quality, probably depending on whether or not the sun was shining directly on the subject, among other factors. They were taken at exposure times of several seconds, so water motion appears blurred and, in one instance, a human figure has been caught as a ghost. Other artefacts from photographic reproduction are visible on the pictures used in subsequent chapters, such as fibres from the paper. A large plate camera was used judging by the size of the prints, and the depth of focus visible in most of the photographs suggests a small aperture.

Weather Experts

One important set of witnesses heard in the early sessions of the Inquiry were local meteorologists and observers, including many seamen who had direct experience of storms. Meteorology had expanded fast as an observational science in the Victorian period with the development and widespread use of the barometer, especially Admiral Fitzroy's popular mercury barometer, but wind speed was more difficult to measure accurately since there were few instruments widely available. Interpretation of wind speed was commonly made using the Beaufort tables, where qualitative observations of the state of trees or other indicators can be correlated with wind speed *(5.1)*. It had been widely adopted, first by the Royal Navy in 1838, and the Merchant Navy in 1852, judging by a Board of Trade circular. It was actually based on experiments first performed by the civil engineer John Smeaton in 1759. He was interested in helping windmill owners to adjust their sails for different wind speeds, so he measured the pressure at different speeds and established the simple relation between the two variables. It was a simple matter to adopt it for use by ships, and so measure how much sail to use under given wind conditions.

A strong breeze, for example (Beaufort scale 6), produces a whistling sound in telegraph

(5.1) Beaufort table of wind speed on land

Beaufort force	Specification of Beaufort scale for use on land, based on observations made at land stations	Mean pressure (at standard density) on a disc $1ft^2$	Limits of speed at $33ft$ in the open
		$lbf\ ft^2$	mph
0	Calm; smoke rises vertically.	0	<1
1	Direction of wind shown by smoke drift, but not by wind vanes.	0.01	1–3
2	Wind felt on face; leaves rustle; ordinary vane moved by wind.	0.08	4–7
3	Leaves and small twigs in constant motion; wind extends light flag.	0.28	8–12
4	Raises dust and loose paper; small branches are moved.	0.67	13–18
5	Small trees in leaf begin to sway; crested wavelets form on inland waters.	1.31	19–24
6	Large branches in motion; whistling heard in telegraph wires; umbrellas used with difficulty.	2.3	25–31
7	Whole trees in motion; inconvenience felt when walking against wind.	3.6	32–38
8	Break twigs of trees; generally impedes progress.	5.4	39–46
9	Slight structural damage occurs (chimney posts and slates removed).	7.7	47–54
10	Seldom experienced inland; trees uprooted; considerable structural damage occurs.	10.5	55–63
11	Very rarely experienced; accompanied by widespread damage.	14.0	64–72
12	Widespread structural damage.	>17.0	≥73

wires, makes large branches move and use of an umbrella is difficult. It corresponds to wind speeds of 25 to 31mph. The equivalent scale for use at sea is shown in *(5.2)*, and force 6 produces some large waves with breaking foam and some spray.

(5.2) Beaufort scale for use at sea

Beaufort force	Description	Features at sea	Knots
0	calm	Sea like a mirror.	less than 1
1	light air	Ripples with appearance of scales, no foam crests.	1–3
2	light breeze	Wavelets, small, but pronounced; crests with glassy appearance, but do not break.	4–6
3	gentle breeze	Large wavelets, crests begin to break; glassy-looking foam, occasional white horses.	7–10
4	moderate breeze	Small waves becoming longer, frequent white horses.	11–16
5	fresh breeze	Moderate waves of pronounced long form; many white horses, some spray.	17–21
6	strong breeze	Some large waves, extensive white foam crests, some spray.	22–27
7	near gale	Sea heaped up, white foam from breaking; waves blowing in streaks with the wind.	28–33
8	gale	Moderately high and long waves; crests break into spin drift, blowing foam in well-marked streaks.	34–40
9	strong gale	High waves, dense foam streaks in wind, wave crests topple, rumble and roll over; spray reduces visibility.	41–47
10	storm	Very high waves with long overhanging crests. Dense blowing foam, sea surface appears white. Heavy tumbling of sea, shock-like. Poor visibility.	48–55
11	violent storm	Exceptionally high waves, sometimes concealing small and medium-sized ships. Sea completely covered with long white patches of foam. Edges of waves blown into froth. Poor visibility.	56–63
12	hurricane	Air filled with foam and spray, sea white with driving spray; visibility bad.	≥ 64

An important feature of wind is the pressure exerted on solid objects. The wind pressure increases as the square of the speed, so that doubling the wind speed quadruples the pressure. At force 6, the pressure on a 1ft-diameter disc is about 2.3 pounds per sq.ft (psf) for a maximum speed of 31mph. But at force 9 (strong gale), the wind speed rises to a maximum of 54mph. The wind pressure has increased to about 7.7psf, causing slight structural damage such as loss of chimney pots and slates from roofs. A force 10 storm will uproot trees and cause considerable structural damage on land, with a maximum wind speed of 63mph and a pressure of about 10.5psf. At sea, visibility will be poor, the sea will appear white and there will be very high waves.

So what were conditions that night on 28 December 1879? Among the early witnesses called was Captain Scott of the training ship *Mars*, moored about three quarters of a mile below the bridge. He noticed that the barometer had been dropping from about midday when it stood at 29.6in, until it reached its lowest point of 29.0in at about 7.00 p.m. A strong gale was thus indicated and he had lashed the boats:

1268. Will you describe it, how you would describe it? – We describe storms in the navy by numbers from 1 to 10, 12 would be the maximum, 1 to 12.

1269. Twelve represents the maximum strength of the wind pressure or disturbance? – Yes.

1270. On this occasion how would you describe this gale on the Tay by figures? From 10 to 11 in a squall.

1271. The whole squall made so by a continuous gale, what figure would describe that? – I should call it 10; a whole gale.

Captain Scott went on to say that he had experienced one or two storms equal to that on 28 December in the last two or three years, and at least three in the last ten years. The wind was blowing steady, with gusts every ten minutes or so. During the day the wind had shifted from south-south-west to due west at the height of the storm, at right angles to the line of the bridge. He had extensive experience of violent storms and hurricanes, such as on the river Plate, in China and the West Indies. His statements were confirmed in the ship's log by the gunnery instructor of the ship, and the seaman instructor on watch from 4.00 p.m. till 8.00 p.m. The ship was anchored east-west, so headed into the wind to minimise damage.

Admiral Dougall (retired) was then called to give evidence. He lived about 3 miles from the bridge at the mouth of the river, 200ft above sea level. He noticed the drop in the barometer and the gustiness of the wind as it grew in strength. He reckoned the squalls at 75 to 79mph and an old walnut tree in his garden was brought down by a severe gust between 7.15 p.m. and 7.20 p.m. A neighbour had lost six chimneys. Another witness, Charles Clark, lived at Magdalen Green, so was much closer to the bridge. The storm on 28 December had been equalled before, two or three times in the last fourteen years.

William McKelvie, superintendent of cemeteries in Dundee, also gave evidence. He had kept records for the Scottish Meteorological Society for the last twelve years. His barometric readings were similar to the others, allowing for being taken at 167ft above sea level. He was in church from 6.30 p.m. until 8.00 p.m., and noticed a tremendous noise from the ventilator in the roof at around 7.15 p.m. On his way home after the service, he saw broken chimney cairns, slates and zinc from rooftops as well as a door blown from its hinges. However, he appeared confused over wind pressure when he said that winds could have the same speed but yet exert different pressures! Counsel went on to make a key point:

1521. Are there a great many chimneys in Dundee? – Yes.

1523. Did any of those chimney stalks come down that night? – I do not know; not to my knowledge.

1526. Can you account for the fact that if the force of the wind brought down the bridge, it did not bring down some of the chimneys? – I cannot answer that.

The point Trayner was making here can be demonstrated by a blow-up of the picture of the bridge after the disaster, showing numerous very high stacks of factories behind the remains of the bridge *(5.3)*. If the wind blew down the bridge why did it not also blow down the many chimney stacks in Dundee town?

(5.3) Stricken bridge seen from the south bank with chimney stacks in background.

Several large gravestones were blown down that night in Balgay cemetery on the hill above the bridge *(4.4)*, but McElvie admitted that he had no anemometer, and knew of none in Dundee for measuring wind speed. The credibility of the witness was at a low ebb, and the final question was devastating when he admitted to Rothery that evaluating the force of the wind was a 'guess'. The present cemetery possesses many old and very large graves, especially near the crown of the hill, which would have been exposed to the full force of the wind that night.

Captain Wright of the *Tay* ferry steamer told the Inquiry about conditions in the estuary that night. He had made several trips across the estuary on 28 December, the last being at 5.15 p.m. from Dundee, when conditions had worsened. The wind had increased in strength with heavy showers of sleet. He was due out again from Dundee at 8.15 p.m., but took the decision to delay passage owing to the storm, which was at its height at around 7.10 p.m. He had not seen the Edinburgh train attempting to cross the bridge; the night was dark although when the clouds cleared there was bright moonlight. He thought that conditions were the worst he had seen but admitted that he had delayed the service for bad weather only twelve months previously. John Greig was principal keeper of the lighthouse at Tayport, and was on duty the night of the accident. He was up in the 67ft-high tower from 7.00 p.m., and he had felt a tremulous motion in the tower at the height of the storm, but there had been no damage to the light. He had felt such tremors once before in a storm in 1859.

The picture which emerged from the local witnesses was of a severe storm which had sprung up suddenly and abated later in the evening. It appeared to be at its height when the Edinburgh train was crossing. There was minor structural damage in the town, such as loss of chimney pots and tiles or slates. But there had been no major damage and certainly nothing on the scale of the fallen bridge. Those closest to the bridge and best able to judge conditions were the crew of the *Mars* training ship. They were experienced seamen, and thought that the storm was force 10-11, and not of hurricane force as some had claimed. This picture is consistent with the Beaufort scale, with one tree uprooted in Admiral Dougall's garden and some roof damage in the town. However, further evidence on the storm would be heard at later sittings of the court.

Victims

Numerous railwaymen were called in the initial stages of the tribunal to assess the state of the equipment, as well as the estimate of the number of passengers on board the train. All agreed the condition of the train had been checked and approved, and there was nothing apparently amiss with the state of the track. The ticket collector had collected stubs for those intending to alight at Dundee and was able to estimate the total number of passengers. There were seventy-five individuals, including driver, stoker and guard, who were unaccounted for after the disaster, although the total was probably larger on account of the young children travelling with their parents.

The first body was found down the Fife coast late on 29 December. It was Ann Cruikshank, a maid. No more bodies were found for several days yet, and the search by the divers continued at the site of the bridge. The train itself was found the following day between pier Nos 4 and 5, but no trace of the victims was found. Around a week later, several more bodies were found, all having been washed downstream by the powerful currents in the river. By the end of January, thirty-three bodies had been recovered, and more were to be found as the months went by. But twenty-nine of the victims had disappeared forever, and have never been found. Presumably they are buried in the silt of the estuary or the surrounding coast.

The court was adjourned until 26 February while more witnesses were called for, and a wider and deeper examination of the causes of the disaster instigated. In its final day in Dundee, the court discussed the experts who would need to give evidence about the design of the bridge and the testing of the materials of the piers, to see if they came up to specification.

Second Session of the Court

The next session of the court, over a month later on 26 February 1880, lasted two weeks in all and enabled the court to examine a range of witnesses who had been involved in the construction or maintenance of the bridge, and use of the bridge when built. It included the complaints about fast trains, and the worrying testimony of the painters on the bridge in the summer of 1879. There were, as well, the foundrymen from Wormit where most of the iron for the columns had been cast, and the constructors who built the piers on the bridge. Given the amount of broken metal left on the pier heads, it was inevitable that both groups would be examined at some depth. The focus of attention was the cast-iron columns and their bracing elements, especially the tie bars. Although the full state of the girders themselves had yet to be fully determined, reports from the divers showed that damage was much more limited than that to the towers which supported them.

Foundrymen

Richard Baird was a moulder who worked for nineteen months in the Wormit foundry, set up to provide the columns for the bridge. He described the way the columns were cast using a sand mould placed horizontally on the floor. A model of a column was available in court for him to demonstrate various points. The mould was made from wood with sand creating the hollow shape of the column such that, when molten iron was poured into the mould, it flowed into all the parts. When it had cooled and solidified, the container was stripped away and the sand removed to reveal a complete column. But such a large object as a column was itself hollow, so needed a core of sand, which was essentially a cylinder of the required diameter. The size of the outer part of the sand mould was such as to give a wall thickness of 1in in the 15in-outer diameter columns, which formed the great majority of those used in the high girder section of the bridge. The hollow into which the metal was poured was itself created by ramming sand around a wooden pattern made to the shape of the final product.

There were problems not only in maintaining an even wall thickness (caused by a shift in position of the internal core), but also in the critical design features of these columns, especially the lugs at the top and bottom of the columns (2.6). For example, since the lugs were at the extremities of the mould, molten metal might not always penetrate into this part, so leaving either no lug at all or a partly formed lug. To avoid scrapping the entire column, a lug could be attached to the column in a secondary operation known as 'burning in':

5484. Will you explain what the process is of burning-in the lug? – I will try; that part of the column which wants a lug is heated up to cause the column to expand first, and then a portion of the mould to form the new lug is placed on and metal is poured over the column that is wanting the new lug until it is properly softened and becomes amalgamated with the metal going on.

5485. In short, you the mould to the side of the column, after the column had been heated, and poured in metal into the new mould with the view of attaching itself to the column? – Yes.

He went on to explain that it was almost impossible to make the new burnt-in lug as strong as a fully cast lug, owing to the different temperatures of the molten lug and the hot column. There was frequently a rent formed between the lug and the flange.

Another problem experienced in moulding was known as 'scabbing'. This occurred when sand was detached from the inner surface of the mould by moving molten iron, and shifted to another part of the mould before solidification. Since the sand was much lighter than the iron (by a factor of about three), the sand floated on top of the moving iron and solidified into the metal towards the top of the horizontal mould, so distorting the shape of the column. He also mentioned that his speciality was making the lifting columns; columns fitted with wings to which the lifting apparatus could be attached when in position on the pier. They were not intended to stay in the final tower but would apparently be removed and replaced by conventional columns.

He was well aware that columns which were found to be defective, such as those with uneven walls or which were too short, were stacked separately to be broken up and the metal recycled. However, he had not seen columns with burnt-in lugs put into the scrap stack. He personally had seen about thirty such columns, but did not know whether they had been used in the bridge. The sand for casting had been collected from the shore and separated from gravel and, when reused for another casting, had been wetted with water from the estuary. The men complained of the acidic fumes produced when the hot metal met the wet sand. He also mentioned that the iron was mainly from Cleveland and not so good as local Scotch iron, tending to be less mobile and containing more impurities. When re-examined by Mr Trayner, he said that the columns went on to be machined in another part of the factory. It applied to the bolt holes in the flange, but the bolt holes in the lugs were cast and not bored.

Another moulder, James McGowan, repeated the complaint about the quality of iron used for casting, and added that it could produce 'cold-shuts' in the columns. This was where two streams of molten metal in the moulding did not unite correctly where they met. He saw columns which had been broken up for scrap which showed the marks of cold shuts, and he thought that all columns with cold shuts had been recycled. He agreed with Baird that burnt-in lugs had frequently been made and thought they were weaker than new lugs. But 'good' lugs sometimes broke by handling since they were exposed on the outer side of the columns. Just such a lug had been burnt-in as with partly formed lugs made by poor casting conditions. Cracks could often be seen at the lugs due to poor joining during burning-in, but were frequently puttied up and painted over. Like Baird, he was critical of the plant foreman, Fergus Ferguson, who had replaced Hercules Strachan, the previous foreman. He had been sacked for drunkenness. The excess iron on scabbed columns was chipped off using a chisel.

A third moulder, Alexander Hampton, was called next. He was not impressed by the quality of the iron used in the columns because it formed a thick scum floating on top when melted. It was also sluggish and columns scabbed easily. Production rate was about two columns per day. Andrew Foreman worked at the furnace or cupola, melting the iron ready for casting, but had initially worked at dressing the columns. He supported the previous allegations about the poor quality of the iron. He mentioned the use of cement or putty to fill holes in the casting. Such holes (known as blow holes) were formed from gases formed during casting. They could be up to ½in in diameter. Where they met a free surface it was common practice to fill the holes and paint over so as to give a smooth finish.

At a slightly later date, Fergus Ferguson, foreman in charge of the moulding shop, was called. He was thirty-five years old and had twenty years' experience in moulding. He attested that many columns were faulty but that they 'always got the hammer', meaning that they were always scrapped and recycled. He confirmed that lugs were sometimes burnt-in if they had only been partly formed. But none which had cracked were put in the high girder section, and he had this to say about brittle cracks:

7967. Did you always use your eyes to see? – Often the hammer.
7968. The eyes at least? – Yes.
7969. In your judgment could cracks either of the 32nd or the 16th of an inch have existed without your seeing them? – No
7970. Is it impossible? – Impossible. A 16th is a large part.
7971. Even if it had been what you call a hair crack, would your eye and hammer [have] detected it? – The hammer would have detected it quicker than the eye.

He went on to deny that any of the blow holes he had seen could have affected the strength of columns. It then emerged that the material used to fill visible blow holes in the outer surfaces of the pipes was '... a stuff called Beaumont's Egg':

7997. What stuff is that? – It is a composition; it is beeswax, rust and other things mixed up together.

He maintained that it was only used on small holes, however. The term he used is vernacular usage of 'beaumontage', a French word for a filler, and familiar to most house owners with rotting window frames.

There was some more detail about the criteria for scrapping or mending a column with a partly formed lug. If it had not formed above the bolt hole, he would burn-in the rest of the lug, but if below the bolt hole then the whole column would be scrapped. He agreed that burning lugs in was a common practice in the casting shop, but such lugs were of equal strength to original complete lugs.

One of the major reasons why the court were obsessed with lugs was simply this: they had all been out to the wrecked piers and seen with their own eyes the large numbers of broken lug wings present on the platforms (5.4).

Moreover, they had seen some of the broken lug ends *in situ* still on the columns of pier Nos 1 and 3, where two and three tiers still survived, almost miraculously (5.5).

(5.4) Broken lug ends and other debris on the masonry platform of pier No.3.

(5.5) Broken lugs on the bases of the columns at left and right of the lowest tier of pier No.1.

They were seeking an explanation of the reasons why the lugs were so weak, and whether or not it was caused by the practice of burning-in of only part-formed lugs during casting, or whether or not they were weak because perhaps they had cracked in the moulding shop, or contained blow holes or other defects. If they were the weakest link in the chain, could this simple design feature explain why the entire high girder section fell on the night of the storm? What was so special about the lugs? It must somehow be related to the importance of the diagonal tie bars which braced the towers together. It was to Henry Law, their investigator, that they would eventually turn to for answers to these key questions.

But they had also seen other signs of poor casting practices on the same piers, scattered among the debris which had fallen on the night of the storm, such as columns with uneven walls, caused by small shifts of the core within the mould. So many questions put to Mr Ferguson were also directed to this problem, as well as scabbed columns and blow holes. He estimated that about 200 columns had been rejected and recycled, such as those with blow holes 1¼in in diameter and at least ¼in deep. He had not seen cracks in the columns apart from the lugs. Such columns were condemned for scrap. However, no written records had been kept of scrap rates in the moulding shop. Lugs were often cracked by simply dropping them accidentally, since they were exposed at either end. It seemed that Mr Ferguson was an enthusiastic wielder of 'the hammer'. As for burning-in of the lugs, the only columns with such lugs had been used in the two low sections of the bridge and never in the high girder section. All the columns had spigots and recesses for positive fitment together when assembled. He had not seen cold shuts in finished columns.

Hercules Strachan was another of the foremen moulders examined, and he had preceded Fergus Ferguson in the shop. Blow holes, in his experience, ranged generally in size from 'a pin-head to a half a pea' in size, but he had only seen two broken lugs mended by burning-in. He gave a precise description of the operation:

8364. How do you burn-on part of a lug? – We have the whole lug, we have the broken lug. I chip a piece off the lug so that there would be ⅜in in space between the broken lug and the part of the lug that was on the column; I heated up the column to a red-hot heat, a blay heat.

8365. Which is it, a red heat or a blay heat? – A red heat. Then I put the two lugs together, the ⅜in part and the other part and pour about 5cwt or so of as hot iron as you can get into the part between the two, and scrape it with a rod all the time, and you feel distinctly where the two sides melt, and the three irons get, as it were, amalgamated.

Only two columns had been scrapped while he was foreman, a remarkable record compared with his successor, Fergus Ferguson. Why there was such a discrepancy was not revealed by the Inquiry.

Machinists

After casting, the columns would be turned on a lathe, to smooth the rough-cast surface at the ends of the flanges. In addition, there was a spigot or projection which was designed to mate into the socket of the column below. The columns would be seen close-up and therefore any serious defects would have been readily apparent. Could any of the machinists shed light on the problem of faulty castings or 'burnt-in' lugs? From questioning George Fender, an iron turner and foreman of the machine shop, it became clear that such defects as blow holes or cracked lugs were indeed found and reported, and those defective columns were scrapped: to be broken up and recycled back into the furnace. Fender used his discretion with blow holes, since small ones ($\frac{1}{16}$in diameter) would not affect the strength, whereas large ones (up to ¼in diameter) could. He had also seen scabbed columns where excess iron had been chipped off with a chisel. No faulty columns had been passed for fitment in the bridge to his knowledge. But he had seen blow holes which had been filled with 'cement' and, if the blow hole was large, he picked the cement out, and showed the column to a superior. If sufficiently large, the column would be rejected. The cement was dark, so matched the colour of the columns, but could be seen when the columns were inspected closely. He had also seen burnt-in lugs (many times) but had rarely seen cracks in the lugs. When he asked two colleagues, Hercules Strachan and Fergus Ferguson, about their strength, he had been assured that the lugs were as strong as original castings. The weights of the castings were:

18in-diameter column	12–14cwt
15in-diameter column	17–18cwt

In addition to smoothing the flanges, they had drilled bolt holes in the 15in column flanges using a boring machine, but those in the flanking 18in columns were cast in like the lug holes. They had no machine for boring the larger columns.

The Erectors of the Bridge

William Oram, by contrast, was a rivetter working on the Tay Bridge who also checked and corrected poor fitment on the columns of the high girder towers. For example, he replaced service or temporary bolts on the columns, and caulked the nuts to stop them working free. But he also saw some broken lugs:

6554. Did you examine the condition of any of the columns themselves? – Yes.

6556. Did you see any of them at all damaged in any way? – I saw two I think with the lug broken, and it was replaced with malleable iron put on its place.

6567. (Mr Barlow) You said there were one or two cases of a lug being broken off and put on by malleable iron; how was that malleable iron lug put on? – By screw bolts; what we call pincing screws. The holes were bored in the column, that lug was broken off and the holes were tapped, and the bolts screwed in through them and fastened on the lug in that way.

Clearly, lugs were a sensitive part of the column and could be broken relatively easily in the foundry and when fixed in place in the towers of the high girders. Whether or not the two broken lugs Mr Oram found had also been burned-in, we shall never know.

Further evidence of the state of the bridge emerged during examination of Edward Simpson, who had not only been diving on the remains, but had supervised the painting of the bridge in the summer of 1879. One of his duties was to inspect the painting and, clearly, if any defects in the metalwork found, to report them to Mr Noble. He had found two diagonal tie bars loose for 'want of screws' and the matter had been fixed the next day. When the staging needed for the painters had been removed, he was satisfied that all the tie bars were correctly fastened. Indeed, they were used for climbing up and down, like ladders. He had also observed the effect of passing trains on the bridge, and had only noticed a tremor. However, he modified his evidence in cross-examination when presented with contrary testimony from the painters who were working full-time on the structure:

6737. The motion you felt produced a kind of tremble? – A tremble.
6738. Nothing more than that? – No, nothing more to my feeling.
6739. Rather a strong tremble, was it not? – Well it was pretty heavy in the centre of the girders.
6740. Would you go to the length of saying that it was a shake? – It was a kind of shake.

Moreover, he admitted that the shaking could be felt at the north end of the high girders when a train entered the south end, around half a mile away, and the shaking increased as the train approached. The high girders were, in his opinion, more sensitive than the low girders in this regard. He was currently being employed by the NBR for work on the bridge.

William Newcombe was a foreman erector who had worked on the high girders before the bridge was open. He climbed them three to five times a day for three months. He could have seen defects, but never did so. It was very slow climbing the towers. He had been working on the towers of the high girders when ballast trains passed over (each weighing about 112 tons), and felt a slight motion. But he had not felt their approach, and no lateral motion. It was a slight jar or shake that he had felt, but nothing more.

The next erector called was William Dixon, who continued work on the high girder section after Newcombe. He was currently employed on a new railway bridge at Arbroath for Sir Thomas Bouch. He had overhauled the joints of the high girders, tightening bolts and caulking them:

6998. What was the last job that you did upon the bridge, generally? – Overhauling the bolts and seeing that they all had a full nut and were properly caulked, and the bracing bars and the channel bars tightened up.
6999. That was done on the piers after you had finished the girders? – Yes.
7000. What do you mean by caulking the nut? – After the bolt is taken out she gets a full nut and we use a tool, a hammer, and caulk the bolt into the nut to prevent it coming out and getting slack.
7001. Is that done with a blunt chisel? – No, a caulking tool.
7002. After that is done, could the bolt possibly unscrew itself off the nut? – No.

He had thus apparently examined every nut and bolt, and hence every lug in the piers he had worked on, so could he have seen any cracks in the lugs? He replied in the negative, rather surprisingly for someone who would have been close to the lug when caulking and tightening the bolts which held the tie bars in position. He must also have been close to the columns when doing this work, and been in a good position to examine their state too. But he had seen no blow holes or scabs or cracks whatsoever. Caulking the nut and bolt would have involved applying tow or tar-soaked thread to the bolt thread or shank, and screwing the nut home hard so that the fibre was trapped in the joint.

Edward McGovern was employed as a foreman in finishing the ironwork of the bridge, especially bracing the tie bars by hammering in the cotters in the joint. He had no idea of the degree of strain he applied, but tested a finished tie bar by the sound it made when struck with a hammer. After tightening, the ends of the cotters were opened out so that they could not fall away from the joint. He also bolted columns together at the flanges. If he had seen any cracked lugs he would have reported the matter, but had not come across any faulty lugs at all. However, he had reported a cracked 'lifting column' because they were only intended to be used during the lifting phase with the hydraulic lift, and should have been removed before completion of a tower. Such columns had a wing below the flange and lugs to which the lift could be attached, but they were temporary and were meant to be removed in the final structure.

After a very vigorous session on the stand, it was now the turn of George Macbeath, also then working on the new Bouch Bridge at Arbroath. Macbeath had been instructed by Bouch himself to overhaul all the ironwork on the bridge, 'from end to end'. It transpired that Macbeath had the authority to instruct the contracting engineers to make good where poor work had been found. It is interesting that the Inquiry chose to question senior workers or supervisors after they had questioned the workmen themselves, a policy applied uniformly to the painters, railwaymen, foundrymen and erectors. Perhaps the Inquiry felt that questioning the workers first would be more likely to yield answers unsullied by any possibility (however remote) of influence by their superiors. In any case, it was judged vital to assess first-hand evidence as fast as possible to prevent the inevitable relapses in memory or colouring of the evidence as time passed. Indeed, there was an indication that the supervisors and foremen tended to bias their evidence in deference to their superiors in management, whether subconsciously or otherwise.

Macbeath had tested rivets with a hammer and, if any were loose, had them replaced. No doubt, he said, the rivets found much later by the painters on the pier platforms were those thrown away by his workmen. In answer to questioning by Mr Balfour (counsel to the NBR), he affirmed that he had inspected all of the diagonal bracing tie bars by climbing from the base of a tower and examining each tier in turn. The hammer was indispensable for testing the joints. He had found that some of the bolts were too short, and had had them replaced. He had discovered that three lugs were broken, and they were replaced by wrought-iron lugs as already described by a previous witness (Oram). But only one had been in the high girder section, on pier No.9, the others being in the low section of the bridge. He had continued inspecting the bridge till the end of May 1879, but had not seen any weakening of the structure, even after many trains had by then passed over it. He had felt no strange vibrations when high wind forced the workmen off the bridge.

Mr Trayner attempted, with some success, to squirrel into his testimony. He admitted for example, that he had tested less than 10 per cent of all the rivets in the structure, although there was some confusion over rivets and bolts. But Trayner went to the heart of the issue when he started questioning about the diagonal tie bars:

7287. Were the diagonal bars of any use in the bridge, or were they merely ornamental? – They would be intended for some use, I believe.
7288. What was the use of them? – To stiffen the end posts.
7289. And to stiffen the end posts I suppose was a material thing in stiffening the whole length of the high girders? – No, just to prevent the end posts from getting together.
7290. And if those end posts were not prevented from getting together, would that not have materially weakened the structure from end to end of the high girders? – No.
7291. Then they were of no use? – No.

Macbeath thus appeared unclear of the precise role of the diagonal tie bars of the towers. However, if he had been over all the connections in the high girders, he would have been in a position to examine the columns as well as the critical lugs. He had apparently not found any which had been burnt-on, although he had admitted that three lugs were found which had cracked and been mended. It must have been serious cracking to have broken the paint film on the lugs and presumably he could not detect hairline cracks which had been painted over. In cross-examination, he too admitted that he felt vibrations in the structure when trains passed over.

The Managers

Gerard Camphuis was the assistant civil engineer to Grothe in charge of the bridge, and had been there from the beginnings in August 1873 to October 1879, when the bridge was carrying passenger traffic. He therefore had a good overview of the project as well as the finished structure. He was responsible for producing monthly progress reports, for example. When asked about the practice of burning-in the lugs, he said that only ten or twelve had been treated while he was in charge of the foundry. He had tested the burnt-in lugs with a hammer and found them to be of satisfactory strength. The damage had been caused during transport of 12in columns used in the low section, which were actually cast in Middlesborough:

8666. Will you kindly mention to what test you subjected the lugs? — By hammering them, and in one instance, which is distinctly before my eyes, when I expressed some doubt to the foreman about the solidity of the snug, he took a sledgehammer and gave it a good swing round, which would have knocked off a perfectly sound lug, and that lug stood it perfectly well.

He went on to deny that defective columns had been installed in the bridge towers, whether the defects were cold shuts, wall thickness variations, cracks, scabs or blow holes. He also resisted the suggestion of any unusual tremors (such as oscillations) when trains passed over the structure. However, he did admit that passenger trains had travelled at around 30mph over the bridge and so exceeded the speed limit imposed by the NBR:

8868. Do you think that you ever saw a higher speed than that on the bridge? — No, I do not think so. I have been standing by the side when they passed with ladies and dogs.
8869. Was anybody frightened? — No, except the dogs.

Following this rather blasé answer, he was questioned about the role of the diagonal tie bars:

8875. Would you kindly tell us as an engineer, whether these diagonal bars had much or any strain to bear? — I think not.
8876. What are they there for? — I suppose they are there more for ornament than for anything else, because I often found them slack, and they should have tightened themselves if they had been of any use. Occasionally one was slack.

8878. Does it appear that they could have any strain upon them except that of keeping these upright things apart? — Not even that; I do not think that there was a tendency for these upright things coming apart at all. The structure of this end post and of the top boom is exactly the same, and they both have to sustain a compressive force, and the top boom has not these diagonal bars and does quite well without them.

So we now have an engineer in charge of the project denying that the tie bars are of any use whatsoever.

On the second day of his cross-examination and after having denied the presence of defects in any of the metalwork, he was presented with exhibit No.1. He was asked to measure it with callipers and it was ⅝in thickness (the specification called for a 1in-wall). He was then handed exhibit No.2, and performed a similar exercise, the sample having a wall thickness of ⅝in again. A third specimen (exhibit No.3) had a maximum wall of 1in. We are not told who provided these first exhibits to the Inquiry, but they had presumably been collected from broken columns on the piers during one of the visits the court itself had made to the ruins in the centre of the estuary. Could a variation of ⅝in to 1in in wall thickness make a difference to the integrity of the towers? It depended how many such columns had been made and erected, but since most of the columns were now lying at the bottom of the estuary, it was difficult to determine the defect rate. Exhibit No.1 also possessed a large blow hole which lay in the fracture surface of the sample. The witness was asked to measure this as well, and it formed a significant proportion of the wall, being ³⁄₁₆in deep. However, it was much wider as seen on the fracture — ¾ x ⅞in. Both witness and counsel agreed that it was a serious defect, and they also discovered that it was partly filled with a cement. Exhibit No.2 showed a honeycomb of small blow holes associated with a brittle crack, together with contamination by 'cinders' and 'scum', presumably slag from casting. Both again agreed that the strength of the column would be lowered by such defects, as well as the integrity of the bridge.

Mr Trayner then read out to him that part of the original contract which specified that a bar (1 x 2in) cut from a casting should be tested to 3,000lbs (1.34 tons) bending load at the centre of a 3ft-length. Camphuis did not know of any such bend test being performed in the foundry, and indeed knew of no tests carried out on samples at all.

It also turned out that the wrought-iron bolts holding columns together at the flanges were a rather loose fit: the bolts were 1⅛in wide to fit holes of 1¼in, so there was ⅛in slack. They agreed that vibration could loosen any bolt, given time. The argument could be extended to the joints on the tie bars:

9237. If these bracings gave way through defective fastenings, what would the effect of that have been on the stability of the girders? – It would surely not increase the stability; it would diminish the stability.

9238. If these were not properly fitted as regards the surface of the cotters to each other, and properly driven home or fastened by spreading out at the split at the end, would these cotters have a tendency to come away through vibration of the bridge? – I would think so if they were not opened up.

Camphuis is now contradicting himself, because he said earlier in testimony that the diagonal tie bars were only ornamental features of the towers, yet here he is saying that the stability of the towers would be lowered if the joints became loose.

Trayner then turned to the spigots machined or cast into the ends of the columns so as to give a secure fit with other columns. Previous testimony from the machinists and moulders stated that all the columns had spigots, but now Camphuis says that this was not so:

9257. Were these male and female attachments on every column? – Not that I am aware of. They were on all the columns except the bottom length, the 18in columns and there they were left out purposely, why I do not know.

9258. But with the exception of the bottom lengths, the lowest lengths on the piers, and with the exception of the lowest columns of 18in-diameter, all the other columns, so far as you are aware, had the male and female attachments? – Yes, on the high girders so far as I am aware.

9259. Would you be astonished to hear that there are a great many of the columns standing now where the high girders once stood which show that there never was such a male and female attachment at all? – Yes I should be very much astonished.

9260. If that is the case, how could that have happened? – I cannot account for it.

Mr Trayner was simply describing what the court had seen for itself on the wrecked piers, as seen for example in the etchings published by the journal *Engineering (5.6)*, and based on the Valentine photographs taken just after the disaster *(5.7)*. The broken lugs are similar to those from most other piers, at extreme left and right. The remains on pier No.9 are interesting for showing uplift of the masonry foundations.

Camphuis had not visited the ruined piers directly but had only observed them from a distance, on a boat used for the occasion. For a manager in charge of these basic engineering operations of making and finishing the hardware of the towers, he seemed remarkably unaware of the key details which held the towers together. Trayner went on to cross-examine him about the tie bars, and specifically his expressed belief that they were largely ornamental fixtures, which he maintained. Next came the vibrations which might have been responsible for the deterioration of the high girders structure. He did admit that a train could be felt approaching from some way away, and that there was an obvious and perceptible movement of the bridge.

Frank Beattie was the assistant mechanical engineer under Grothe, and was also the draughtsman for the project. He had designed much of the ironwork of the bridge. He was in charge of the foundry at Wormit, having suggested that it be constructed in the first place. He

Opposite above: (5.6) Etching of the west views on pier Nos 7 and 9, published in *Engineering* magazine.

Opposite below: (5.7) Valentine photograph of the west view from pier No.9, showing how the etcher used it for making his picture.

THE TAY BRIDGE; REMAINS OF PIERS Nos. 7 AND 9.

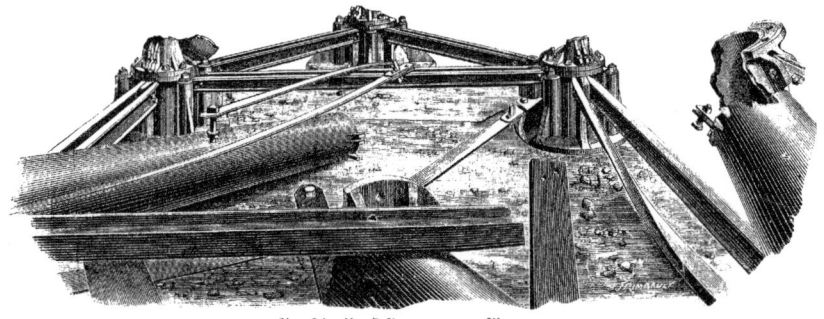

[FIG. 16. No. 7 PIER, LOOKING WESTWARD.

FIG. 17. No. 9 PIER, LOOKING WESTWARD.

Pier No. 9

looking West

was able to give first-hand evidence of the way moulding was conducted in some detail. The pattern they used for the columns was a cast-iron shaft turned down to the correct diameter and fitted with flanges, pockets and lugs. The flanges of the 15in columns were bored by a dedicated machine tool, but that did not extend to the 18in columns, where the holes were cast rather than being bored out. He had known about Beaumont's Egg being used to fill exposed blow holes, but deprecated the practice. And he had tested samples of cast-iron bar as required by the contract, and found them to meet the specification load of 3000lb. He had also known of burning-in lugs and approved any such lugs, to the extent of examining them for cracks using a microscope. There were only five or six that he knew about. But such lugs only occurred in the special lifting columns, which would normally be removed before completion of a tower, so did not end up in the finished bridge.

Beattie had answered questions to him from Mr Balfour knowledgeably and credibly, a significant contrast with Camphuis. But now he faced cross-examination from Mr Trayner, who had already established himself as a skilled interrogator. One of his first acts was to present the witness with the three exhibits he had just put to Camphuis, and ask for his comments. The differences in wall thickness – as in exhibit No.1 – would probably arise from a shifting of the core, he said, so that the metal would be thick on one side of the column and thin the opposite side. He would allow only a maximum difference of ¼in between the walls, so would allow walls of ⅞ up to 1⅜in the other side. Beattie thought the large blow holes serious defects, but they were latent defects which were difficult to detect if buried deep in the metal. The cinders and scum only existed in the interior of the column wall, and were not so serious. Blow holes were a serious problem in all casting work, because of the difficulty of detection. Moreover, they would weaken any products in which they occurred. He remembered 150 scrapped columns, about a twelfth of the total production, while he was supervising the shop. Asked about the cast holes in the flanges of the 18in columns, he said that they were 1½in in diameter for a 1⅛in bolt, a larger figure than Camphuis had supplied.

Before the Inquiry adjourned and decamped from Dundee, there were some more witnesses to interrogate. Both Thorntons (for the NBR) and the BoT presented witness lists, the former being passengers who had not experienced undue vibrations on the bridge, testimony which provided nothing new whatsoever. These passengers had never timed the crossings or noticed strange oscillations. However, the BoT produced a most interesting set of workmen from Wormit, the dressers of the columns, who were to provide key details of the defects already mentioned by the moulders and others. Some even more interesting details of the working conditions at the foundry were also to emerge.

The Dressers

After casting, the columns were examined and 'dressed' before being passed to the machinists. They would examine the columns for defects and, if severely faulty, reject them or send them back to the moulding shop. But they could also chip off offending parts, or hide recesses with Beaumont's Egg. Finally they painted the columns after machining. Their testimony was to give yet more direct evidence of what was being made at Wormit for the new bridge.

The first dresser to be heard was Alexander Milne, who had worked mainly under Fergus Ferguson, and for only a week under Hercules Strachan before he left. He had worked as a dresser for two and a half years at Wormit:

10,830. Did you find any of the columns defective? – Oh, yes.

10,832. What were the defects? – There were blown holes and lugs off.

10,833. Blown holes in the columns and lugs broken off? – They were generally blown between the hole and the top of the lug.

It seemed then that blow holes were actually very common, especially in the lugs, which could explain why they fractured so easily. In some cases, the blow holes were very large indeed, ½in at the skin of the metal, but 2in wide inside. The larger holes were filled with molten iron, the smaller ones with Beaumont's Egg. The turners used the same material to fill blow holes exposed by machining before painting with white lead/grease paint, and then being sent to the bridge. The material was a composition of: beeswax, fiddler's rosin, finest iron borings, and a little lamp black. It was melted with a hot iron bar into the blow hole. It solidified there and set against the metal before a final rubbing down to match the surrounding surface. The egg was kept in a cupboard in Ferguson's office, and he supplied it when needed. It was used more frequently in the later stages of the project, when Mr Trayner asked him about frequency of use:

> 10,879. *Did he ever give it to you?* – Two or three times; more so at the finish of the foundry; there was a great number of burns and one thing or another puttied up that way. There were a great many columns that were damaged on the outside with lugs knocked off, and they got lugs burned-on, and where there was any part of the burn that did not melt together we just gave it a fill up with that.
> 10,880. *At what part of the burning did you most generally find the defect that you had to fill up with Beaumonts egg?* – Near the body of the column at the tail of the lug.
> 10,881. *Was there any crack observable?* – It was always cracked on the solid metal; not the burn; below the burning generally; out round the flange.

Here then was very positive evidence for defective lugs being burned-on, the process creating yet more defects like brittle cracks before being hidden with the filler. He also chipped any excess iron from the lugs so as to make them more presentable. Such was the rate of burned lugs that he had chipped six in only two days. The Beaumont's Egg was hidden and, if anyone came by, a cloth was thrown over the stuff to hide it from view. All the workers knew it was used, but the practice was frowned on by management, and could result in dismissal.

Peter Tuite was a dresser at the foundry for somewhat longer, serving under both Hercules Strachan and Fergus Ferguson, and working to the end of the project there. He had also seen blow holes in the top of the lugs, and hairline cracks up to ½in in length in the lugs. Similar evidence was given by John Gibb, another dresser, who had been with the project for two and a half years. He had seen even bigger holes in columns, 3in-diameter in the shaft and 1in in the lug, in a column which was scrapped. The maximum hole he had filled was about ¼in in diameter and ⅜in deep. He had filled holes formed by faulty burning-on, at the junction of the lug and flange, with molten lead. Holes in lugs were filled, as were cracks in the column shafts near the lugs. Defects were hidden from the management by throwing a poke (or sack) over them. The evidence was generally corroborated by John Tasker, who had worked at Wormit for twenty months. He was the dresser who prepared the Beaumont's Egg for the whole team, using money provided by Fergus Ferguson to buy the ingredients. He had seen 'hundreds' of blow holes in the lugs of cast columns, but had not seen any cracks. He had also seen many columns scrapped because they were beyond repair, such as those with large holes through the walls. A finger could be put through the largest he had seen. Others were plugged up and filled, and sent on for machining. In the end he had been dismissed for taking time off work for drinking, and had been drinking today before coming into the witness box!

Adjournment

So what had the Inquiry achieved before adjourning to Westminster, after examining the many people who had been involved in making the columns for the bridge? The lines of questioning adopted by Trayner, and to a lesser extent, Balfour, were very clearly based on what they had seen on the wrecked piers, of which there were no less than twelve. Some of the piers were cluttered with debris from the lowest columns which had fallen on the night of the disaster *(5.6)*, but others, especially two piers (Nos 1 and 3) were relatively free of the large broken columns. The debris accumulated on those platforms during the collapse was minimal, but revealing. There were numerous broken lug ends, almost always broken across the bolt hole, as perhaps one might expect, given that this represents the minimum section area *(5.4)*. In other words, any load applied to the lug will be greatest across the bolt hole. There were also broken and bent bolts, some of which must have come from the same broken lugs. The corresponding fractured lug bases were still in place on the piers, and their shape matched those of the separated pieces *(5.5)*. While the photographs from the other piers are not so easy to interpret owing to the amount of other debris present, broken lug wings are visible in most of them. Whether they were present before the accident or were caused by the accident is difficult to say. The investigators, trawling through the mountains of debris left accessible on the piers, faced a serious problem in interpretation. Most of the ironwork of the towers lay buried in the estuary: very little of the original ironwork remained to be examined. It is true that the high girders themselves were relatively unscathed, and were lifted over the coming months as the weather improved. But the cast-iron columns and bracing members would generally be left where they were, since all accounts from the divers suggest that they were in a similar state to those parts left on the piers. That meant that recovery would be difficult and expensive.

6
Henry Law Investigates

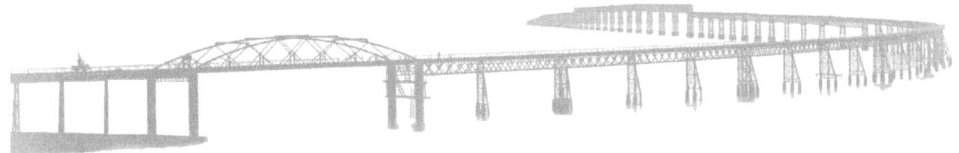

The chief investigator for the Inquiry was Henry Law, a well-known civil engineer who had published manuals on the subject. With assistants, he visited the piers in February and March 1880, collecting samples lying freely on the masonry platforms. It was to his investigation that the Inquiry would turn for detailed description of the damage, and more importantly, his interpretation of what that evidence showed. He would be followed by a train of other experts whose interpretation of the same evidence gave quite a different picture of the events on the night of the storm.

The Inquiry reopened on 19 April at Westminster Hall in London, nearly six weeks after adjourning in Dundee. Disraeli had lost the general election in early April to a Liberal landslide, and W.E. Gladstone would shortly be appointed Prime Minister. The disaster was still a political hot potato, however, since the bridge had been approved by the BoT, and the inspector, General Hutchinson would appear as a witness. Mr Rothery requested in an opening address that meteorological experts be called, including Sir George Airy, the Astronomer Royal. Professor George Stokes of Cambridge University, a noted expert on fluid dynamics, would also be called. He had been involved in the Royal Commission on Iron after the Dee Bridge disaster. Rothery expressed concern at the delay in testing samples which had been taken from the three surviving tiers of the high girders by Henry Law. Mr Kirkaldy of Southwark had been retained to test the samples using a hydraulic tensometer. There were more barristers present, including Mr Bidder, representing Sir Thomas Bouch.

There were still some important witnesses of fact to be questioned, including Henry Noble, and a raft of toolmakers and machinists from the Cleveland Nut and Bolt Co., who had supplied the project. The debris on the piers showed many fractured bolts and it naturally occurred to the court whether or not they too might have been defective. The totality of their evidence did not raise any particular problems with defective bolts, but Noble's evidence was vital in understanding how the bridge failed. However, it was Henry Law who was to bring the many threads of evidence together in producing a credible explanation of how the bridge fell on 28 December.

Court Instructions

The court had written to Mr Law on 22 January 1880, requesting his assistance with the disaster. He duly complied and was in Dundee the following day. His instructions included investigating:

1. The state of the piers and scour in the river bed caused by the piers.
2. The dimensions of the diagonal tie bars, mode of attachment to the columns and the degree of play between the bolt and lug hole.
3. The nature of the fracture of the lugs.
4. Dimensions of bolts in the towers.
5. The state of each of the wrecked piers.
6. Broken column ends to show quality of casting.
7. Quality of fitment between one column and another.
8. Quality of the iron as shown by the fractures.
9. Position of the fallen high girders in relation to the piers.
10. Condition of the standing columns for the possibility of frost damage.

He remained in Dundee until 12 February 1880, again on 24 February until 6 March, and finally from 24 March to 27 March 1880. He had visited the piers several times during those visits, as well as hearing the direct witness evidence in the court at Dundee. He had been provided with a transcript of the hearings and a plan of the train, with weights and areas of the carriages. Mr Noble had given him records of the tests made on the concrete. A section of the river showing depths together with copies of the contracts was provided by the NBR, and drawings of the bridge by Sir Thomas Bouch. The latter had provided an expert report from Dr Pole and Allan Stewart, and the court gave him a set of the photographs taken by Valentines. He had use of a river boat to reach the piers in the middle of the river as well as assistance from a Mr Peddie (one of Bouch's assistants) and Henry Noble. His report had been presented to the Inquiry, but he was asked to describe the bridge in detail for the benefit of the record. Following his description, he then described the damage to the structure as seen just after the accident. The pictures taken by Valentines were to be an important source of evidence for the court, and the witnesses, who would use them to refresh their memories.

Valentine Photographs

The completed bridge was very photogenic, and the subject intrinsically interesting because of the long perspective created by the sheer size of the structure. Many copies of pictures of the bridge survive from before the disaster, and it was photographed by many professionals. Valentines (James Valentine & Sons) was one of the most prominent local companies, but there were others such as George Washington Wilson of Aberdeen. His collection is now kept by the University of Aberdeen, while St Andrews keeps much of the Valentine output, which was vast.

Victorian photography had come far since its inception in the late 1830s and early 1840s. Fox-Talbot in Britain and Daguerre in France had independently developed ways of capturing exact images of nature, but in entirely different ways. It was the Fox-Talbot method which eventually prevailed since a negative image was made initially, and from which any number of positive prints could be reproduced. The daguerreotype, by contrast, was a unique positive recorded on polished metal, so was expensive and impossible to copy. But both methods needed a wet, freshly prepared, film or plate, requiring an extensive stock of chemical developers and fixers (some highly toxic) and a mini-laboratory on site. Technical improvements in the 1860s and 1870s gave the professional photographer dry plates, which could be exposed on site and then developed at leisure back at the studio. It is likely that such dry plates were used by Valentines, given the problems of recording the remains of the towers on each and every pier. Four shots were requested by the court, one from each of the four quadrants, so two were long shots taken from the next pier in the line, and two (the east and west views) were close-ups taken on the pier itself.

Remains of the Bridge

Henry Law started by discussing the towers which stood at either end of the high girders. They were intermediate structures between the smaller towers of the low girders sections, and the massive seven-tier high towers supporting the high girders. The one at the south end *(6.1)* was, however, much taller than that at the north *(6.2)*, owing to the steep drop in the rail line into Tay Bridge station in Dundee.

Each of these towers supported the ends of two girders stacked upon one another, where the train entered the girders rather than riding on top of them. The two structures still stood, but were in a very sorry state.

Although the tower at the north end was lower in height, it showed a much greater level of damage than its southern compatriot, especially in terms of the various bracing elements. All the horizontal struts on the central section, the core of the strength of the tower, had been fractured. The base platform was heaped with debris which had fallen from the top during the accident, including large cast-iron plates and the roller bearings. Their impact with the struts presumably broke them, and weakened the integrity of the structure. However, many diagonal tie bars in the outward facing cells of the structure had also broken *(6.2)*, suggesting that they might have been broken by another mechanism since they were not in the path of debris falling from above *(6.3)*. Both up- and down-wind diagonals had broken, and they had fractured at one end only, at the lugs where they were attached to the columns.

The damage to the south tower was also severe, with many of the core struts broken and hanging freely. The debris pile at the base was not as extensive, and some of the core struts and diagonals survived the fall of metal from above *(6.4)*.

Above, left: (6.1) Last standing pier at the south end of the ruined bridge.

Above, right: (6.2) Last standing pier at the north side of the ruined bridge.

Above: (6.3) Base of the last standing pier to the north of the remains of the bridge.

Right: (6.4) Base of the last standing pier at the south end of the ruined bridge.

Opposite: (6.5) Enlargement of five high girder piers showing remains left on platforms.

All the diagonal tie bars on the side cells of the tower were intact, not a single one being broken. As with the north tower, breakage of both struts and diagonals had occurred at the lugs where they were joined to the cast-iron columns.

The Remains on the Piers

Henry Law then turned his attention to the wreckage on the piers *(6.5)*. Here the damage was almost total. Not a single tower of the twelve originally there still stood, the entire high girder section having been destroyed. The girders themselves were nowhere to be seen, and most likely rested nearby at the bottom of the estuary. The boat seen near the South tower is presumably searching for survivors by sending down divers in the first few days after the disaster. Each pier platform could be reached by boat and would be surveyed in detail by Law and his team of helpers, as well as being photographed by Valentines. There were piles of collapsed columns on most of the piers, some seemingly still partly attached to their bracing elements. However, there were also two piers where the debris was less daunting, pier Nos 1 and 3 *(6.5)*. It was to be those two piers which would provide key clues as to the way the towers had fallen on the night of the accident.

Partly Standing Piers

The first pier was that one adjacent to the south-standing tower. It was two tiers high, the upper part having appeared to have broken cleanly away on the night of the storm *(6.6)*. But there was subsidiary damage to the diagonals and a few of the struts. Both the core cells and the side cells exhibited fractured tie bars, those on the western side being in a worse state than the eastern side. In the core cell, it was those diagonals which braced the tower against movement to the east which were broken. In the upper tier, one of these diagonals had broken away with the strut, and hung down almost vertically into the lower tier. The other – at the

Left: (6.6) Two tiers on pier No.1 looking north from the last standing pier in the south.

Below: (6.7) A single tier on pier No.3 looking north from pier No.2.

rear in *(6.6)* – had fractured cleanly at the lug, and had dropped a few inches as it swivelled from its still intact upper lug. The diagonals in the side cells showed the opposite effect, some of those bracing the structure against movement to the west being broken in precisely the same way at the lower lugs.

Some of the columns had also been damaged, that at the corner of the lowest cell – right-hand side of *(6.6)* – showing that a large scab of cast iron had fallen away to reveal the inner concrete core.

In addition, the flange at the top of the same column had broken away, as had the next column. Equally significant was the state of the platforms below the metalwork. There was very little in the way of fallen debris, much less than had been seen at the bases of the still standing towers. Only one large strut can be seen in *(6.6)*, lying near the centre of the platform. It seemed clear that the upper five tiers had been sheared away very cleanly, and little had fallen on to the platforms.

Six tiers on pier No.3 had been swept away on the night of the accident, leaving just one tier intact on the platform *(6.7)*. This picture was taken from the next pier along looking north, so the last standing pier can be seen in the background. West is now on the left-hand side of the picture, and east to the right. The damage to the cells is similar but not identical to that on pier No.1. The first thing that strikes the eye is the rod hanging down in the core cell, still with its cast-iron connection attached at its free end. Both east bracing diagonals have been broken and are resting freely on the platform, yet the other pair of tie bars are intact. The diagonals in the side cells appear almost entirely unbroken. Some damage to the tops of two columns is apparent, that on the extreme eastern side being broken, in addition to a column top in the centre cell. Some small debris piles are visible on the platform, but nothing by comparison with the standing piers. The similarity in damage suggest that both towers failed in a similar way, with the top tiers being completely swept away. But what did detailed examination of the damage at the bases of the piers show Henry Law?

Close-ups

We are very fortunate to be able to see what Henry Law saw when he climbed onto the platforms for his first inspection of the damage. Excellent quality close-up pictures had been made by Valentines, and can now been easily enlarged at will from scans of the originals. The photographs from pier No.3 are the most convincing evidence for the sequence of events during the collapse, the shot looking upstream to the west being shown in *(6.8)*.

The details are easily confirmed by comparison with the previous long shot *(6.7)*. The hanging tie rod with its cast-iron attachment piece is, for example, just visible behind one of the tie bars in the immediate foreground. The intact tie bars in the western cell are also clearly seen in the picture. More significant are the details visible at the bottom of the picture. One of the broken cast-iron lugs is shown in close-up in *(6.9)*.

The southernmost broken lug *(6.9)* shows a set of four fracture surfaces, two each on the two wings of the lug on either side of the central bolt hole. The four surfaces seem featureless, although closer inspection shows a highlight on the front left-hand surface. There is another white highlight on the outside of the right-hand bolt hole. Most obvious of all is the conical taper to the hole, showing that the entire load from the diagonal bars will have been concentrated on a very small part of the lug. Normal practice would have been to drill the bolt hole after casting so as to ensure that the bolts would fit snugly and the load distributed evenly over the section.

An intact lug at the right provides a section of the original state of broken fitting, with the ends of the wrought-iron tie bars entering the inner space between the lug wings. The hexagonal nut (without any sign of a washer to spread the load) is seen at the centre of the facing wing, together with the ends of a cotter prised open to fix the joint at the right.

There is the top of another cotter adjacent to the prongs of the open cotter, the end which ould have been hammered to tighten the joint. Close inspection shows there to be a gap between the side of this cotter and the rectangular slot into which the cotters have been inserted. This gap must be around ¼in in width in order for Mr Noble to have hammered a shim during his 'maintenance' activities in silencing rattling joints, although the gap in this particular one appears empty, so the joint is apparently tight. The damage to the lug on the northern side of the centre cell was very similar, with an almost identical fracture on the lug *(6.8)*.

Debris Fields

Although there appears to be very little debris on the masonry base of the platform, the reverse view shows an interesting set of parts *(5.4)*. It is worthwhile summarising what can be seen in this view of the eastern part of the platform of pier No.3. The first, and most common, piece of metal is a horseshoe-shaped fragment: a semi-circular fragment with a central hole. It is not difficult to see that they are the corresponding parts of the broken lugs, especially when compared with *(6.9)*. There are no less than eight or nine such fragments scattered over the base of the pier. The second kind of debris present is either intact or broken bolts, a complete but bent bolt being seen in the left foreground of the picture (even with two washers). The rest are bolt parts, broken on their shafts, with and without nuts. Finally, there are some stone or possibly cement fragments which may or may not have been there before the accident. It is hardly likely that the bolts or lugs were there before the accident, but at what stage did they come to fall from the tower?

It must have struck Henry Law quite quickly that here was a feasible explanation of the way the tower on pier No.3 fell that fateful night. Eight or nine broken lugs could not have been produced simply by breakage of the lugs on the first tier: there were only two broken tie bars in the central cell producing, at the most, four lug ends. They must therefore have fallen from the tiers higher up, but are now no longer present. The damage to the diagonal tie bars on pier Nos 1 and 3 was very similar: those supporting the structures against sway to the east, downwind, were those which had mainly failed. It implied that the two towers had failed by swaying to the east, and toppling over downstream.

Other Piers

When he came to examine the rest of the piers, his conclusion can only have been strengthened, because all show more or less a similar pattern of damage and debris. Without exception, for example, all of the piers show broken east-facing lugs, all fractured in just the same way, across the bolt hole. All the pier bases show small debris comprising broken lugs and bolts, a striking example being that of pier No.10, towards the northern end of the section *(6.10)*. Not only are there more than twelve broken lug ends, but many broken bolts and a broken joint.

It is true that the amount of large debris across the other piers does vary enormously, but even here the pattern is consistent with collapse of the towers to the east. It is also clear from pier Nos 2, 4 and 5, that the towers above collapsed by failure of the centre cell, because the remnant left is just the triangular-shaped cell which originally would have been on the western side of the piers *(6.5) (6.11) (6.12)*.

It seemed natural to suggest the following events occurred on the night of 28 December:

1. The towers in the high girders swayed to the east under the combined loading of the train, being pushed to the east.
2. The lugs on the bracing bars facing east were put under fearsome strains by the movement of the towers, and broke progressively, putting extra tension on the struts of the centre cells, which also failed progressively.

(6.8) View of pier No.3 tower looking west.

(6.9) Southernmost east-facing lugs on pier No.3 with details of fracture surfaces on the wings of the broken lug at left.

(6.10) Debris field on pier No.10 looking west, showing numerous lug ends, bent and broken bolts and a failed joint.

3. Each tower then became effectively two separate towers, and totally incapable of supporting the applied loads, and they fell under the train.
4. The massive high girders themselves were unsupported and fell with the train down into the east side of the estuary.

However, this theory did not explain why all the towers fell, and not just those loaded by the train and the wind forces acting on it. Indeed, the damage to the piers beyond where the train was actually found (between pier Nos 4 and 5) seemed yet more severe than those over which the train had already passed. It included the severely damaged north-standing pier, in a much more damaged state than the south-standing pier. The theory also does not mention at what stage the lugs started to fail. Was it really only during passage of the last train, or had it already started with the last local train before the express?

Why had the lugs failed so quickly? Why were they the weakest link in the chain holding the bridge together? The Inquiry turned to pier Nos 1 and 3 for surviving parts which could be tested under laboratory conditions to determine their strength more exactly.

Testing the Parts

The laboratory chosen for the tests was situated at 99 Southwark Street in London, just south of the river. It was headed by David Kirkaldy, a Scot from Fife who had established a reputation for independent testing of large components using a hydraulic testing machine, or tensometer, built to his own design. He actually advertised his independence in the motto engraved above the front door, 'Facts Not Opinions'.

The testing of components before use in structures had been well established for many years before the Dee Bridge disaster, by independents such as Tredgold, Hodgkinson and Fairbairn. However, it has to be said that their tests were not always rigorous, especially when

(6.11) Wreckage on pier No.4 looking west, showing remnants of the western sub-tower.

(6.12) Wreckage on pier No.5, with remnants of the western sub-tower.

attempting to assess the strength of cast-iron samples. The strength of any product (especially brittle materials) is one of the most difficult to measure accurately, owing to the problem of flaws and defects which lower the strength. One way around the problem was to test many identical samples, and to take an average of the results. It was also important to test samples of the components in as realistic a way as possible. Thus, the cast-iron girders used by Stephenson in the first Dee Bridge were tested at the foundry by hanging weights from the centre in an attempt to replicate usage conditions. The problem was that such a test did not accurately replicate usage. In the real bridge, the weight was distributed over only one lower flange, which itself had been weakened by a cavetto moulding with sharp corners. So had the proposed materials and components been tested before the Tay Bridge was redesigned with cast-iron piers and wrought-iron braces? Yes and no. The wrought iron had been approved by testing, as had the cast iron, but the connections had not. Indeed, Kirkaldy himself had done the tests on the materials, and they were approved for use in the bridge. It was a fatal mistake not to have tested the lugs because if the connections had been tested, they would have revealed the fatal weakness at the heart of the design.

Kirkaldy's Tests

Henry Law extracted as many parts as he could from the demolition of the three tiers on piers Nos 1 and 3 for testing in London. He also included samples extracted from the high girder section, which were only obtained after parts of the girders lying in the estuary were lifted and placed on land. But this took time, not just in dismantling the towers and girders, but in transporting the parts (whole columns, girders and attachments) to London. It would take time to cut the parts up to fit the machine and, in many cases, further machining to make suitably shaped specimens. Kirkaldy planned a series of tests on complete lugs, tie bars and bolts, as well as the materials used in the high girder section of the bridge. It is important to mention that the lugs included both the lower lugs and upper lugs. The latter were of slightly different design and incorporated lugs for the horizontal struts in each tier (which were not actually tested). The tests were mainly conducted in tension (the most crucial since the tie bars were designed to act in tension), but he also tested the cast iron in compression and bending. To overcome the problem of selectivity, he tested as many as Henry Law had collected, but it was inevitably a small sample. Even some of those connections he did test were seriously flawed, but whether or not because of, or in spite of, the disaster, we shall never know. Although the rate of straining was very slow, his machine would produce comparable strengths for the several components, which would be of great value to the court.

Results of the Tests

So what were his results? They are summarised in *(6.13)*, a set of histograms which show individual results for lower and upper lugs, and the wrought-iron bars respectively. The vertical axis of the graph shows the breaking load for each of the complete components when tested by pulling in his 300-ton capacity tensometer. From his tabulated results, we know that the lugs failed from around 0.57in to 0.98in extension. The conclusions confirmed first of all, that the lower lugs were the weakest link in the load path. The graph shows the mean load for each component, and there is considerable scatter for all the parts concerned, although least for the wrought-iron tie bars. The scatter for the lugs is large and similar for both top and bottom attachments. Kirkaldy recorded the nature of the way each sample failed, whether for example it included failure of the hole through the tie bar or the bolt. What he does not state is where the break occurred, perhaps because it was obvious that they all broke across the lug diameter across the bolt hole. Neither does he describe the flaws he found, or mentions in his tables, but perhaps we can assume that there were voids and small cracks present in the samples, which would account for the lower strengths shown in *(6.13)*.

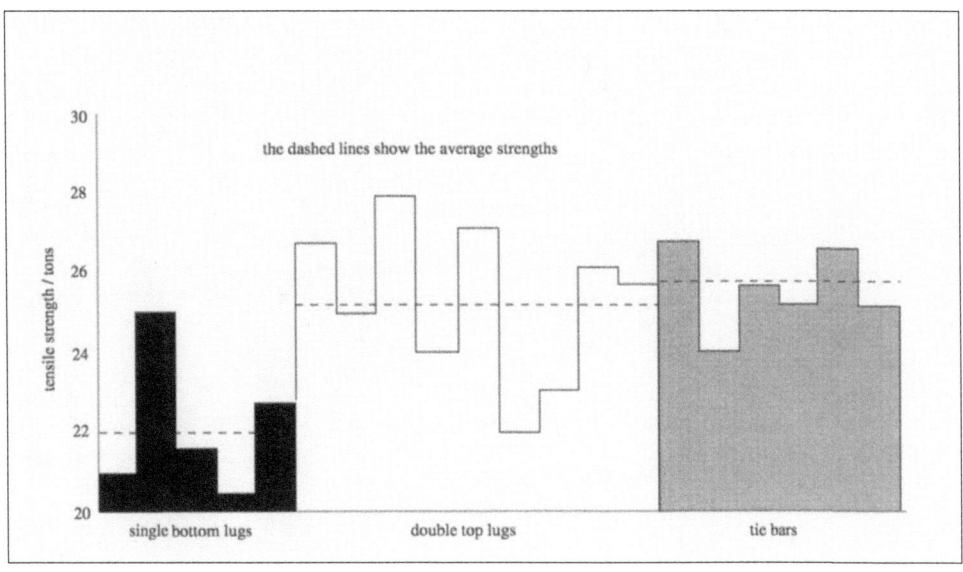

(6.13) Histogram of tensile strengths produced on diagonal tie bars, by David Kirkaldy.

It is true to say that he provides small drawings of the way cracks grew in the holes of the wrought-iron samples he tested, because they all failed there, but in slightly different paths when compared with one another. The cottered joints all proved stronger than the bolt holes at the ends of the tie bars, and the bolts of wrought iron showed reasonably consistent and high values given their intrinsic ductility. The ultimate strength of the wrought iron was equivalent to approximately 20 tons per sq.in (tsi).

Kirkaldy had tested the cast iron of the columns as well as the lugs. He had machined cylinders of diameter 1.128in, and tested them in bending, compression and tension using his giant tensometer. The results of fourteen identical tests for each form of strain produced a tensile strength of 20,473lbs per sq.in of section, compared with a compressive strength of 77,524lbs per sq.in. Only one of the samples proved 'unsound', suggesting that serious defects were not widely present in the cast iron. These results are equivalent to:

Tensile strength of cast iron = 9.14tsi

Compressive strength of cast iron = 34.6tsi

The cast iron he tested was of reasonable strength for the time, showing its normal characteristic of being around four times stronger in compression than in tension. It is interesting to translate the tensile strength into what would be expected of a lower lug. Given that the lug was about 4.5in wide and each wing was an inch thick, this gives an area of around 9 sq.in. The bolt holes were around 1.125inch in diameter, so the area (about 2 sq.in) must be subtracted to give the net section area. So the lugs should have a tensile strength of 7 x 9.14 = 64 tons. In fact, they were only about a third of their expected strength, suggesting a stress concentration of about three. This is well in line with modern expectations of the stress-raising effect of a hole. However, the drastically lower strength of the lugs was well appreciated by all at the Inquiry.

But it is jumping the gun to bring in the test results here because in reality they were so late in being produced that the court was not able to hear them until the final stages of the Inquiry. Indeed, they were produced so late that Kirkaldy was not called as a witness, either to attest to their validity or to be cross-examined about their interpretation. In his biography published much later, it was said by his son that he felt aggrieved by this decision. He had often acted as an expert witness, and would normally be required to attest to the veracity of experimental results. More importantly, he felt that the lawyers had misinterpreted his results. Be that as it may, the significance of his results was very clear to the court, since the judges were well qualified to assess the tests. It was already fairly clear from inspections made by both Henry Law and all the Commissioners that the lower lugs held the clue to the way the bridge had fallen. They had all visited the wrecked piers, and seen the many broken lugs, especially on pier Nos 1 and 3, which were relatively clear of other debris. When the results did appear, they confirmed what the Court had already figured out for itself.

Design Defects

But Law went on to catalogue many more design defects, as well as defects in the castings and the way the high girders had been built. The design defects are summarised in *(6.14)*, starting with the problems of the cast-iron lugs.

(6.14) Tay Bridge defects: design defects

Design	Defects	Number	Inquiry Reference
1	Lugs of low strength.	All lugs	14,193
2	Bolt holes with conical sections, so bolts act only against a short length of the hole.	Almost all Bolt holes	12,619
3	1.125in bolts for tie bars fitted to 1.25in bolt hole in lugs and flange.	–	12,580
4	Strut not abutting column wall.	All struts	14,669, 12,608
5	Strut bolts difficult to tighten.	All struts	14,553
6	L-girders not continuous across pier head.	All high girders	12,665
7	Pier base too small.	All piers	12,712
8	Batter on 18in columns too low.	All piers	12,717
9	Girders resting only on piers.	Most	12,655

In addition to the low strength of the lugs, he observed that the bolts were undersize, having a diameter of $1\frac{1}{8}$in compared with a smallest diameter of $1\frac{1}{4}$in to the hole in the lug. There was play of $\frac{1}{8}$in, giving a loose fitting. When tightened, the side of the bolt would meet the lug, meaning that the contact zone was smaller than expected, so concentrating stress over a very small area. It would mean that if the joints loosened for whatever reason, lateral movement of the towers was a real possibility.

The horizontal struts were also a problem because bolts were difficult to tighten against the rough, 'as-cast' surface of the adjacent lug. These were of a different design to the lower lugs, two holes being cast into the larger lug at the top of each cell of a tier. Some broken top lugs can indeed be seen in the debris field present on pier No.10 *(6.10)*, judging by the two holes visible in the broken parts. Breakage of the top lugs in terms of the fall theory presented above must represent the final stage of degradation of a tower, because once the struts have failed, each tower becomes two separate towers and therefore much more unstable against lateral loads.

The absence of a lateral girder at the top of each tower just below the spans *(6.1 and 6.2)* destabilised every tower in the high girder section. This design defect is visible in the long shots of the intact bridge shown earlier, and is present only in the twelve towers of the centre section, the lower towers either side being supported by lateral girders *(2.11)*. What is its significance? All the towers were space frames where each and every bracing element in the structure held it together. The bases were bolted into the masonry, and so held in a fixed position. The tops should also have been fixed rigidly to one another by the top girder, but if the laterals were omitted would be of lower strength against lateral loads. This was just another structural defect only present in the high girders and, together with the other defects noted above, would contribute to their fall on 28 December 1879. Just why those critical lateral girders were not fitted remains a mystery.

Other factors were at work in destabilising the central towers of the bridge. The pier bases were much too small for supporting such high structures, a feature which must have been obvious to all who saw the intact bridge. It had originally been envisaged that there would be eight columns on each pier, but it was reduced to six at an early stage in the project. Even then, the six columns only just fitted the base, and meant that there could be little lateral batter to the tower, a matter of about 12in over the 88ft-height of the highest tower in the centre section. No doubt the extra costs of providing much wider bases weighed heavily in the discussions of the bridge designers. This feature went against all prior practice in pipe bridges, such as Belah and the earlier Crumlin Viaduct. Those and other iron viaducts were given a batter measured in feet, and not inches. It provided them with much greater stability against lateral forces, and helps explain why they survived for so many years.

Defects of the Cast Iron

Henry Law described in his testimony many other faults found in the wreckage on the piers. They included variation in wall thickness caused by a shift of the inner core in the casting box. There were also axial lines on the outer surfaces of the columns caused by slight opening of the external part of the casting box. Much time at the tribunal was spent discussing the many casting defects found in the ruins after the accident. However, their haphazard occurrence could not be linked directly to the fall of the towers. Another kind of random defect found by Henry Law was the absence of spigots on many column ends. The purpose of a spigot was to stabilise the connections between columns, mating with the central hollow core and so providing extra support at the junction, in addition to the bolted flanges. Where the spigot was absent, the junction was less strong against separation, the columns only being held by the flange bolts. There was ample evidence of broken fractured bolts in the debris fields *(5.4 and 6.10)*.

He found other evidence of defects in the castings. They included blow holes buried within the bulk structure of the cast ironwork, only revealed at the breaks. More sensationally, where a blow hole impinged onto the free surface of a column, it formed an obvious flaw, many of which had been filled with beaumontage or 'Beaumont's Egg' as it was termed by many witnesses. John Prebble made much of the problem in his book about the disaster, but the significance of the defect is more difficult to pinpoint. A hole filled at the surface of a cylinder would clearly represent a point of weakness, but it is unlikely that such defects caused the fall of the bridge. None have been seen in our survey of the photographs of the wreckage, although they would be difficult to spot, given their nature. Such flaws must have occurred in a random way, which suggests that they were unconnected with the disaster. Similar comments apply to the much discussed possibility of 'burnt-on' lugs present in the structure. Slag inclusions in the castings, said by Henry Law to be 'very extensive', have not been observed in any photographs of fracture surfaces.

Faults of Construction

The investigation also uncovered many faults of construction, such as enlarged and damaged bolt holes, presumably created by the fitters during erection of the towers. If a bolt could not easily be passed through mating holes, it would be a quick solution to widen it with a chisel.

The base bolts securing the towers to the masonry piers were said to be poorly embedded, and there does appear from the pictures to be a variation in height of the bolts, suggesting varying depths of bedding. The mating surfaces of some columns were sometimes left rough, so that a poor junction was formed between them, often resulting in cement being extruded at the joint. Henry Law confirmed the poor design of the cottered joint. The slot for the gib and two cotters was simply too wide, so encouraging looseness when vibrated, and allowing Henry Noble to apply his infamous shims.

Such a large-scale failure left enough debris on the piers to be subject to very close scrutiny, and would inevitably expose defects commonly found in cast iron. It does not follow, however, that those defects were the cause of the failure. The poor design of the joint was a much more serious matter since all joints were so affected, and would form an important plank to Law's explanation of why the bridge fell. There were enough design defects present in the high girder section to explain why the centre section, and it alone, fell that night.

The Law Report

There were two parts to Law's published reports to the Inquiry. The first described construction of the bridge and the problem of lateral support of the piers. The second was a detailed set of calculations attempting to estimate what wind pressure would cause the piers to topple. It was reproduced at the end of the official report (together with Kirkaldy's tables and a similar report from Pole and Stewart acting on behalf of Bouch). The method Law used was essentially one known to generations of schoolboys as the method of moments, used in assessing the state of static equilibrium of a body. If a body is in equilibrium, then all the moments of the forces acting on it are balanced, the moment being defined as the product of force and distance of that force from the centre of gravity of the body.

The known forces on the bridge on the night of the storm were the force of the wind acting on the solid area of the train plus the wind acting on the surface of the bridge. The latter is relatively small since both the piers and the girders are open lattice structures. Those wind forces are opposed by the weight of the bridge acting about its centre of gravity plus resistance from the bracing elements and bolts holding the structure together. The surface area could be estimated from the bridge and train plans, so the net force attempting to push the bridge over calculated (for one pier at least) for various wind pressures. The opposing forces of the weight of the pier (plus girder) and the strain of the tie bars could be estimated and compared with their known strength to give a critical wind pressure needed to topple one pier. The same method could also be used to calculate the wind pressure needed to topple a carriage on the line. Law's calculations produced the following critical wind pressures:

To overturn a pier with a train on it, and columns bolted down	$P = 64.4\,\mathrm{psf}$
To overturn a pier without a train on it, and without columns bolted down	$P = 36.38\,\mathrm{psf}$
To overturn a pier with a train and without bolts	$P = 32.69\,\mathrm{psf}$
To overturn a pier with a train with all bracing elements and bolts	$P = 30.84\,\mathrm{psf}$
To overturn a second-class carriage, exposed	$P = 35.69\,\mathrm{psf}$
To overturn a carriage within girders	$P = 41.2\,\mathrm{psf}$

Thus his results showed substantial variation, but all the wind pressures were rather high, especially when the rigid columns were fully bolted down to their bases. They also showed, as one would expect, that it was easier to overturn a single pier when a train was upon it, simply by virtue of the extra exposed area of the train itself. The pressure needed to overturn a light carriage (the second-class carriage was chosen for being the lightest on the train that night) was surprisingly high, and it seemed an unlikely possibility.

The difficulties of a theoretical approach to the problem are, however, fundamental to the credibility of the analysis. There are many assumptions which must be made to simplify the calculations. All the joints, bolts and bracing elements must be exactly identical in resisting the wind moment, for example. This assumption was not supported by the evidence of the broken remains found at the scene, and was specifically refuted by Mr Noble's evidence of joint modification. When weaker joints or bracing elements are present, then a pier will fail from the point or points of least resistance in a chain reaction. Moreover, the entire calculation focused on just one pier in the high girder section. It was abundantly evident that the whole section of twelve piers had collapsed in sequence, most of them without having experienced the train moving upon them at all.

7
Disaster Theories

Following Henry Law's evidence, a credible explanation of how the bridge fell was beginning to emerge from the welter of information. There would, however, be another quite different interpretation of the sequence of events on the night of the disaster, to explain the fall of the high girder section. Central to the Inquiry was the location of the damage when seen just after the accident, the remains located in the estuary and their condition. To remind witnesses of the contemporary state of the visible material evidence, the large collection of photographs taken by Valentines was made available to the Inquiry. Plans of the position of the high girders had also been made, and included the exact position of the carriages within them. The state of both train and girders would be scrutinised for any evidence that the train had left the tracks, collided with the bridge and possibly started the collapse.

Many experts gave their opinions on the causes of the fall, including many eminent engineers of the day. They were employed by all sides in the Inquiry and, indeed, some of those engaged by Bouch and the NBR were to provide important evidence which helped clarify causation. Dugald Drummond, the locomotive superintendent of the NBR, would give important evidence of the condition of the train and permanent way on the bridge. John Cochrane was able to help pinpoint how the towers fell, and Benjamin Baker produced a practical survey of the effects of wind speed on the local surroundings. Their opinions did much to influence the court on the way it interpreted the massive amount of information on the remains from the disaster.

The Pole/Stewart Report

Being so closely associated with the design of the Tay Bridge, Dr Pole and Allan Stewart were questioned closely about their involvement with the project. Dr Pole was a Fellow of the Royal Society and a distinguished mathematician, while Allan Stewart had some experience of bridges as a civil engineer. Prepared using the same methodology as Law, Pole and Stewart produced a report which calculated the loads at various points in the bridge under live locomotive loads and wind loading at various pressures. Stewart was employed by Bouch to perform the original design calculations for the bridge, while Pole was brought in as an independent expert. He had extensive experience of use of different materials in bridges and indeed, had written a standard text book for engineers on the subject. The Court of Inquiry asked the two experts to supply all design calculations made for the bridge, before and during construction, in a letter from the three Commissioners. Seventeen points of detail were mentioned in their formal letter of instruction, including: the weights of the different parts of the structure, estimates of the surface area exposed to the wind and the maximum pressure which the piers could withstand the maximum stress on the diagonal tie bars for various wind pressures.

Pole and Stewart attempted to respond to the enquiries by noting that: '... they seem to refer to the calculations originally made for the structure...'. Although they stated that the bridge parts were designed: '... with full regard to all the strains likely to come upon them, the calculations have not been preserved in such a form as to be available for our present purpose...'.

This is a curious way of answering the request. Were the calculations made when the bridge was built or not? If any calculations were made, then surely they would be important evidence for the enquiry. Perhaps no calculations were made at all, and the bridge was built simply on previous experience, by 'make and do'. Whatever the case, the two experts said they would perform new calculations from the original design drawings. In a later section of their detailed report, they stated that the calculations are difficult: '... seeing that the strains are borne by the concurrent resistances of many bars in different positions'.

How true is this remark in the light of current knowledge? It is impossible to calculate the loads in the bracing bars without considerable computing power combined with rather gross assumptions regarding the uniformity of the structure. Law realised this and did not attempt the calculation. However, Pole and Stewart (no doubt having to respond to the request posed by the court) did estimate the loads, which was more than Law felt able to do. Using a wind pressure of 30lbs per sq.ft with a train on the bridge, they produced a figure of about 10tsi. Given that the cross-sectional area of a bracing bar is around 2.25 sq.in, it equates to a force in the bar of about 22.5 tons, similar to the breaking load of the bottom lugs.

Their calculations were duly performed for various wind pressures, although it is important to say that the approach of both Law and the two experts acting for Bouch and the NBR was highly theoretical and made little attempt to relate their results to the practical measurements made by Kirkaldy. Both analyses were static in nature, and made no allowances for dynamic effects, despite the evidence for oscillation of the bridge prior to failure, and the crucial evidence of Mr Noble about the looseness of the joints on the bracing bars. In their defence, it is also true to say that neither engineers nor analysts of the day had much appreciation (theoretical or practical) of the dynamic effects of winds on large structures. Their results were subject to severe criticism in the subsequent oral examination by the court. In vigorous cross-examination, neither expert would admit that the piers were faulty, and Mr Stewart was caught in a trap, as the following part of the transcript shows:

19,143. Take the hypothesis that is put to you, that these tie bars were giving to the extent of a ¼in, do you say that would add to the stability of the structure, or that it would detract from the stability of the structure? – Of course you mean this and the one opposite (pointing to the model)? It would add to the stability of the structure.
(Mr Bidder) Do you mean giving by extension, or by bolt bending?
(Mr Trayner) I mean giving by extension.
(Mr Stewart) I still hold to the view I have expressed. If Sir Thomas Bouch could have put in some kind of spring that would have allowed a yielding of a ¼in it would have added to the strength of the structure. It would have been very difficult to do.
19,144. It would have been something like building a castle in the air? – Perhaps.

19,156. When these bars chattered in the way we have heard described, it was again a piece of unnecessary work on Mr Noble's part to fill them up with packing pieces? – You have already asked me that question. I do not know that it is always wise to increase the stability of a bridge by looseness, I think it wiser to pack it up. It is difficult to answer that question.

Mr Stewart was clearly caught on the horns of a dilemma: he said that loose tie bars would make the bridge stronger, but yet supported packing them out with shims to tighten them!

Remains of the High Girders

By the time the tribunal had reconvened in London, most of the high girders had been located on the bed of the estuary. A plan was made available to show its relation to the piers *(7.1)*. Some had been recovered, especially the section containing the train *(7.2)*. It was that part of the girders lying between pier Nos 4 and 5 where it had been found, and was in remarkably good condition considering the height from which it had fallen. The locomotive, like all the rest of the train, was found lying on its side, like the high girders themselves. The first evidence of the state of the train had of course been obtained early in the year from the divers in their search for possible survivors. But it was when the remains were hauled to the surface (with some difficulty owing to their size and weight), that they would be subject to intense scrutiny.

Although the high girders lay seemingly intact on the floor of the estuary, there was some damage, especially near to points where it had been attached to the piers *(7.1)*.

It lay surprisingly close to the pier bases, extending in a lazy wave across the river bed. At some points it was so close to the piers that it seemed to have just dropped vertically down before rolling over to the east. Those points were at the south-standing pier (22ft 6in) and pier No.1 (16ft), followed by pier No.5 (21ft), pier No.9 (25ft 6in) and then the north-standing pier (23ft). Allowing for the width of the girders at 14ft, it had only just cleared the easternmost point of those piers. Since the towers were up to 80ft tall, the possibility of simple toppling had to be excluded. That would have left the high girders some 80ft away from the edges of the piers. On the other hand, if the high girders had simply fallen through the towers, they would have landed on the piers themselves. The actual position of the girders showed that the towers had broken up before and/or during the fall, to land so close to the tower bases.

Part of the fifth girder was photographed when it had been hauled to shore *(7.2)*. It came complete with carriages in greater or lesser states of damage. The first shows a door swung away, and some damage, although the following carriage is just a chassis. The rails are at the right, showing distortion where they have been bent by the fall; there is the water pipe at the lower right, buried in the corner of the structure. To what extent the damage was caused by

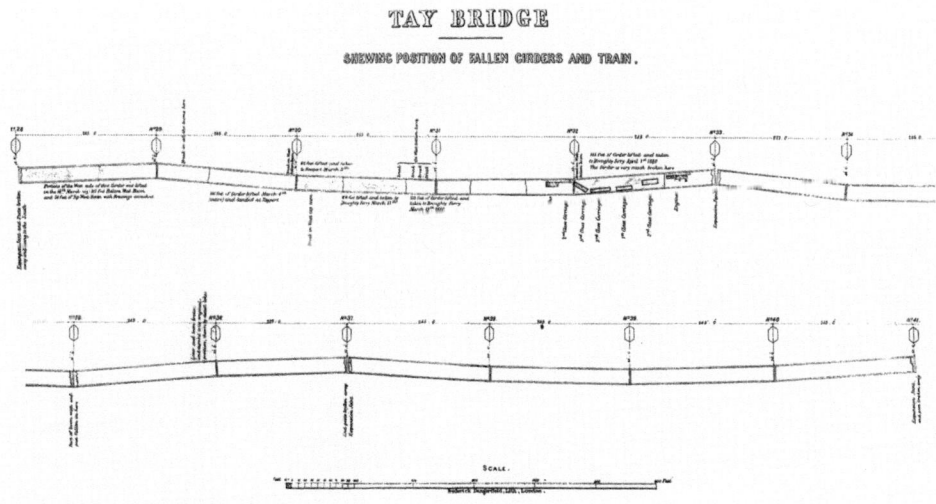

(7.1) Plan of the high girders in the estuary, made for the Inquiry. The plan has been split, so the upper right links to the lower left.

(7.2) Part of the high girder still containing the carriages.

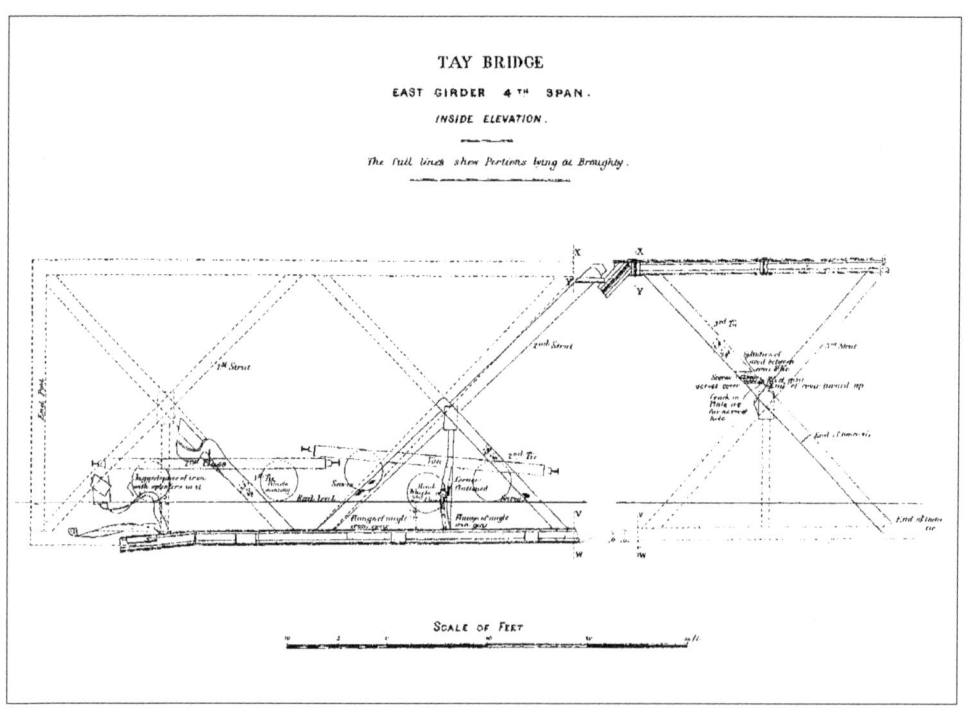

(7.3) Section of part of the high girder showing marks allegedly caused by contact with the moving train.

the fall or during recovery, remains undetermined. Dynamite had been used to cut the high girders into smaller, more manageable parts. When the fourth span was examined in detail, marks were found on some of the girders *(7.3)*.

The section shows the chassis of the guard's van and final carriage, but whether it represents their final position is unknown. Comparison with the plan *(7.1 and 4.5)* seems to show them just at the edge of span 4. The fine detail added to the diagram, shown in the section at the right, describes superficial damage to the large cross-girders forming the sides of the structure *(7.2)*. Horizontal marks have been drawn on one of the diagonal struts, and there appear to have been splinters of wood caught in the metalwork near the marks. This evidence would be the basis for a defence argument that the carriages toppled over and hit the sides of the girder, and initiated the whole collapse sequence.

A Second Theory

On further examination, Pole and Stewart admitted that they had not, unlike Mr Law, made a detailed survey of the fallen piers and examined the fractured and failed component parts of the columns. So what, in their opinion, was the cause of the failure of the bridge? They suggested that the train hit the high girders, and the shock was transmitted to the piers, which then fractured and brought the bridge down. There was indeed some evidence (two girders were damaged), as just described. But the heavy locomotive and tender had never left the line, so they advanced the theory that one or more of the last and lightest carriages had caused the critical damage. The theory was to be challenged, not least by Dugald Drummond, the NBR locomotive superintendent, but also by many of the expert engineers.

Train derailment was of course the same argument advanced by Stephenson to explain the failure of the Dee Bridge much earlier in 1847. The natural question was then put to the experts: if the bridge could be brought down by the train hitting the high girders, was it not then a faulty design? Stewart had apparently approved all the design changes made to the bridge by Bouch (cast-iron piers instead of brick piers, pier tops not strongly connected, six columns instead of eight etc.). He had done calculations at the time but could not produce them to the Inquiry. Indeed, their calculations in their joint report were done entirely from scratch and without reference to any calculations done before construction was underway.

Also of some interest was their calculation of the wind pressure needed to overturn an isolated carriage when on the rails. Using the known surface area presented to the wind (acting at right angles to the surface) produced the figure of around 30psf, but would clearly vary according to the total weight of the carriage and its surface area. When in a train, the connections with other carriages would increase the resistance to toppling.

Dugald Drummond

The trace evidence which Pole and Stewart interpreted as coming from sideways impact of the train with the girders was questioned by several witnesses. In particular, Dugald Drummond maintained that there was no evidence to suppose that the train ever left its tracks. He pointed out that the marks were around 11ft above the level of the rail and, although the carriage was about 10ft above the rail, the girder was about 3ft horizontally from the rail, so was unlikely to have made the marks in question *(3.4)*. If it tilted over, its height relative to the girder would have been lower. Moreover, if the wheels of any carriage had left the track, there would have been damage: none had been found on any wheels. He concluded:

18,233. Looking to the state of the tires and buffers and the couplings, and the whole state of what remains of the second-class carriage, have you formed an opinion as to whether it had left the line or not? – I do not think that any of the carriages left the rails until the girders had left their place on the pillars.

He was challenged in his examination by Mr Bidder (acting for Bouch) but refused to modify or change his opinion, despite extremely aggressive questioning by counsel. He was, however, ably defended by the Commissioners, who had taken exception to Bidder's increasingly aggressive tone with Drummond.

He was also asked about the state of the engine and its controls. All evidence showed the suddenness of the calamity which overtook the train:

18,376. Was there anything to indicate that there had been time to do anything after the appearance of the accident? – There was every indication that there was no time for acting. The reversing lever was standing at the third notch from the centre, or six notches from the full forward gear; the regulator standing full open, and the brake screw on the tender was full off; the brake screw on the brake van in the rear of the train was also off.

18,377. Those would be indications of great suddenness. The first thing for a driver to do if there was anything wrong would be to shut the regulator if he felt any jolting with his engine, and the next thing would be to apply the brake...

The train had been fitted with the new Westinghouse air brakes and, only under the control of the driver. Whether they had been applied was not possible to ascertain. However, he did notice that all the axles on the locomotive, tender and carriages were bent to some degree, a feature he attributed to the fall while still in place on the rails. Indeed, he could place the position of the locomotive exactly at the point of impact with the floor of the estuary from marks on the rails made by the wheels.

Benjamin Baker

Working in the offices of Sir John Fowler, Benjamin Baker had a well-established reputation as a civil engineer and bridge builder. He had actually worked in an iron foundry in South Wales, and had helped design and build the first underground railway in London, the Metropolitan. He had recently designed the Staithes Viaduct, and he estimated that he had designed some 12 miles of bridges and viaducts. He had worked on the first elevated railway in New York (the so-called 'El') in 1868. It had been built on a continuous viaduct over the streets and was around 14 miles long. Although now much truncated and mostly in Brooklyn, where it originally crossed the famous Brooklyn Bridge, the El has attracted film-makers for its visual qualities, especially for the car chase sequence in *The French Connection* (1971). The 'loop' in Chicago still acts as a tourist magnet for its superb views of downtown city life. The various Els were mainly built of wrought-iron girders and supports. Baker had published a small book in 1870, which demonstrated the superiority of steel over wrought iron in long-span bridges.

When questioned at the Inquiry, he referred directly to the problem of the missing superstructure which had not been raised from the estuary bed.

He agreed that the conical lugs were serious defects but felt that the stress from the tie bars would be ameliorated by the wrought-iron bolts being bent into the cone, so spreading the applied load more evenly. He thought that the bridge was capable of withstanding high winds, and had made a detailed survey of the remains for any evidence of the effective wind pressure that night. He had been interested in the topic for some time, especially during the successful transport from Egypt and raising of Cleopatra's needle on the new embankment on the Thames in London. The subject was clearly relevant to the court, given the problem of assessing the wind speeds and pressures acting on the structure during the storm the night of the disaster. There were many much smaller structures close by and on the bridge which should have suffered severely if the winds had been excessive. They included the signal box, walls near the bridge *(7.4)* and ballast lying on the track itself.

The photograph was taken by Valentines shortly after the accident, and shows the signal boxes and railway cottages below, none of which show any storm damage. The boxes retain

(7.4) View of the ruined bridge from the south, with the fateful signal box in the foreground.

their chimney stacks and no tiles or slates have been lost from their roofs. An intact wall and fence is seen at the bottom of the picture, and the ballast under the track seems completely undisturbed by the storm. It may be compared with a similar photograph taken by George Washington Wilson of exactly the same field of view in the summer of 1879. There is very little difference, even to the position of various planks on the side of the embankment to the right. The only substantial difference between the two pictures is the state of the cottage gardens and a (presumably new) fence at the front of the cottages.

This what Benjamin Baker said about the wind pressure that night:

> 19,460. You have said that, in your judgment, the base was perfectly safe, having regard to wind pressure as a whole (I do not mean any isolated point of it) it had to meet? – I do not think the ruling maximum pressure of the wind on that night exceeded 15lbs per sq.ft.

He explained that he had performed experiments on window glass panes, and examined the undamaged panes on the windward side of the signal boxes *(7.4)*. None of the windows or glass-paned doors had suffered significant damage. Although ballast on the track had moved, the state of the track at the edge of the fallen section was identical with that at the south signal boxes. Similar comments applied to the north signal box (although it seems that the north box lost its chimney that night), and other large structures near the Tay Bridge station (although again, the glass roof of the new Tay Bridge station had been blown out that night). He reiterated his opinion on further questioning:

19,480. Taking all that into consideration, do I correctly understand that in your judgment there could not have been an average wind pressure per sq.ft over the span of the girders greater than about 15lbs? − No, I think not. I may say that for the past fifteen years I have looked very carefully for evidence of any structure capable of standing a uniform pressure 20lbs per sq.ft which has been blown down. I issued a challenge in a letter to The Times *when the question was raised about Cleopatra's Needle, and those heavy pressures were brought forward, about 80lbs, and so on, and I said I had been a very careful observer myself, and I should be very glad if anyone could give me an instance of a chimney or a wall, or anything capable of standing a pressure of 25lbs, which had been blown down. I think the most violent storm I ever experienced was in Brighton, when I saw a man blown down. I looked out for fence walls, some of them on the edge of the cliff, and some of them on the downs, and I measured them and calculated their stability, and there are miles of walls there which would distinctly tumble over with a pressure of 13lbs per sq.ft, and they have been there for thirty or forty years, and have not been blown down.*

Here then, was powerful evidence against the idea that the bridge had simply been blown down by the force of the wind that night.

John Cochrane

John Cochrane gave evidence on the way the towers fell at pier No.5, the pier just ahead of the train when it fell. He had wide experience of using cast iron in very large structures, and had himself worked on the Crystal Palace, as well as the Westminster, Charing Cross and Cannon Street bridges. He was one of the first experts to indicate the sheer scale of the problem faced by the Inquiry. Since only three tiers of eighty-four had survived anywhere near intact, the rest of the metalwork was buried in the estuary, and thus unavailable for direct inspection. All the work of Henry Law had focused on the wreckage surviving on the piers, a very small proportion of the original towers. All the work of the divers focused initially on locating survivors, and when none were found in the train or nearby, efforts transferred to determining the position of the high girders and retrieving them. This was, by the sheer size of the girders, a long, difficult and expensive task. It effectively meant that retrieving the wreckage of the piers would not be attempted. After all, the wrought iron of the girders was valuable as scrap, while the cast iron had very little value. The high girders would be rescued and examined, but the cast-iron columns were left where they were. The former could provide some new evidence for the way the bridge failed, and would be exploited by Sir Thomas Bouch when it came to his defence. The latter would remain *in situ* at the bottom of the estuary, and much information about its state would be lost forever. John Cochrane's evidence before the court would, however, yield a little extra information on their state, especially their relationship to the high girders at the bottom of the estuary:

15,001 (Mr Trayner) Did you notice that on some of the piers the lower tier of columns had been forced to the westward? − I did.
15,002 The great mass of the superstructure we know went over to the east? − Yes.
15,003 In your opinion, what led to the forcing of theses columns westward? − At No.5 pier the eastern set of columns is underneath the eastern girder crushed up.
15,004 The eastern set of columns is under the eastern girder? − Yes, as it lies on its side, or as it did lie on its side at the bottom. The western columns are lying over the top of the western girder, and that renders it absolutely clear to my mind that the three eastern columns gave way first, that the structure went over sufficiently quickly, and that then the three outer columns or western columns fell over onto the top of the girder, and so they are found.

15,007 (Mr Barlow) Showing that the eastern and western parts separated from each other? − That they separated from each other. I think the probability is that the separation would not have taken place had the angle girders or L-girders at the top been connected together so as to have brought the whole six columns in unison.

15,015 (Mr Barlow) If those columns had been strongly cross-braced, strongly fitted and strongly held down by holding-down bolts, do you think the bridge would have been sufficient? — I believe that it would be standing at the present moment; it is a question of the bracing of course.

The upshot of Cochrane's answers was clear: the western set and eastern set of columns had separated at the start of the collapse, the eastern set falling first, followed by the high girders and then, finally, the western set, so as to form a sandwich on the floor of the estuary. It followed that the tower on pier No.5, at least, had failed when the lateral bracing tie bars and struts had broken.

Having seen both the recovered train and the girders, Mr Cochrane went on to refute the theory that the train had derailed and caused the fall:

15,033. (Mr Trayner) You heard the suggestion that the train had gone off the rails and knocked over the bridge; have you formed any opinion as to whether the train had gone off the rails, and by so doing had contributed in any way to the result? I think it did not from all I saw. I do not believe the train left the rails.

Sir George Airy

As Astronomer Royal since 1835, Airy was a pre-eminent astronomer with interests well beyond the official remit, such as standardisation of weights and measures. He reformed the Observatory at Greenwich, introducing the famous dropping ball which signalled to ships on the Thames the time of twelve noon, so that their chronometers were synchronised. He held strong views about the weather, rather surprisingly for an astronomer, but then English astronomy had for many years been of direct practical interest to mariners for celestial navigation, for example. He was deeply involved in the standardisation of time, a problem created by the railway system, and the need for accurate timetables. He was no stranger to railway problems, having been a member of the Gauges Commission in 1847, when the problem of reconciling Stephenson's narrow and Brunel's broad gauge was discussed (without resolution, although Airy had driven one of the test locomotives himself!). Most significantly, he had criticised the design of the Crystal Palace in 1851 for the possibility of structural damage in strong winds combined with large numbers of users. He was worried about the strong gales which struck London with a pressure of 20-25psf every year, and their effect on the structure. His concerns focused on the 'snugs', the connections that joined the columns with the horizontal girders as well as the foundations of the columns in the Crystal Palace. Could a gale uproot the structure? His fears were put to rest by tests at the time, but the Tay Bridge disaster seemed to echo earlier fears.

However, he was not to be reminded of his scepticism of 1851, but rather address a very specific issue of a report he had made for Bouch, when asked for advice on wind pressures. He had been consulted not about the Tay Bridge, but about Bouch's plans for a new Forth crossing by means of a suspension bridge. The height and length of the suspended way could be affected by strong winds, so what was Airy's advice? In his report, he advised that a pressure of no more than 10psf could be expected, but with localised gusts up to 40psf. He was questioned very aggressively about his estimates, given the wind pressures suggested by both Henry Law and Pole and Stewart. In his report he had qualified his opinion about expected pressures on the proposed Forth Bridge, saying that:

> ... the fairest estimate of the pressure on the entire bridge would be formed by taking the mean of the recorded pressures on the entire bridge at one point of space for a moderate extent of

time, as representing the mean pressure on a moderate extent at one instant of time. Adopting this consideration, I think we may say that the greatest wind pressure to which a plane surface like that of the bridge will be subjected on its whole extent is 10lbs per sq.ft.

He was effectively saying (in a long-winded way) that the design of the suspension bridge should allow for an average pressure of 10psf, but could experience much greater, momentary, gusts of 40psf. The point at issue was, would he make the same recommendation of the Tay Bridge? He pointed out that a long suspension bridge would swing back after being moved laterally by high pressure, while a rigid structure like the Tay Bridge would not return to equilibrium so easily. The Commissioners were left with the impression that his range of pressures could apply just as much to the Tay as the proposed new Forth Bridge. So the situation was left in an unsatisfactory state, largely owing to the absence of reliable wind speed data, not to the opinions of Airy.

Sir George Stokes

Another eminent scientist of the day, Stokes, had been a member of the Royal Commission of 1847 (Iron in Railway Structures), and had conducted many experiments into fluid mechanics. He is remembered today for his law governing the fall of spheres through viscous liquids, and for other analyses in what is now known as fluid mechanics, the study of the way fluids move. But he was much more the Victorian polymath, making substantial and significant discoveries in optics (such as fluorescence and light polarisation) and even in medicine (for his analysis of haemoglobin in blood). His mathematical skills were justly famous, perhaps as one might expect for a successor to Sir Isaac Newton at Cambridge.

He was also to be questioned on a very narrow range of issues, and certainly not engineering questions about the bridge structure. His testimony was related to the problem of measuring wind pressure accurately, there being few instruments available. He was concerned about the formation of eddies at the edges of flat plates, for example, which had been used to measure pressure in the past. There was also concern about a partial vacuum formed behind the plate and its effect on the readings. There appeared to be a dearth of research, since serious instruments were not widely available, and systematic recording of both wind speed and pressure was absent. He felt that theoretical statements were not advisable in the absence of further research, although did confirm that wind pressure was dependent on the square of the wind speed, so pressure rose very quickly as wind speed increased. It would of course explain the destructive power of cyclones and hurricanes, as well as tornadoes. There were practical problems of assessing local variations in wind speed and gusting, where again, instrumentation was lacking. Stokes' approach to the court was academic, with rather long answers to very short questions. Given the nature of the problems he was asked about, it was inevitable that the lawyer's questions needed extensive explanatory responses. He was followed by a meteorologist, who admitted that there was no anemometer at Dundee which could have provided critical and quantitative information on wind speeds that night, so the tribunal could only rely on estimates from local observers.

Sir Thomas Bouch

The questioning of the bridge proponent, designer and builder would inevitably be foremost in the minds of the Commissioners. More than any other, it was his project, a plan he had developed over many years and had then put into action.

First, he was asked about the design of his Belah and Deepdale viaducts. Their supporting cast-iron towers were about twice the height of those on the Tay Bridge. They had given satisfactory service but their towers were much closer together, since they had been built on land rather than in an estuary. The history of the Tay Bridge project was reviewed, and the problem of the foundations for the piers dominated the questioning. The initial borings had indicated solid rock all the way across the estuary, but the survey was found to be faulty towards the centre of the bay. He had consulted Colonel Yolland (one of the Commissioners sitting in judgment) about bridge and wind loadings during the design phase, and had been advised that '... we do not take the force of the wind into account when open lattice girders are used for spans not exceeding 200ft.'

It was pointed out that the letter from Yolland to Bouch referred only to the girders and not to the piers which supported them. So Bouch (supported by Allan Stewart) had not performed any calculations of the effect of wind on the structure, despite the fact that he had changed the length of the girders in the centre from 200ft to 245ft (with two spans of 225ft). He admitted that he had changed the bracing system from that used at Belah to the Tay piers:

16,482. Were you also satisfied as to the strength of the bridge with regard to the wind? – I was. I may mention that when I built the bridge at Beelah I used to have rather a high opinion of the force of the wind there, and the bracing is somewhat different to what I had adopted afterwards...

However, there is no explanation of why he changed the bracing method for the Tay Bridge, with lugs cast as one with the columns, rather than separate lugs, as at Belah. He had changed the design of the bases of the towers from a set of eight to six, arranged as a hexagon, and it also emerged that he was working simultaneously on the project to build a suspension bridge across the Forth. On the latter design, he had consulted four eminent engineers, one of whom was no less than Mr W.H. Barlow, another of the Commissioners sitting in judgment. Barlow worked with Dr Pole and it was they who consulted with the Astronomer Royal, Sir George Airy.

Some troubling details of the early history of the Tay project emerged:

16,620. To go back to history. As we know, about the beginning of 1874, I think it was, Mr De Bergue became incapacitated by illness from attending to business? – Yes.
(The Commissioner) What time in the beginning of 1874?
(Mr Bidder) March 1874 is the date I had given to me.
(The Witness) He became insane.

Bouch repeated the assertion:

16,622. Messrs Hopkins, Gilkes & Co. of Middlesborough, were originally, I think, the third lowest in the list of tenders? – Yes, in the original tender.
16,623. And when the contract was given up by Mr De Bergue they were invited to take on the work? – Yes.
(Mr Webster) I am told that the death of Mr De Bergue took place on the 10 April 1873.
(The Witness) But he was insane before that.

Such an extraordinary assertion appeared to pass without further comment from the court.

The questioning now turned to the details of the column designs. At some stage (apparently on 13 March 1873) it was decided to increase the wall thickness from 1in to 1¼in, but only for the large 18in-outer columns. Concrete was to be added to the hollow interiors, but only to prevent rusting:

16,657. You did not calculate upon the concrete for stability? – Not in the slightest.

The great weight of concrete added to all the columns would of course increase their weight, and hence lower the centre of gravity of the towers, although by a marginal amount (from 88 to 110 tons) when compared with the massive weight of the girders (288 tons eventually, when ballast was added to the track) which they supported. Mr Bidder then turned to the problem of testing the materials and the connections to be used in the bridge.

16,670. Did you take steps to have all the malleable iron that came from Middlesborough properly tested, whether it was for girders or tie rods? — Not all the malleable iron, but I sent specimens to Mr Kirkaldy to be tested.

The result of those tests showed the wrought iron to be strong and up to specification, but the connections were never tested. The cast iron had apparently been tested, as it emerged a few minutes later:

16,679. Have you anything to say with regard to the cast iron? — The cast iron was tested with a transverse strain; that is always done in the foundry.

But when repeatedly questioned on the nature of the foundry test, to which he gave evasive answers, a direct question from the Commissioner elicited the response:

16,685. (The Commissioner) The question asked you is: are you aware that the cast iron was tested at all by anyone at Wormit? — No, not any special test.
16,686. (Mr Bidder) That is to say, of your own knowledge? — Not of my own knowledge; it was only the talk at the time at those meetings.
16,687. (The Commissioner) Did any of your assistants say to you 'We have tested the cast iron'? — It is seven years ago, and I really cannot say; but I can say positively that they told me that the cast iron was satisfactory.

He said that he had visited the bridge regularly and had not received any adverse comments about defects in the cast iron or other parts. He was apparently not aware that the lugs had been formed with conical holes:

16,714. Were you aware that there were any conical holes? — I was not. If I had known I should certainly have had them drilled out square, though that would have reduced somewhat the quantity of metal in the lug, but I should have done that certainly.
16,715. You will so far agree with what has been stated that there was a thing you would not knowingly have passed, and you would think it disadvantageous? — You could not see the thing by inspection; you could not see the conical shape of the hole.
16,716. It would be very difficult to see, even if you were looking at the lug itself before the bolt was in it? — Yes; my own theory is, that the rattling which Mr Noble spoke to was due to the bolt bent in the conical hole. It would be drawn from the straight, and it would take its bearing on the cone.

But the bolt bending into the cone cannot have happened immediately, because he had accompanied General Hutchinson when he inspected the bridge in February 1878. The tie bars then were tight and secure in preventing movement of the columns when the heavy trains passed over. The loosening must therefore have happened later. The issue is important because if they had bent into the cone, it would ameliorate the stress-raising effect of the hole. It may have happened when Kirkaldy was testing the lugs owing to the very slow rate of test, although Kirkaldy never says so in the tables of results, or anywhere else for that matter. The point is this: if the bolts had not bent into the cone on the bridge, the stress raising could be more serious than a simple factor of three. It might mean that the tie bars broke sooner than expected from Kirkaldy's results. Their effective strength would have been lower than the results shown in the previous chapter.

Bouch was also asked about his relationship with his inspector, Mr Noble:

16,729. There were a good many letters upon this, Mr Noble, as we know from his evidence, continued to be employed upon the bridge with certain staff? – Yes.

16,730. And Mr Noble stated that as regards his examination of the piers of the bridge, I think, that he simply did it of his own motion; is that correct? – That is not true. The staff was given him of two men, and when they were not sounding, and finding out about the scour, which was the principal thing I was afraid of, they were to be employed upon the piers seeing that the nuts were all right.

The evidence was not just Bouch's opinion, but was supported by the written evidence of Noble's contract with the NBR, where Mr Walker, the general manager of the NBR, said in an internal letter of 22 June 1878:

> Referring to your letter of the 20th instant, I have today seen Mr Bouch, and arranged that the maintenance and repair of the piers and foundations of the Tay Bridge shall remain in his hands for the next nine or twelve months...

This was not all, though. Noble made many personal reports to Bouch about the condition of the bridge in the subsequent months. Thus, in a letter of 31 July 1878, he says, *inter alia*, that:

> I am happy to say that the piers are not only secured at the price named, but upon a strict scrutiny made every day there is not the slightest sign of settlement at any of the piers. My staff of men who work the steam-boat are always busy overlooking the bracings, &c., while I am attending to the Newport branch.

It was quite clear (at least in Bouch's memory) that inspection of the bridge included bracing elements:

16,751. Is it within your understanding that his staff were continually engaged in overhauling the bracings and ties throughout the bridge? – Yes, that was the arrangement I made, that they should devote their spare time to examining them.

In a letter-report to Bouch from 18 December 1878, he asks for a reduction in the number of staff he employed:

> There will be no more rubble required at the piers unless something occurs very different from what I expect. The superstructure stands the traffic first class; there is not the least defect in the entire length of the bridge, nor any sign of settlement at any one of the many piers.

It may be noted that Noble, in his evidence to the court, said that he heard the first 'chattering' tie bars in September 1978, so why does he not mention the problem in his December report? Why did the tribunal not put the new evidence to him directly, since it clearly contradicted what he had said before? Both Bidder and Trayner made just this comment before the court, but he was not to be recalled. Bouch was asked whether or not Noble had reported the chattering tie bars if not in the written report, verbally, at any time. Perhaps more important, what would he have done if he had known of the problem.

16,763 (Mr Bidder) Did Mr Noble ever report to you as to any of the tie bars chattering? – No, never. I was very surprised at it when I heard it.

He then went on to the period just before the accident, when two cracked columns had been reported by Noble to Bouch. They were not actually in the high girder section, but they had been hooped with wrought iron to limit the further growth of the cracks. He had visited the bridge to inspect the cracks:

16,785. You told me that in consequence of Mr Noble's letter you visited the bridge and saw these cracked columns? — Yes.

16,786. Your visit, therefore, must have been subsequent to the 13 December last year? — It is possible; I cannot tell.

16,787. That letter is dated the 13 December; it was after that letter? — It must have been after that last letter.

16,788. It must have been a very few days before the accident? — Yes; it went over very soon after I got that letter.

16,789. At that time were you on the pier yourself? — I was.

16,790. With trains passing over? — Yes; I thoroughly examined it.

16,791. Was there any looseness, or chattering, or perceptible slackness of any of the tie bars? — Not the least.

After the accident he had hurried to the scene and seen the debris. What was his opinion of the cause or causes of the fall? It was the second-class carriage near the end of the train which derailed when toppled by a violent gust of wind and smashed into the girder, leaving the marks shown in *(7.3)*. But why such a small collision could have brought the whole bridge down was left an open question. It might have been a different matter if the locomotive had derailed, since it was much heavier, but Bouch did not go so far in his explanation.

In cross-examination, he was asked about the cost-savings of using cast-iron columns rather than a brick pier. Bouch agreed with Mr Trayner that cost-savings would be made, and would also apparently bring stronger piers. It emerged that he had regularly visited the building of the bridge about once a week, but had fallen ill at one stage and retired to recuperate in the south of France for three months. He said that his unspecified illness was caused by the anxiety of building the structure. He reiterated his ignorance of the conical bolt holes in the lugs, and maintained that when the bolts bent into the cone, the tie bar would be just as effective, provided it was correctly tensioned up again. There was no evidence that Noble did tighten them at all, but nevertheless Bouch seemed to believe that he had done so.

The collision theory naturally came up for more serious scrutiny than when Bouch had been examined by Mr Bidder. Not least of the many objections to the theory was the utility (or otherwise) of the guard rail: surely this was meant to prevent just such an event? There also appeared to be no grinding marks on the tires of the second-class carriage. The east side of the carriage would be presumably seriously damaged by the impact with the girders, but in fact it was the west side which showed worse damage. Perhaps the carriage crossed the track to be transverse to the line, and the guard's van then smashed into it. This too was difficult to imagine because the carriage was actually longer than the girders were wide. And why was the axle of this carriage bent in the middle, just like all the rest of the wagons? Perhaps it was bent when the carriage hit one of the angle irons protruding from the corners of the girder *(3.4)*. If the carriage had derailed, there would be a mark on the wheel, but none was found. Bouch admitted that he had not examined the tires, but he did mention that a plank had recently been washed up at Newport and bore the mark of a wheel upon it. However, the plank was not positively identified as coming from below the rail track, or being a sleeper, and anyway had been washed away by the tide. Bouch floundered when put to the test and was clearly flustered by the cross-examination, judging by a sympathetic comment made by the Commissioner afterwards. He himself had some pointed questions for Bouch, however. One of these concerned the conical holes. The contract for the bridge contained the following clause:

> All bolts to be made of Low Moor iron, or such as shall be specially sanctioned by the engineer, and to be neatly finished, head and nut, and not projecting more than ½in through the nuts; to be carefully forged and screwed, and made to fill the bolt holes.

Bouch admitted that it was a serious defect to have conical holes, and they weakened the action of the diagonal tie bars against the lateral forces exerted by the wind and passing trains. He showed the strain he himself was under by his vigorous examination in the witness box when he exclaimed in answer to a question about the cracked columns outside the high girders:

17,166. Do you not recollect that there was some suggestion made as to how theses pillars could be better protected? – I have no recollection. I have thought of a plan for strengthening all that part of the bridge.
17,167 Why? – On account of the public feeling since the fall of the bridge.

General Hutchinson

The inspector who approved the bridge was called to give evidence. His inspection in February 1878 had been thorough, involving loading the bridge to the greatest possible extent with no less than six locomotives weighing over 400 tons, travelling at speeds of up to 40mph. He had examined the piers by landing from a launch, and had seen no movement of the structures when the test train ran overhead:

15,966. I observed nothing at all to give me an uncomfortable impression about the stability of the columns. There was naturally a slight vibration in the tie bars as the engines ran over, but nothing more than you will always find in every structure.

So he had felt vibrations in the tie bars but did not think it unusual. He was questioned further about the state of the tie bars:

15,970. You know how these tie bars are fastened with jibs and cotters? – Yes.
15,971. Is that a matter which, in your opinion, required careful attention after the bridge was opened? – I should think so, certainly. Of course the object of putting the cotters in was to have the means of tightening as slackness occurred.
15,972. In a bridge of that construction tied together in that way, did you anticipate that would be a matter receiving careful attention from those in charge? – Certainly, it seemed a very important point.

15,974. Would the action of trains passing over the bridge naturally tend to loosen these cotters to some extent? – I have no doubt that it would; and especially the higher the speeds, the more racking motion, so to speak, would be produced on the structure.

He went on to explain that he had recommended a speed limit of 25mph for passenger trains to limit the deleterious effects of vibrations on the tie bars:

15,975. Had you that in mind when you suggested the limit of 25mph which should not be exceeded? – I had that in my mind; that it was not a structure with a wide base, and that therefore it was very desirable to limit the action of passing trains to as great an extent as was reasonable; and I therefore thought it prudent to suggest a low speed, because, of course, the higher the speed or the higher the momentum brought to bear on the columns, the more tendency there would be to give them a rocking.
15,976. But even with that limited speed uniformly observed, would there have been from natural action the probable result that I have pointed out of loosening these cotters? – There must have been a certain amount of vibration and oscillation introduced into the columns, and hence a tendency to loosen all the different joints of the structure.

The court was now getting to the heart of the problem, and the line of questioning proceeded to the remedial actions adopted by Mr Noble.

15,978. If you had found any of these cotters in a condition which would have admitted of the insertion of a packing piece, would you have passed that as being sufficiently tight to warrant the bridge being used? – I should have called attention to it if I had seen it, and requested that the bar in question should be tightened or replaced by a proper one, but the presence of two or three loose bars, had I seen them, would not have led me to think that the bridge was an imperfect bridge, and could not be passed.

15,979. But supposing that you multiply two or three into one hundred? – It would have very much depended upon the amount of looseness which I found. So much depends upon what you see when you examine a structure.

The consequences of vibrations on the structure and the 'racking' motion of the towers as trains passed overhead would be a focus of attention for the court when they came to their final judgment. There was just one more issue which the court wished to examine. There were eighty-four diagonal tie bars in each of the towers, and the 100 loosened bars over the twelve high piers were significant. General Hutchinson had recommended in his report that he wanted to have an opportunity of observing the effects of high wind when a train was passing over:

15,981. What induced you to make that observation? – During the time I was at Dundee, at the end of February, it so happened that there was no high wind blowing, and I was therefore anxious in order to see what additional or what perceptible effect a high wind on a train of carriages might have had, to have another opportunity of observing that; but, unfortunately, before the railways came forward for inspection, when I might have had that opportunity, I was taken seriously ill, and the final inspection of the railways north and south of the bridge devolved upon another officer.

But that officer never came, and he personally was never able to see the effect of a high wind on the structure. In his original report he also made some interesting comments about the track, that the gauge (or width) needed preserving using ties between the rails, and that '... slack places in the rails require adjusting'.

8

Finale

The final submissions to the tribunal were the closing speeches from the various counsel. As is normal, both then and now, the speeches presented a careful selection of the evidence which favoured their own clients. It was up to the three Commissioners to decide which witness evidence they preferred where there was any conflict. The Inquiry finally ended on 8 May, adjourning while the Commissioners sifted the evidence. It was a mountain of evidence: not just in the volume of direct testimony heard (569 close-printed pages of transcript from 121 witnesses), but in the expert reports and the material evidence of the fall. Henry Law had brought many broken parts for direct examination, such as a bagful of broken lug ends he had found on the piers. There were more than fifty photographs, the results of Mr Kirkaldy's tests (some of which were witnessed by the Commissioners in person). There was a model of part of the high girders, and numerous drawings and sketches prepared by the NBR, Bouch's assistants and other witnesses. Even then, they did not see all the evidence because the witness prognostications had been sifted by the solicitors involved in gathering them.

The final judgment was delivered less than two months later, on 30 June 1880, in two separate reports, one by the Commissioner himself, the other a joint effort by Yolland and Barlow. They agreed on most points, bar one: the personal responsibility of the engineer in charge of the project, Sir Thomas Bouch. Since Rothery spoke as chairman, it is to his report that we turn to read the conclusions of the tribunal. Rothery was also completely independent, not having been involved (as far as is known) with any of the parties before the disaster. Both Yolland and Barlow had been involved with either Bouch or the NBR in giving engineering advice before the fall, a feature of the Inquiry which would not be countenanced today. Rothery's report was forthright and uncompromising on this, the worst structural disaster to have affected the railways since their introduction in Britain.

Rothery's Report

The Commissioner prefaced his report by saying that all three agreed on the major points, and where they disagreed, he would summarise them at the end of his report. After reviewing the way the Inquiry proceeded, he discussed the irregular way the Tay Bridge project had developed over the years. The key change in the contract involved the use of cast-iron piers instead of brick for the centre of the bridge, where the foundations were not of solid rock. He describes the fall of two of the girders during a storm in 1877, and the completion of the bridge, followed by inspection and approval by General Hutchinson. His description of the bridge makes a point about the lack of a continuous girder at the top of each tower, so that instead of a unitary structure, each tower was effectively composed of two separate triangular structures connected by struts and diagonal tie bars.

Wreckage and Lugs

The condition of the wreckage on the piers was an obvious and immediate focus of attention for trying to reconstruct the sequence of events during the fall. The position of the high girders was interesting, lying a short distance to the east in the form of three distinct arcs corresponding to each of the three girders, and coming closest to the piers where there were expansion joints. There was no evidence that the piers had settled owing to poor foundations, the main concern of Bouch and his inspector, Mr Noble. However, there had been some damage to the masonry in two cases: the masonry having been upended by the fall of the columns *(5.7)*. Most of the piers had gone into the east side or downstream in the estuary, with the exception of the two tiers on pier No.1, the single tier on pier No.3, and the shattered wreckage on the bases of the piers. Column flanges had broken, sometimes carrying part of the shaft. The wrought-iron parts (struts and tie bars) had survived unbroken, although in many cases grossly distorted, while the cast iron showed multiple brittle failure. What was remarkable was the almost universal failure of the cast-iron lugs, especially noticeable on the centre parts of the south and north-standing piers. The lack of a girder connection (the so-called L-girders) at the top of these two towers produced a structure akin to 'two three-legged stools', attached only by struts and diagonal tie bars *(2.11)*. All the fallen towers in the high girder section lacked this connection. The train itself had been found in the girders between pier Nos 4 and 5, the locomotive and tender, guard's van and last carriage on their sides, the intermediate carriages in an upright position.

Causes of the Casualty

Rothery then considered the various theories put forward to explain the disaster, the first being that initially presented by the NBR in response to a request by the tribunal. They had pointed to the '... overpowering violence of the wind...', but were not yet aware of '... any circumstances which in themselves would account for the disaster.'

They had come to this conclusion more than two months after the accident, during which time they must have obtained knowledge of the facts in consultation with Bouch and the officers of the company.

The second development of this theory came in April during examination of Mr Grothe, the resident engineer and manager for the contractors. He said that the girder on pier No.5 had been blown off its bearings and crashed down through the tower supporting it, smashing everything in its way. But this hypothesis did not account for the girder lying a substantial distance way from the base of the pier, and there was little backing for the theory from any witnesses.

The third development occurred during questioning of Bouch, when the derailment theory was advanced. It was suggested that the last or last two wagons (the guard's van and second-class carriage) canted over in the violent wind, and impacted on the girder. But how the tower at pier No.5 fell was yet to be explained by the impact above, let alone the collapse of the entire high girder section, which remained obscure.

Then a further hypothesis was advanced by Dr Pole, a close adviser to Bouch. Pole's contribution was to add the idea of shock loading of the lugs which initiated the collapse. It was the impact of the last two wagons of the train against the girders which produced the shock, which ran down through the tower at pier No.5 and started the whole sequence. Pole was clearly convinced that something extra, and additional to the purely static loading from the wind, was needed to cause the collapse. His colleague, Allan Stewart, gave more details of the theory under questioning. He said that it was the 'sheering action' of the wind which first broke the lugs supporting the tie bars, leaving the columns unbraced. They then fell, and initiated the fall. Benjamin Baker backed the hypothesis, pointing out that the lugs were the weakest link in the chain, and probably broke by shock loading, which itself came from a collision between the train and the high girders. So only two forces are said to have caused the disaster: the force of the wind and the impact of the train against the girder.

Which End Fell First?

The whole theory of train collision supposed that it was the southern end of the girders which fell first. But if the northern end had collapsed first, then the theory must be invalid. The three Commissioners had looked very carefully at the evidence of the fall that night to try to determine the issue. The way the rails were wrenched away might give a clue to the collapse sequence, and they had asked for photographs of the ends of the girders at pier No.9 to be taken, simply because it was better preserved than the others. They showed that the rails had been torn away to the east, so it seemed that collapse from the north end was a distinct possibility. Rothery's chain of reasoning, however, seems rather weak, because if the whole section of girders had fallen to the east, there seems no particular reason why the direction of tearing should explain the exact sequence of the collapse. Nevertheless, it was a hypothesis which could be explored further by, for example, seeing what the eyewitness evidence revealed.

Unfortunately, the witness evidence that night was inconclusive. Alexander Maxwell saw three great flashes which appeared to him at Magdalen Green to travel from south to north. On the other hand, William Clark, standing close by, saw the same flashes at the north end of the bridge. William Robertson, ex-provost of the city, saw 'two columns of spray, brilliantly illuminated' at the north end from his viewpoint near Newport. Peter Barron at Magdalen Green said that a girder on the north end fell first, followed by the middle, and then that the south end was last to fall into the estuary.

Henry Law had found that the girders, as they lay in the estuary, were 18in displaced to the north, and the fallen columns (those presumably left visible on the piers) also appeared inclined to the north. If the collapse had indeed started at the north end of the high girders, the train derailment theory was redundant. But what about the direct evidence for a collision?

Did the Train Strike the Girder?

Several score marks and abrasions had been found on the east side of the high girder section between pier Nos 4 and 5, in which the train was located. They had been found by Thomas Arnit, one of Bouch's assistants, when the girder had been lifted and beached. The marks were between 11ft and 12ft above the line of track, but if the second-class carriage was only 10ft high, it was difficult to see how its tilting over could have damaged the girder. The east side of the carriage would have produced marks much lower down owing to the tilt. Since several similar marks had been found at a similar height on adjacent girders, why didn't the 22ft-long carriage simply fall out between the 25ft gaps in the girders? There was another objection: if the guard's van and carriage had leant over and impacted the girder frame, is it possible that such light wagons could have caused serious damage to the wrought ironwork? Any impact was much more likely to have smashed the light wagons than the heavy metalwork of the girder. To suggest that the light roof of the carriages could have caused the fall of 1,000 yards of bridge seemed highly implausible. The nature of the marks was also very slight, with the paint rubbed off, and some scratches in the iron. It was inconceivable that such minor damage could have created such serious consequential damage to the whole structure of the bridge. It was much more likely that the marks were caused after the fall, rather than before. Similar comments applied to marks lower down the girder, allegedly made by the chassis of the carriages, but they themselves were untouched, judging by the photographs taken of the chassis concerned.

Finally, Dugald Drummond reported that the controls on the locomotive were in full forward travel position. If the vehicles behind had tilted and hit the girder, the driver would have reacted by applying the brakes or by throttling the engine back. The evidence showed that he had not taken any action at the controls, suggesting that he was taken completely unawares by the collapse of the bridge under him.

Wind Pressures

The second force operating on the bridge was said to be the high wind blowing from the west that night. According to Pole and Stewart, the bridge had been designed to resist a pressure of 20lbs per sq.ft, although Bouch said in his testimony that he made no special allowance for wind pressure acting on the structure. The results of consultations with Airy (10psf average, 40psf maximum) were made much later when he was considering the design of the Forth Suspension Bridge, and could not have been used when he was designing the Tay Bridge. Moreover, Benjamin Baker insisted that his survey of the bridge and its environs showed that wind pressure could not have exceeded around 15psf on the night of the accident. The evidence from a variety of eminent authorities, such as Professor Stokes, was mixed. There seemed, however, to be little doubt that wind pressures of up to 50psf could be experienced in Britain. The practice in France was to allow for a maximum pressure of 55psf, and in the USA 50psf. Whether such pressures actually occurred on the night of the accident remained doubtful.

Once again, the evidence from witnesses was mixed. The evidence they preferred was that of Captain Scott on the training ship *Mars* located only about three quarters of a mile downstream of the bridge. He described the storm as being force 10 on the Beaufort scale, perhaps gusting to force 11. He personally had experienced more severe storms in Britain, and one or two of equal force to that on the night of the disaster within the last two or three years while stationed on the Tay. He had, while on duty overseas, experienced more violent storms of force 11 to 12, in the West Indies and China Seas. His testimony had been confirmed by instructors on board the ship. Although the court would admit that it was a violent storm that night, it could hardly explain the overthrow of a nearly new bridge. So the issue now arose of what lateral force could act against the structure.

The static analyses both by Henry Law and Pole/Stewart had produced broadly similar results of the forces tending to overturn a pier in the high girder section, the exact critical pressure depending on the assumptions of the calculations. If the columns were all correctly bolted down, and the tower of rigid construction, then a pressure of just over 64psf was needed to topple the structure, a figure well in excess of estimates of the maximum pressures ever experienced in Britain, and well above reasonable estimates of the pressures acting on the bridge on the night of the disaster. So it was difficult to see how the wind alone could have caused the accident. Rothery then turned to the reasons why the piers might have been weaker than originally intended, the many defects found in the ruins after the accident.

Defects in the Metalwork

For a start, evidence was presented about the Wormit foundry, the conditions under which the columns were cast and the general running of the enterprise. Defects were certainly introduced into the columns, but did they weaken the towers to a point where they could not withstand even moderate wind loads? The molten metal had proved more difficult to cast than Scotch iron, and defects such as scabs and cold shuts were incorporated into many columns. Blow holes were present in the metal, and where they met the free surfaces, had been filled with Beaumont's Egg. The walls of many columns also showed unequal thickness, owing to shifts in the core. However, many of these defective columns were detected during inspection and rejected for use in the bridge. Some defective columns did end up in the bridge, according to Henry Law from his examination of the remains still visible on the piers after the accident. The proportion actually built into the final structure could never be known for certain, since most of the piers had ended up in the river and had not been recovered.

The most serious defects were associated with the lugs cast integral with the columns. They were often imperfectly made, and attempts had been made to burn-on new lugs, although there was little evidence that they were present in the piers of the high girders. More dangerous was the conical state of the lugs caused by using a tapered core during casting. It was the most serious of all the defects since the tie bar bolts would not be resting against the walls of the hole, but rather against the outer edges. Bouch had admitted that they were most serious, and had he known, he would have had the holes drilled out. But the bolts themselves were a poor fit to the imperfect holes, having a diameter of 1⅛in to fit a 1¼in minimum-diameter hole, so giving a clearance of ⅛in. The combination of problems meant that there was substantial play in the joints which, in the end, held the columns together. When tested by Kirkaldy, they produced a breaking stress around a third of what they should have exhibited based on the sectional area.

A similar problem existed with the 18in columns which also had conical bolt holes, since a machine needed to drill the holes was not purchased, despite the fact that there was a machine for the smaller 15in columns. It meant that there would be less effective joints between adjacent columns. In addition, the bolts were 1⅛in in diameter while the holes were cast with a minimum width of 1½in, giving a play of ⅜in.

The Wormit Foundry

The management of the foundry left a great deal to be desired, several individuals being in charge at different periods of time. From 100 to 200 columns were made under the supervision of Hercules Strachan, who was dismissed, and then the rest by Fergus Ferguson. Mr Beattie was in overall control but could not effectively manage the foundry, owing to his other duties elsewhere on the site. It was his responsibility to test the columns using hydraulic methods, but he did not do so. He should have inspected the columns and rejected defective work, but his tests were limited to what he could discover visually on external surfaces and by tapping them with a hammer. When he left the foundry Mr Camphuis was in charge, but, having no practical knowledge of ironwork, he was more of an administrator. He was unfit to supervise the works.

But what role did Bouch and his staff have in overseeing the work of the foundry? As far as the Commissioners could see, none whatever. His immediate staff were Paterson, Ralph and Butler, but none appeared before the Inquiry. Mr Paterson was apparently paralysed and 'of advanced years', while they did not know where either Ralph or Butler were. None of these assistant engineers appears to have ever inspected the foundry.

Bridge Maintenance

The main perceived maintenance activity was to monitor the foundations and ensure that they were not undermined by the rapid currents in the estuary. It was done by depositing large amounts of ballast around them by Mr Noble, a man appointed by Bouch for inspecting the piers. When standing on one of the piers, he heard the tie bars 'chattering' and, without telling anyone, fixed the problem by putting around 150 small iron packing pieces into the affected joints. He was not apparently instructed by Bouch to inspect the metalwork, although here Rothery clearly did not believe the evidence of Bouch and the various reports sent to him by Noble.

Using the packing pieces in this way could not return the tie bar joint to its correct tensioned state, and merely served to preserve its distortion, with little bracing action then possible in holding the columns together. There had been some extraordinary evidence from Allan Stewart in his testimony, which suggested that loosening the tie bars actually increased the strength of the towers! If that were so, then loosening the shrouds would improve the stability of a ship's masts.

The speed of trains using the bridge was also very relevant to the problem. General Hutchinson had recommended a maximum speed limit of 25mph. The engine drivers had, however, interpreted it as an average not to be exceeded, and had well exceeded the limit when travelling north across the bridge, where the gradients in the line allowed them to build up speed from a near standing start at the south signal box where they received the baton. The best evidence of excessive train speeds was given by William Robertson, who had timed the trains. He was a frequent traveller and had recorded speeds of 36 up to 43mph when passing through the high girder section of the bridge. The drivers then applied their brakes at around the third or fourth span from the end of the high girder section, in order to descend the steep downward gradient on the bend coming into Tay Bridge station. They believed that part of the momentum lost here would be transmitted to the piers, and severely strained them. It was those piers on the northern side of the high girders which were probably weakened as a direct result, and support the contention that the north end of the bridge was the first to collapse.

True Cause of the Fall

Rothery concluded that it was the defects built into the high girders which led to the downfall of a badly built and badly maintained bridge in a strong wind. The bridge had been badly strained, partly by previous gales and partly by speeding trains going north into Dundee. The central tie bars (the so-called wind ties) were so loosened by the night of 28 December 1879, that a 'racking' motion was set up between the two triangular groups of columns which made up the towers on each of the twelve pairs of the high girder section. Rothery expected the bases of the towers to yield first, unless there was a weaker place above (as was visible on pier Nos 1 and 3). Once one set of wind ties had broken, an additional strain would be placed on those remaining, and the tower would simply keel over to the east, just like a pack of cards.

That separation occurred at the base was, in his opinion, confirmed by the curious shape of the final resting place of the girders, in three arcs. The girders were furthest away where there was a fixed bearing, owing to the tower carrying the girder with it as it fell. On the other hand, where they were resting freely on the rollers, they slipped off the collapsing tower, and so fell much closer to the base of the pier. At the south end, the girder was closest of all since only the upper tiers failed.

Design Defects

But were there defects in the original design which, in spite of the poor workmanship and maintenance, would have inevitably caused it to fail? It was usual to design such structures with a safety factor of 4 to 5, that is to say it should be able to withstand 4 to 5 times the maximum stress it may be expected to bear in practice. This very generous safety factor is to allow for inevitable material defects such as blow holes, which are extremely difficult to remove entirely from any casting, however well it is made. To build a structure which could expect to receive wind pressures of up to 50psf could, according to Henry Law's analysis, not withstand more than 64psf, a much narrower margin of only about 1.3. The new bridge to replace the ruins should thus be built in such a way as to have a much larger safety factor.

Bouch had neglected to check the results of the first borings made for the foundations, and should have determined the nature of the river bed before changing his design to accommodate what he found in fact to be relatively insubstantial conglomerate. The bases he built up were far too small to support high piers, and he could only fit a hexagonal shape of columns to fit them. Having only two single outer columns of 18in-diameter meant that they bore more of the mass above than the smaller 15in inner columns. He should have used two outer columns rather than one to provide the extra support they would provide. In his design of the Belah Bridge, for example, although each pier had only six columns, they were arranged as four outer raking columns with only two inner columns to support the mass of the girders, the reverse of what he used on the Tay Bridge. This improved plan could have been used in the Tay Bridge. Such a plan would also have provided better support from the wind ties, which would then protect each tower to a greater degree from lateral pressure, since all would be aligned at right angles to the axis of the bridge. The hexagonal plan gave two outer sets of wind ties which were aligned at a less favourable angle.

Equally serious was the omission of a complete circle of girder at the top of each tower in the high girder section. Connecting the two L-shaped girders would have given much greater support to the towers than was actually the case. Many of the columns in the centre section lacked a spigot and were thus weaker as a direct result, lateral movement being only resisted by the flange bolts. The most serious design defect lay in the cast-iron lugs, especially in moulding them integral with the columns and with integral bolt holes. The conical holes were the single most important defect in the columns, and the single most important cause of the fall of the bridge.

Belah Viaduct

Rothery thought it instructive to compare the Belah Viaduct built by Bouch at the western edge of the Stainmore pass, with the Tay Bridge. It was built about 4 miles from Brough for the South Durham and Lancashire Railway, across one of the wild mountain gorges of the Pennines. The viaduct as described in a recent (in 1880, that is) edition of Humber's book of iron bridges was 1,000ft long and was carried on fifteen piers around 50ft apart. They varied in height according to the depth of valley below. The hollow columns were set out in three rows of two parallel to the axis of the bridge, and tapered by no less than 22ft from top to bottom of the tallest tower of around 195ft (compared with a taper on the outer 18in columns of only 12in on the 80ft-towers of the high girders). The columns were machined so that ends fitted one another perfectly, and no cement was used in the structure. All the bolt holes were drilled by dedicated machine tools, and fitted well together when the viaduct was built without the need for chipping and filing of any parts. The vertical and horizontal wrought-iron braces fitted cross-girders which encircled the columns rather than being attached directly. Bouch was asked why he had changed his tower design so drastically on the Tay, and replied that he was not aware of wind severity until he received the report on the proposed Forth Bridge. Then he made an astonishing admission in a direct question from Rothery:

> 17,218. *(The Commissioner). Is that the only reason why you did away with those ties? – They were so much more expensive; this was a saving of money.*

Responsibility

The three Commissioners had come unanimously to their judgment:

> The conclusion then, to which we have come, is that this bridge was badly designed, badly constructed and badly maintained, and that its downfall was due to inherent defects in the structure, which must sooner or later have brought it down. For these defects both in the design, the construction and the maintenance, Sir Thomas Bouch is, in our opinion, mainly to blame. For the faults of design he is entirely responsible. For those of construction he is principally to blame in not having exercised that supervision over the work, which would have enabled him

to detect and apply a remedy to them. And for the faults of maintenance he is also principally, if not entirely, to blame in having neglected to maintain such an inspection over the structure, as its character imperatively demanded.

He went on to discuss the various wind pressure standards used by other countries, and the way Bouch had effectively ignored the effects of wind on his bridge. It had been brought down solely by the action of the wind, which though violent, was not at all excessive. Either the safety factor was too low or the number of defects too high: either way Bouch could not escape responsibility. But blaming Bouch personally in such an uncompromising way was still not enough for Rothery. He went on to apportion some of the responsibility for the disaster on others, especially Hopkins Gilkes & Co. who were considered responsible for the poor state of the foundry, and its questionable output. The NBR allowed trains to drive at speeds greater than recommended by Hutchinson, so must be culpable for part of the disaster. Even the government would not escape his admonitions.

In particular, the Board of Trade had approved this bridge for public use, so what was the legislative position? It was surprisingly weak. Under the relevant Act, no new line of railway could be opened until notice of one month to the BoT of the intent to open the line had passed. Then a further ten days' notice of completion and being ready for inspection was required. No plans or drawings were required to be sent to the BoT before the ten days' notice had been served, and they were frequently sent after the line had opened. An inspector then had to examine the plans, inspect the line, and make a report. If a copy of his report were not lodged with the company within the ten-day period, the line could be opened anyway, whatever its condition. Owing to the pressure of work on the Inspectorate, it was clear that inspection was often superficial.

In this case, Hutchinson had inspected and tested the bridge with a very heavy load of six engines coupled together with a mass of 438 tons, running at high speeds across the viaduct. He apparently found the structure to be stiffer than expected. Accordingly, he then approved the bridge to be opened to the public. However, when questioned in the Inquiry, Hutchinson had admitted that his inspection of the structure had been superficial, and many of the defects were in any case well concealed from anything but a detailed examination, pier by pier. Rothery felt that if railway inspectors were to be held responsible for defects in a line, then they should be allowed to inspect during the construction phase of a project. Hutchinson had made no test of lateral stability and indeed, there was no such specific requirement for an open lattice bridge. Rothery emphasised that this position should be amended so that, in future, inspectors would need to evaluate the effect of winds on railway structures.

The final questions concerned the remaining part of the bridge and its condition. Henry Law had condemned most of the structure as being inherently unstable, especially the south and north piers still left standing after the disaster. He commented: 'That it will be rebuilt there can be no doubt, for the interests of the large and thriving town of Dundee imperatively demand it.'

Areas of Agreement and Disagreement

Two reports having been made, it remained for Rothery to comment on the areas in which they agreed and disagreed. They were relatively minor points (so he thought), and concerned the issues of how much explanation was needed of specific decisions they had reached, and the issue of personal responsibility and 'naming of names'. They included the following points:

1. Whether or not engineers should be responsible for the results of boring tests for foundations.

2. To what extent they should explain why they thought that the train had not derailed and hit the girder.

3. The management of the foundry and naming of those who were responsible for its insufficiencies.

4. The detailing of all the structural defects in the bridge, and comparison with the Belah Viaduct.

5. The naming of that person (Bouch) who was mainly responsible for the disaster.

6. The establishment of BoT rules governing wind pressures on structures.

Strangely enough, Rothery would not go so far as to legislate for rules on wind pressure, preferring that it be done by the profession rather than by the government. Yolland and Barlow clearly thought otherwise.

Barlow and Yolland

In fact, Rothery was understating their differences. The Barlow–Yolland report was shorter, and decidedly more technical. For example, they discussed Kirkaldy's experiments in considerable detail for the light the results shed on the condition of the lugs. Thus, of the fourteen lower lug samples from pier Nos 1 and 3 he tested, no less than four were said to be 'unsound' (whatever that meant). They also pointed out that similar attachments were widely used for other structures, and engineers should therefore be wary of the joint. This was wise advice for engineers, who would later become much more aware of the importance of stress concentrations in design. Automobiles and aeroplanes would later provide many examples of premature failure from stress concentrations.

They also put more emphasis on Noble's activities in repairing loose cotter joints on the tie bars, which effectively locked each tower of the high girders into an increasingly unstable state. They wrestled with the problem of how to explain why all twelve towers in the section fell in such an apparently similar way. This single fact surely pointed towards a common mechanism of failure for each of the quite separate structures, but they attempted instead to show that the high girders themselves did most of the damage as they fell first on the south side (not the north, as Rothery had said), and dragged the rest of the towers down. Surely, if that were the case, the towers concerned must themselves have been intrinsically weak. Barlow and Rothery suggested, presumably on the basis that four cracked columns had been found by Noble just before the accident, that a cracked outer 18in-column in the high girder section could have initiated the collapse. These columns bore a proportionately greater share of the dead load from the girders so, if one failed, a tower could collapse. Apart from the fact that only one of the cracked columns had been found in the high girder section, the hypothesis fails to explain why the whole section fell like 'a pack of cards'.

However, the suggestion seemed almost an aside when the main drive of their report focused on the wind ties of the centre section. They rightly pointed out the weakness of the cross ties, especially in the absence of a connecting girder at the head of each tower. The cross ties and struts in these lateral braces only weighed around 5 tons, compared with a total metal weight of about 88 tons in each tower. They did not think the bases were too small, as Rothery had suggested, and a much stronger structure could have been built on the same area than had actually been constructed by Bouch.

Like Rothery, it is curious to observe that none of the Commissioners referred to the oscillations of the high girders, which had been experienced by so many workers on the bridge (the painters and carpenter) as well as travellers on the northbound trains. At one point in their report, Barlow and Yolland do refer to oscillations, but it was an isolated reference and the argument was not taken any further.

It was hardly surprising that the Commissioners arrived at different conclusions as to the sequence of events on the night of the disaster. The destruction of the central section was so severe, and so much evidence lost into the estuary, that quite contrary opinions were almost equally credible. What was certain, however, was the overwhelming evidence of bad design, construction and maintenance.

Public Reaction

The reports were finally delivered to an eager and still angry public on Saturday 3 July 1880. By Monday 5 July, *The Times* had written an extensive summary of the main points, amidst stories of atrocities in Afghanistan, the Irish problem and claims of electoral fraud and skullduggery in the recent general election. The leader column quickly got to the heart of the matter:

> ... Such being the initial defects of the bridge its practical supervision was intrusted to a person very imperfectly qualified in the opinion of the Court, to undertake such a responsibility. What defects he observed he did his best to remedy promptly; but he does not seem to have been sufficiently alive to the serious indications of weakness and danger shown in the loosening of the ties of the cross-braces to the effect of which, as seems most probable, the disaster must be immediately attributed. In fact, it is impossible to resist the conclusion that the bridge was an unsafe structure from the very beginning...

The criticism of Mr Noble was powerful stuff. The leader writer went on to criticise General Hutchinson and the Board of Trade for the inspection which proved it could resist vertical loads, but they never tested it for its lateral strength. It went on:

> ... The moral of the Tay Bridge disaster is that railway construction is now approaching recklessness, and that inspection in certain circumstances affords no adequate security even at the outset; that of the Hay Bridge accident is that inspection, however efficient at the outset, affords no permanent security against subsequent deterioration; and, perhaps, the most palpable lesson to be drawn from recent experience is that the whole system of inspection as at present practised by the Board of Trade is formal and perfunctory, and is capable of overlooking the essential conditions of security.

The Hay accident involved the sudden collapse of a bridge on the Hereford, Hay and Brecon Railway, and had occurred within the previous few months.

In a later item in the paper, Bouch's solicitors sent a letter they had received from Yolland and Barlow. They denied that they had agreed with Rothery on every matter not discussed in their own report. It implied that they had not agreed to his naming and shaming the engineer. There had clearly been some strong disagreements within the triumvirate.

9
Hindsight

So the Inquiry finished. It had used the best professional witnesses of the day, had seen and inspected much personally, and employed excellent photographic coverage of as much of the remains as they were able to retrieve, rescue or record. Looking back 125 years to the Inquiry, is there anything new that can be added to what they said? Although the methods of the lawyers have changed very little (if at all) over this period, engineering skills and methods have changed almost beyond recognition. Forensic skills have also improved dramatically with the many different modes of transport available today compared with the 1880s, and the accidents which accompany them. But the numbers of casualties have increased dramatically with larger passenger numbers. The loss of over 1,500 passengers and crew when the *Titanic* sank in 1912 was a foretaste of what was to come. Our Victorian forebears would be shocked by the enormous waste of life from this and other disasters to follow. However, much has been learnt about the materials of construction, their failure modes and means of inspection to detect defects before they become life-threatening.

It is possible to look back at the Tay Bridge disaster not just for its historical importance, but also for any inconsistencies, ambiguities or lacunae in the final conclusions. The Commissioner said, for example, that the bridge fell from the north end, and not the south where the train was passing. He suggested that this end of the high girders had suffered serious long-term damage from speeding trains. However, they failed to mention exactly how failure had occurred, suggesting that fractures occurred at the well-known very weak lugs in the towers. So this was not the shock action suggested by some witnesses at the Inquiry, but rather a slow and continuous deterioration, presumably focused at the loosening cotter joints and the lugs. There was no explanation of what specifically caused lug failure that night, and not earlier, for example in one or other of the severe gales that had battered the new bridge since it was built. A well-known failure mode which has been intensively studied in recent times is fatigue, so is it possible that brittle fatigue cracks grew slowly over time and reached a critical size by late December 1879?

Photographic Evidence

The photographs from just a week after the accident are of sufficient quality to provide further information on the many defects which Henry Law and others had discovered in the wreckage on the piers. They can be enlarged to show details of specific components, as earlier pictures in this book have shown. It is thus with the known defects that a broad survey of the wreckage on the piers is possible, and it reveals direct information about defects which the Inquiry did not research in detail at the time, probably owing to the speed at which it operated. At the same time, many of the defects they did discuss can be seen exposed to the light of day. At the time of the Inquiry in 1880, the public were denied access to these photographs, and many are published here for the first time in their appropriate context.

Lower Lugs *In Situ*

A starting point for this survey has already been started in earlier chapters, especially concerning the state of the lugs. It was possible, for example, to compare broken lug ends with some of the corresponding parts still held by the columns. All of the east-facing lowest lugs on the bases of the piers have fractured across the bolt holes, and many of them show surfaces devoid of detail, where the resolution of the picture is great enough to capture that detail. However, one of the four wings often exhibits some roughness not shown by its fellows. The lower east-facing lug on the north side of pier No.3, for example, shows some interesting detail on the lower right-hand wing *(9.1)*. There is a highlight at the upper right which is crescent shaped, and centred on the far corner. The corner is where the greatest stress occurred when the lug was intact and the tie bar fully tightened. Immediately above is another highlight in the centre of the bore of the bolt hole. One interpretation of the latter highlight is that the bolt pressed against the bore during movement of the tie bar, probably when strained laterally by trains and winds. The bore would be polished at the contact, the surface reflecting light when photographed. By flattening the surface, the bore would increase in diameter and so give more slack to tie bar movement if the cottered joint was free.

(9.1) Close-up of broken east-facing lugs on the lowest tier of pier No.3 (north).

But that cannot explain the other highlight in the wing itself. It is possible that it is the vestige of a fatigue crack which started from or near the highly stressed corner, and grew into the bulk metal at each cycle of strain. Fatigue is perhaps the most common single failure mode of stressed products, and generally starts at stress concentrations like the edges of holes. Such a crack will have grown slowly until it reached a critical size, and then the wing cracked suddenly. The other wings would have cracked soon after, depending on the size of the applied load. The fracture surface bears comparison with the south-facing lug shown in *(6.9)*. This time, there are highlights on both bores, and another highlight in the left-hand wing. Another feature worthy of comment is the presence of a washer on the intact lug at the left (no washer is present in the intact lug of the south-facing intact lug). Fitment of washers would have been important for gaining a secure tight bolt against the rough surface of the adjacent cast iron. The same lug of *(9.1)* also appears to show that it thins towards the outer edge, judging by the shape of the upper surface of the lug. Whether or not this lug is one which was poorly cast, with molten metal not reaching the furthest part of the mould, is highly likely.

Free Lug Ends

Among the many free lug ends seen in the debris fields of the piers *(5.4 and 6.10)*, one small set is of special interest. The set of three ends from pier No.12 (east) is shown in *(9.2)*. The lug in the centre is so placed that its fracture surface was facing the camera, so key details are visible. It is also partly shaded in its position on the pier, so enhancing contrast in the broken surface.

The wing at the right is featureless, but the left-hand wing shows curious concentric arcs which are roughly centred on the corner zone. That this is the critical corner is clear from the taper of the hole, which reaches its most narrow point here. Close by the corner is a circular highlight, which could be interpreted as a small blow hole within the metal, yet another type of defect often mentioned by Henry Law. In this case, the hole could have initiated a fatigue crack since it too represents a serious stress raiser (at a point where the applied stress is high, thanks to the bolt hole and taper). The arcs, if this interpretation is correct, represent successive lines where a growing fatigue crack halted as the stress fell in the load cycle. Debris such as rust will have been formed on the fresh metal exposed by the growing crack, and remains as a kind of beach mark to show one position of the resting crack. The arcs extend a fair way, perhaps half the area of the wing, suggesting that the crack grew over several cycles before becoming critical. The exact origin of the lug will never be known for sure, owing to its separation, although it is likely to have come from one of the lower tiers of this tower.

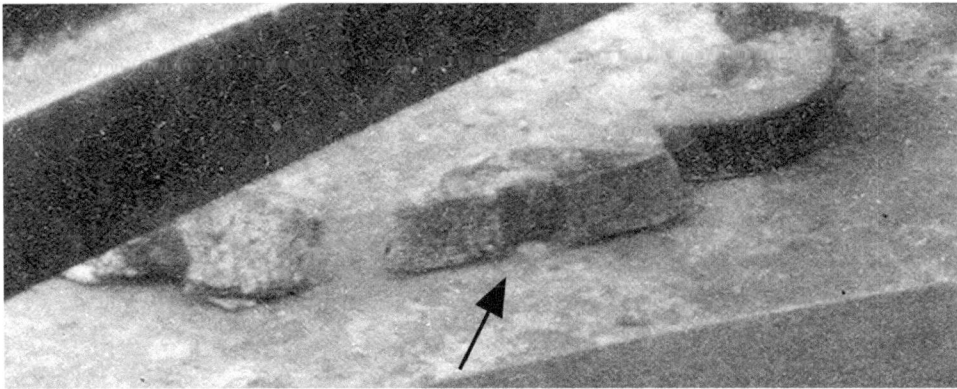

(9.2) Close-up of three detached lug ends from pier No.12 (east), the centre lug seeming to show arcs centred on a blow hole near the inner corner by the bolt hole.

However, this example seems to support the idea expressed in the previous chapter that the bolts were not bent into the cones by tightening the tie bars on the bridge, and that Kirkaldy's results may have overestimated the true strength of all the lugs. In other words, the diagonal bracing bars were likely to snap at significantly lower applied loads than Kirkaldy would have us believe. Fatigue is, of course, a mechanism by which components fail at loads well below their design strength. That would imply that the integrity of the bridge was even more dependent on the diagonal bracing than we have been led to suppose. The origins of the many bent bolts found on the piers are multifold. They could have been produced by several mechanisms, including being bent *in situ* into the cone, but also when one wing of the lug broke, and then stressed again, when the bolt will have been stressed at one end only. No doubt many of the bent bolts were flange rather than lug bolts, which must have been produced in larger quantities since each flange was attached by eight bolts. Most broken flanges on the piers are almost completely devoid of bolts.

It would have been useful to have examined the collection of lug ends brought in a large bag by Henry Law to Kirkaldy's test house. It is likely that Kirkaldy preserved them (and the lugs he had tested to destruction) for posterity in his so-called 'Black Museum' of failures. It was housed on the top floor of the laboratory but, unfortunately, the upper floors were destroyed by German bombers during the Second World War, and all the samples were lost. Many samples, too, were examined directly by the Inquiry, but whether they were saved in some dusty corner of a lawyer's office remains unknown. No doubt much debris also remains at the bottom of the Tay estuary, buried deep in mud and silt.

Upper Lugs

The photographs provide an insight into the state of the upper lugs as well as the lower ones, because many have broken in a not dissimilar way to the lower lugs. For example, *(9.3)* shows just such an upper lug on pier No.4, broken across the bolt holes like the lower lugs.

The bolt holes are tapered in much the same way, although very little is visible on the fracture surfaces. The upper lug also included two bolt holes for the horizontal struts which are still attached, although it shows some distortion, possibly owing to bolt fracture. The picture is interesting for the structure of the column below the lug. A wide flange with a series of holes cast into its surface was intended as a so-called lifting column used to raise the girders by hydraulic jacks. The holes were used to hold the girder before raising to the next higher one, and so on, and such columns were normally removed and not incorporated into the final tower. Why this one remained is yet another Tay Bridge mystery. On the extreme right of the same picture are the remains of a broken flange. It shows the parallel sides of a bolt hole drilled out of a 15in-column by machine rather than cast, one of the few examples of what should have been done on all the bolt holes.

The overall appearance of the wreckage on the piers divides neatly between the wrought and cast iron. Virtually all the wrought iron visible in the pictures and close-ups is intact but severely distorted, while the cast iron shows numerous fractures. This is as expected, because cast iron is a very brittle metal while wrought iron is tough and ductile. One exception to this rule occurs on pier No.2 (looking east) with *(9.4)* showing a close-up of an upper lug and strut, where the lug is intact, and complete with its bolt.

A wrought-iron tie bar would originally have been attached here but must have been wrenched clear during the final moments of the collapse of the tower above. So far the only such example discovered in the pictures, it shows that wrought-iron bars could fail and that, if they had, it was at the hole at the end of the bar. Kirkaldy shows many such examples in his tables of results, where he tested the tie bars alone, and implies that some fractured during his tests of the lugs. The bolt itself shows some slight distortion at the head (at left in the picture), probably caused by the stress which caused the failure of the tie bar.

(9.3) Broken upper lugs from pier No.4 showing conical bolt holes on a lifting column.

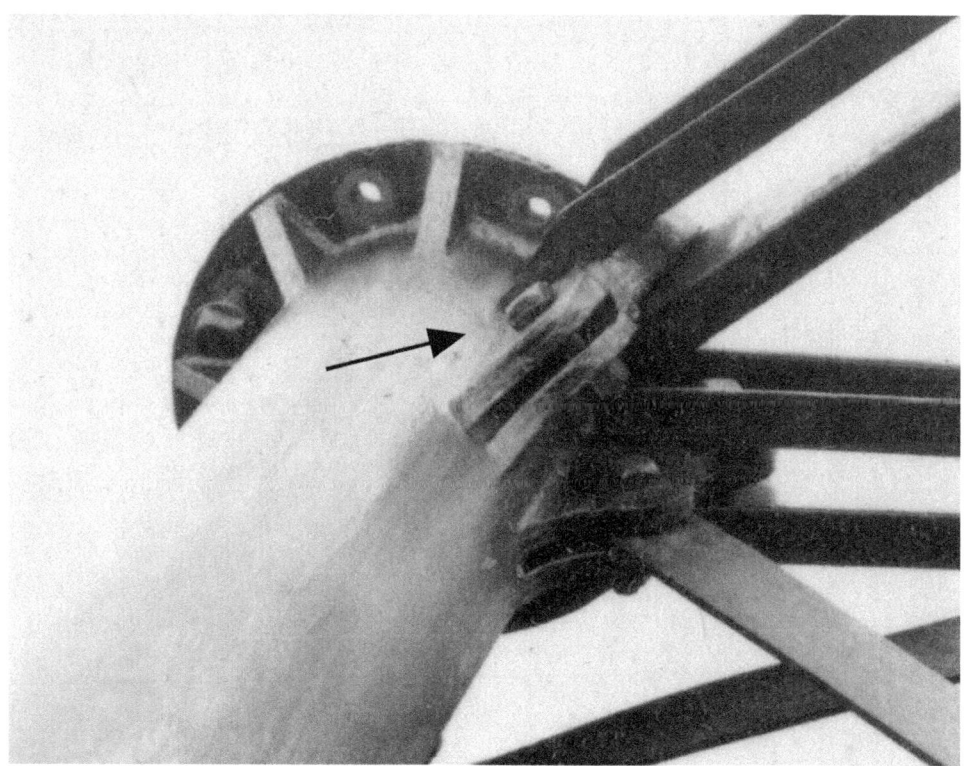

(9.4) Upper lug on a 15in-column on pier No. 2, looking east, showing intact lug and bolt.

Struts

Several broken strut lugs were found while searching the photographic archive. One of the best is shown in *(9.5)*. The close-up shows that the hole is tapered in just the same way as the upper and lower lugs, a point which never emerged clearly at the Inquiry, but is clearly significant for the stability of the towers.

In the same way that a lug taper concentrates stress at the thinnest part of the hole, so stress from the strut will be raised at the edge, weakening the joint, and allowing play in the joint, which was to be crucial on the night of the fall. Two bolts were used to attach each end of the two-channel bar struts, and if play could develop, then movement of the whole structure becomes not just a possibility, but a certainty if the diagonal tie bars start to move. There is a suggestion from some of the close-ups that when an upper lug fractured, the fracture grew into the strut lug *(6.6)*. Since the two lugs were cast as one with the column, it makes their design even more treacherous than was at first believed. At a stroke, two, rather than one, key connections were destroyed. Further critical points about the struts are discussed below.

Partly Broken Lugs

One interesting feature revealed by enlarging of the photographs is the presence of partly broken lugs, especially ones in which just one wing has broken, leaving the other intact, and a tie bar often still attached. A good example is shown in *(9.6)*, on the outer west-facing 18in-column of pier No.3. The right-hand wing on the left is clearly fractured, with the brittle crack running across the lug in the expected path of least resistance. The bolt is still in position, as is the tie bar. From what can be seen of the other wing in the joint, it is uncracked and intact, explaining why the tie bar is still held in position.

Why should such a feature be of significance? The lug must have suffered a cyclic stress for the wing to have broken while leaving the other side intact. If the stress has been maintained, then the other wing would have quickly broken since the load it carries has been doubled. The fact that it has not happened clearly points to a drop in the load to zero. The broken part appears to be held just by friction alone, perhaps at its base, because the crack is wider at top than the bottom. The other point which emerges from this picture is that the tie bar is facing to the west, rather than the east. It implies that the lowest cell was strained to the west or upriver, and this tower was oscillating during the final seconds of its life.

The same picture shows another feature of the poor design and build of the towers, and was referred to directly by Henry Law during his investigation. The four bolts holding the two struts in place are visible at the top of the picture, and they have no washers fitted, so as to ensure that the bolts are fully tightened and gripping the struts. Closer inspection shows that the lengths of exposed thread are different from one from another, suggesting that they have variable tightness. Without washers, it will have been difficult to make a secure fitting against the rough surface of the cast iron, a specific defect mentioned by Henry Law. Inspection of many other bolted joints gives an inconsistent picture – washers being used at some places, but not at others.

There may be an alternative explanation for the variable lengths of exposed thread. Vibrations felt through the structure when trains passed may have loosened some of the bolts, the nuts riding up the thread to make a much looser attachment. Either way, the joint is poor and, along with other defects, induced unwanted flexibility into this tower, as well as all the others, before the accident. Finally, there is a gap of about ½in between the end of the channel sections of the struts and the surface of the adjacent column. Henry Law and other engineers judged the gap to be a serious design flaw, because movement of the struts is not inhibited by abutment.

Apart from completely broken lugs, partly broken lugs are one of the most common features seen in the wreckage of the piers, at least six having already been identified in the debris *(9.6)*.

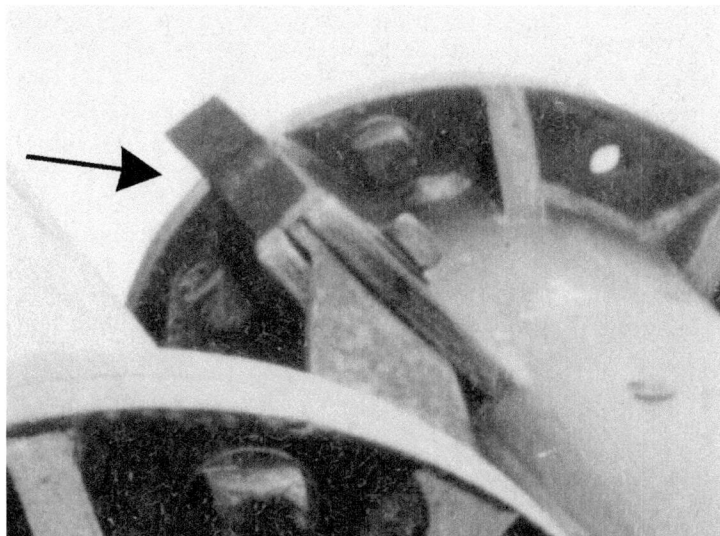

(9.5) Conical bolt hole through strut from pier No.11 (looking east).

(9.6) Partly broken lug from pier No.3 on the left-hand side of an 18in-corner column.

Flanges

With the multiplicity of broken metal found on the piers, it was inevitable that there would be many broken flanges, often cracked through the bolt holes. Just like the lugs, the bolt holes represent an obvious zone of weakness, and a natural starting point for brittle cracks. However, according to the Inquiry, those on the 15in columns were drilled, while those on the larger 18in columns were cast as one, just like the lugs. A good example of a drilled bolt hole from a smaller column is shown at *(9.3)*, one of which has suffered a fracture to reveal the parallel inner sides.

However, the bolt holes in the larger 18in columns were apparently cast, and a check is possible from the westernmost 18in column which fell on pier No.9, looking east *(5.7)*. The end of the column, which was attached to the second tier, faces the viewer in the immediate foreground and there is a single bolt still present in one of the upper holes. The rear of the flange is also visible in the eastward-looking view on the same pier, and the close-up of the bolt head allows the taper to be calculated. Comparison of the two pictures gives a much more precise idea of the fit of the bolt in the hole, as well as the taper alleged by the Inquiry. In the first case, the clearance between the bolt and the hole is estimated at around 0.3in, compared with Rothery's figure of 0.375in (⅜in). This is not bad agreement. Looking at the other side and assuming the bolt has the same diameter of 1.125in, the clearance is now around 0.435in, larger than the clearance on the other side, but still a rather small taper. It certainly seems a smaller taper than the large and visible taper on the lug holes. Unfortunately, nowhere in the Inquiry are the taper angles measured and recorded of any of the conical holes. In this case, the taper is about 10°. A very rough visual estimate of the taper on the lugs, shown in *(6.9)* for example, gives a value of around 20°. However, the estimate is less accurate owing to parallax, and assumes the crack bisects the lug exactly.

Top Heavy Girders

It was never clear from the Inquiry that the high girder section was very top heavy, although it is quite clear from the masses involved, and which were calculated in detail for the two main expert reports on the effect of wind pressure on a pier. The results were buried by a mass of calculations, but are very clear, and in rough agreement between the two reports. The weights of the components are: pier around 110 tons, girders 288 tons and train over 130 tons, so the total superincumbent weight on the 80ft-high pier is nearly 420 tons, a ratio of around 4 to 1. Simple moment calculations show that the centre of gravity is near the top of the tower without a train, and approaching the railway track, with a train perched overhead as well.

So what does it mean? When a structure topples over, there is a net moment pulling it down if the centre of gravity moves past a certain point. The more top heavy it is, the smaller the movement to create a positive moment, and so cause collapse. The conventional view is that if the centre of gravity moves past the base, then that structure becomes unstable and falls. So the higher the centre of gravity, the smaller the movement needed to cause it to fall. Applied to a single tower, movement of the tower past its base will start the process and, if the top moves around half the diameter of the base (around 10ft), it will fall. If the centre section fails, the single tower becomes two separate towers of three columns each, and the critical movement then drops to around 3ft.

This was no leaning tower of Pisa, simply because the centre of gravity of a Tay Bridge tower was so high, that only small lateral movements were needed to cause collapse. In the famous Italian tower, the centre of gravity is about halfway down the structure, so it can lean over to a considerable extent before its centre of gravity falls outside the base foundation. It has actually been pulled back in the 1990s, giving it a more stable configuration, hopefully giving it a longer lease of life.

Vibrations in Structures

Vibrations are a constant companion of engines, as every driver knows. If the engine is poorly tuned, a driver will usually be able to tell simply by the change in frequency or sound of the engine. Sound is simply mechanical vibration of the air within a limited and rather high frequency range. It is similar for any powered device, such as a washing machine or tumble drier. It is obvious when a wash or rinse cycle is over because the machine is silent. Problems can be detected by odd effects such as low frequency vibrations from the machine, causing it

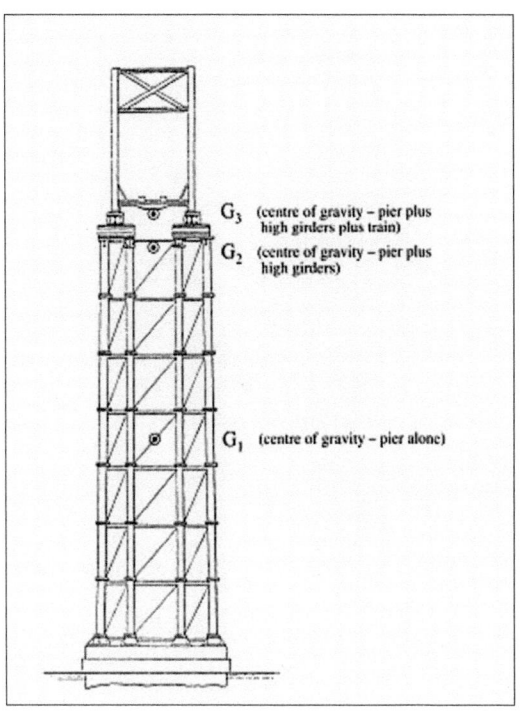

Left: (9.7) Centre of gravity of a single tower with and without a train.

Below: (9.8) Centre of gravity of a single tower when wind braces have been destroyed.

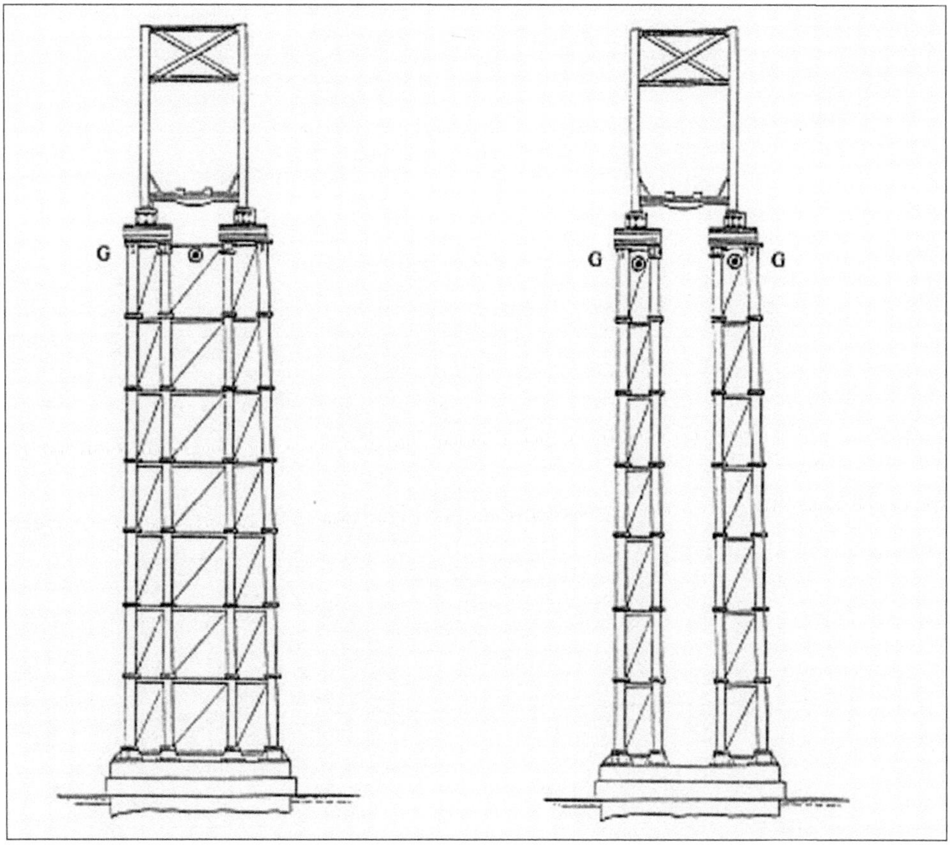

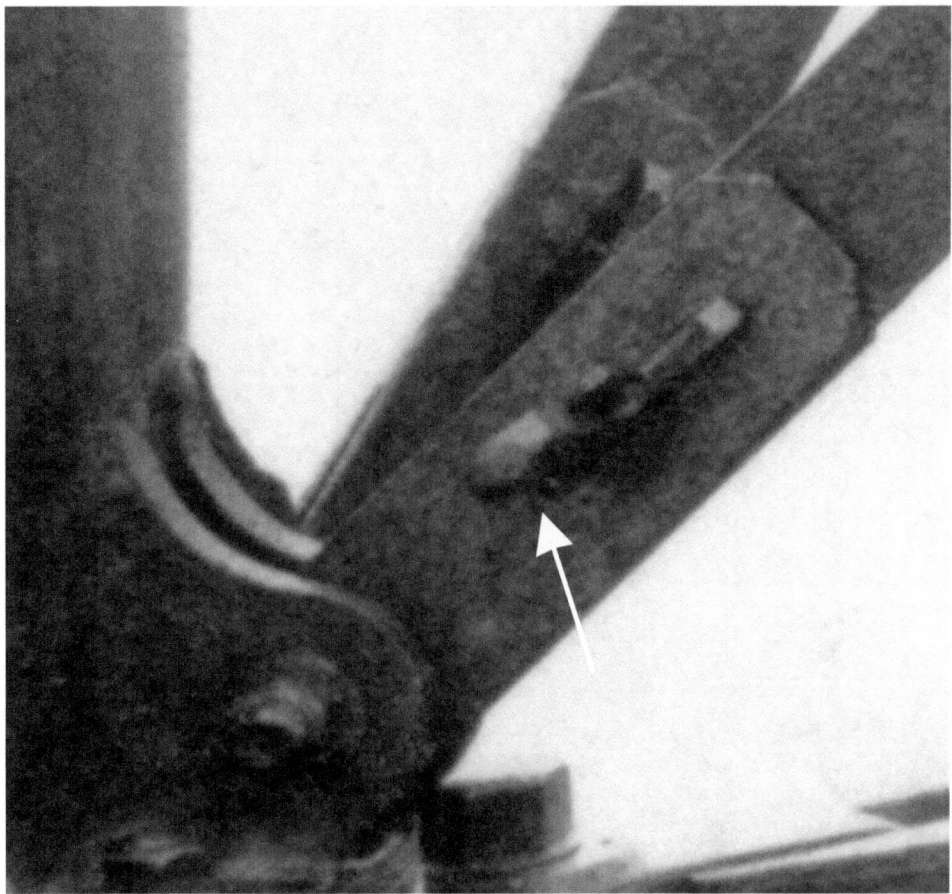

(9.9) Close-up of a joint on pier No.3 with a shim hammered into the side of the cotter by Noble to stop the chattering.

to move bodily. Thus, an overloaded machine or one with a poorly balanced load is readily detected by the wobble induced. However, even constant regular vibrations often produce unwanted effects, a common one being loosening of screws on parts attached to engines (often on parts hidden by the engine, so the user has no warning until he or she cannot start the car because the alternator has drifted free).

Railways and the structures on which they ride are no different in principle, and vibrations can often produce not just unwelcome, but sometimes dangerous effects. The history of the railways is littered with examples of key components wriggling out and causing mayhem. Stationary steam engines frequently produced such effects, which were easily corrected, but when steam engines were moving bodily over a track it was not so easy to detect the problem before a deadly sequence of events was initiated. The disaster at Weedon in 1915 was one of the worst of this kind, when a pin used to lock a screw collar which retained the coupling rod dropped off, the screw unthreaded, and the coupling rod fell free. It struck a sleeper on the opposite track just as another train was approaching. It derailed because the line was knocked out of true, and ten passengers were killed in the subsequent accident.

Eight innocent travellers were killed in 2002 at Potters Bar station when a train derailed at a set of points just before the station. Critical parts of the mechanism such as bolts had worked free, and it failed as the train passed over. There had been some prior warning that this set of points was unstable the previous day, but the maintenance crew were sent to the wrong place, so the defects went uncorrected. The matter of vertical (rather than lateral) vibrations induced by passing trains in bridges was investigated in the 1930s by C.E. Inglis. He showed that such movements increased with train speed and mass, but also depended on the length and stiffness of the girders on which the track was laid. However, an error in the Millennium footbridge over the Thames opened in 2000 allowed lateral oscillations, which were caused by the very pedestrians it was designed to accommodate. When more than around 600 persons were on the bridge, they induced cyclical side-to-side movement from their footfall. They were unconsciously all behaving in the same way, side-stepping at about the same frequency, and the walkway started to sway at its natural frequency.

The Tay disaster is probably an earlier example of the deleterious effects of train vibrations on the structure over which they had been passing. The damage probably started as soon as traffic built up over the bridge, especially with trains moving north at well above the maximum 25mph stipulated by Hutchinson. High frequency vibrations passed down through the towers and loosened the key joints used to tighten the diagonal tie bars. We know that Noble noticed the problem of chattering joints in September 1878, not long after the bridge had opened officially in June that year. It is likely that he only fixed those joints within hearing range, that is in the lowest tiers of the towers, while leaving those higher up beyond earshot and difficult to access owing to their height and the problem of free climbing the structures. This was yet another defect in the design of the towers, one which Eiffel fixed by providing his towers with an inner spiral staircase for ease of access.

The joints Noble did 'fix' was a palliative because, by wedging the cotters in their free position, they no longer acted to brace the columns. An example of what may be one of Noble's wedged joint is shown in *(9.9)*, with the shadow at the right of the cotter (arrow) on the left, perhaps being the tip of one of the packing pieces or shims.

The size is about right for a section of ½ by ¼in, and the joint was readily accessible being on the ground tier of pier No.3 (looking east) of the high girders. It is not a critical east-west joint, but there were many critical joints fixed in the same way, according to Henry Law. The bruised head of the cotter just above shows where it was hammered home originally. The entire high girder section was slowly but surely becoming much more flexible, and the towers were beginning to move as more and more such joints rattled free.

Joint Loosening

It might be expected that the topmost joints in the towers would be affected first, being nearest to the track. As time passed, the lower joints would also loosen, so that between June 1878 when the bridge was opened to traffic, and September, the process had run down at least one tower, because this is when Henry Noble first heard the sound of the joints chattering. By the following summer, when the bridge was being painted, the lateral sway was noticed by the painters working at the top of the towers, whenever a train passed over. What would be the effect of all the loose joints in the centre cells on movement of the whole tower? It is possible to estimate the effect, simply knowing the amount of play in each joint and assuming that all the joints have a similar degree of play.

Consider first a single wind cell of a tower, where the two tie bars are tensioned. However, if the joints loosen, then the tie bars are unstrained. If it is then distorted by lateral forces acting on the tower, it can move from side to side, one tie bar being stretched, the other compressed (although more likely, it just bent, as shown in *(9.11)*).

Movement would be possible if there was some play or looseness in the connections with the lugs, for example. The lug was fitted with a 1⅛in-diameter bolt sitting in a 1¼in-minimum-diameter lug hole, so there was play of about ⅛in. There will be similar play in the other lug, so giving about ¼in. If there was an additional play of ½in in the cottered joint, say, then the total movement of the tie bar becomes ¾in. In a square of side 10ft (the height and width of

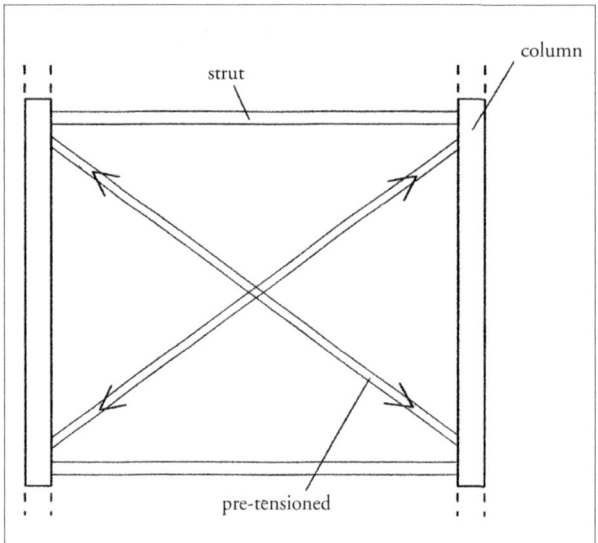

Left: (9.10) Single wind cell of a tower with struts and tie bars.

Below: (9.11) Distortion of a wind cell to the east and west.

Opposite: (9.12) Uniform distortion of a high girder tower under force pushing it to the east.

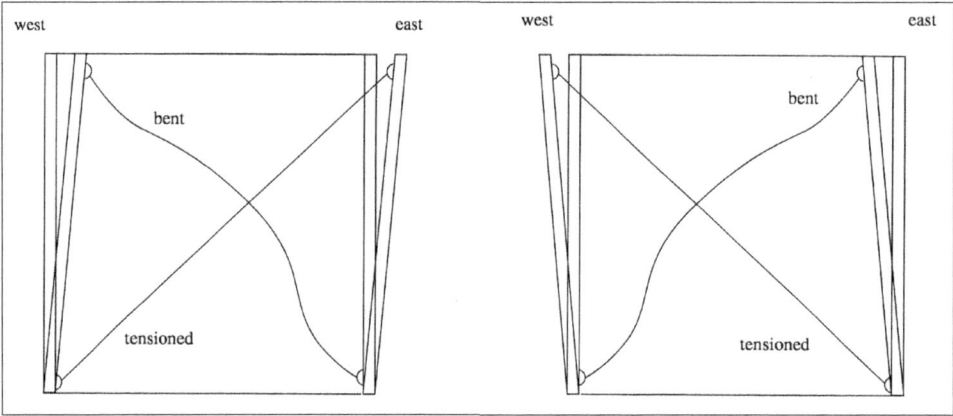

the cell), the lateral movement possible is smaller by a factor of 1.414 (the square root of 2, by applying Pythagoras's theorem), so is around ½in. Now if each cell in a seven-tier tower can each move sideways by ½in, the sway at the top is just (7 x ½), which is about 3.5in *(9.12)*.

This result is of the same order of magnitude as that seen by the painters when working on top of the towers when a train passed over the high girder section. It is only a rough estimate, but is in the right ball park to explain the lateral sway that so frightened them. It would also explain the polishing marks seen on many of the lower lug holes, because if the bolts were moving to-and-fro, it would abrade the cast iron, tending to smooth and polish the surface as shown in *(6.9)* and *(9.1)*.

Deterioration

The evidence for steady deterioration of the high girder section is inescapable. The joints had started to weaken in September 1878, when Noble first noticed the noise made by the loosened cotters. The process continued over many months, and resulted in major lateral movements of the towers when trains passed at speed from south to north. The sway was noticed by the painters when working at height, as well as by passengers on the trains. Fatigue

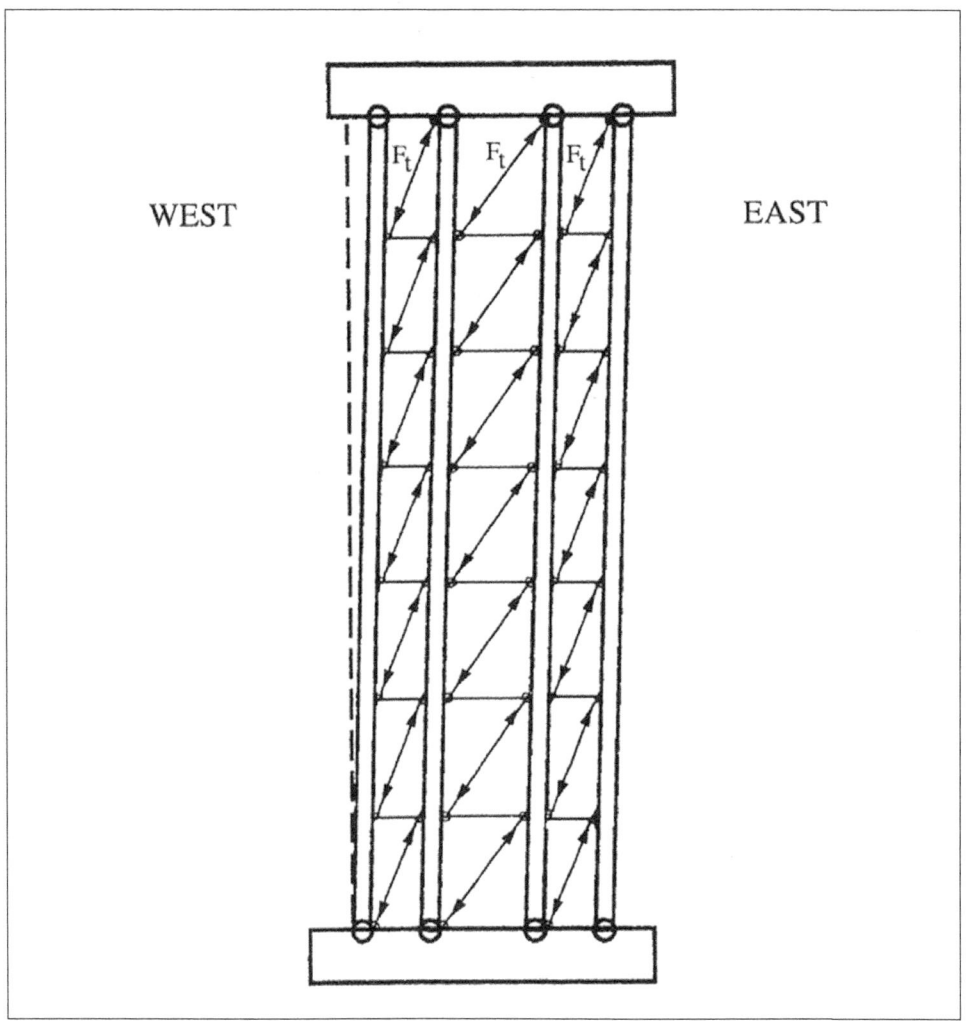

of the lugs of fully tightened tie bars probably started at around this time, since they alone will have been resisting the lateral movement of the towers. The whole section will have been deteriorating and approaching criticality by the time Queen Victoria came to cross over the bridge in June 1879. However, her train was crossing from north to south, and was probably travelling at low speed. The consequences of failure during her crossing can only be imagined, and the thought could well have crossed her mind (and those of her government) after the Inquiry concluded.

It is likely that lug cracking was occurring in all the towers, but the distribution will have varied depending on where Mr Noble had made his 'repairs' and the distribution of original defects such as burnt-on lugs (if they had indeed been installed). The fact that virtually all the towers collapsed is very strong evidence that they were all in a parlous state as the winter of 1879 approached. This feature of the accident has been almost totally ignored by recent commentators, but yet must be explained by any serious failure hypothesis. A derailing train will only have affected one tower and not twelve, while hurricane force wind speeds will have been needed to be over half a mile in width, to carry such a great length of the structure away. Neither theories were accepted by the Inquiry, who blamed the design, construction and maintenance. They stated quite clearly that they thought that the integrity of the bridge had degraded after first use, due to vibrations from passing trains, and the visible evidence fully supports their conclusions. If the express on 28 December had passed over safely, damage to the bridge would surely have been seen the following day, and remedial action taken. The NBR may well have been forced to close the bridge to all traffic while reinforcement was put in place. Indeed, they would surely have had to consider rebuilding the structure, as they were forced to do after the real tragedy.

Missing Evidence

In his book published in 1972, John Thomas made a significant discovery as he was reading the many witness statements produced for the Inquiry. It is a statement taken by Thorntons preparing material to go before the Inquiry from two of the painters, David Dale and John Evans. They said:

> At the junction of the high girders on the south there was a slight twist on the rails. It looked as if the pier had gone to the side a little, and pulled the rail off the straight. When looking at a train approaching you could see the engine dip into the bend, it was to the eastward. You could see this bend quite well.

This evidence was confirmed, according to John Thomas, by several other witnesses, the most important being the inspector of the permanent way, George Murray:

> There was in the first high girder from the south a curve or bend in the line of the rails. The curve started about the middle of the girder and ran to very near the north end. there would be eight metals of twenty four feet in length each affected by the bend. The line should have been straight and the curve was quite perceptible to the eye. The deflection would be about two inches at the greatest.

The Inquiry would not hear the evidence of the kink in the rail (although it examined these witnesses on other matters) because Thorntons thought it might be damaging to their client, so it was suppressed. Alternatively, they may just have supposed the point irrelevant. So how might the kink have originated? This span was that between the south-standing pier and pier No.1 of the high girders, and it fell in the accident in February 1877, when it and another were blown off their temporary pins during a severe storm. It was rescued and apparently restored to shape before being reincorporated into the structure. Bill Dow of Dundee attributes the kink in the rail to damage to the girder created by the fall, the distortion presumably leading to a slight twisting of the track when it was laid later. But the evidence of its origin has been disputed by John Thomas, who claims the fall occurred elsewhere. However, when any vehicle travels at speed, apparently small changes in road contour can produce much more significant effects than at low speeds.

Tower Oscillation

So here is a possible reason for the lateral sway experienced by the painters and passengers in the high girders when trains sped by heading north into Dundee town. If a heavy locomotive dipped into the kinked rail, some of its momentum would be transferred to the track, and from the track to the towers which supported it. The tender and all the attached carriages would follow, tending to reinforce the effect. It could also be the source of the wave of oscillation in the high girders which could be seen and felt as a fast train approached. By the summer of 1879, all the towers in the high girder section would have loosened, and would respond to the stimulus of a fast train in a similar way. Although small at first, the effect could only increase as the wind ties became looser, and the joints

(9.13) View looking north of the wreckage on pier No.4, showing columns perched precariously, facing west, not east as on the majority of piers.

deteriorated.

There are indications that some of the towers fell into the wind, that is to the west, perhaps the best example being that on pier No.4 *(9.13)*. There are two columns facing west, and they may be associated with a third column at around the centre of the pier. The set of columns are probably those from the first tier itself.

By falling to the west rather than the east, as with most of the other towers, the situation suggests that collapse was not at all straightforward. Such features tend to support the idea that the high girders were oscillating laterally, especially when such swaying was reported by workers on the towers in the summer of 1879. The plan of the girders at the bottom of the river also supports the theory, because they lay in a wave, just as one would expect if they had been oscillating to-and-fro in the seconds before they fell. Their position may represent their final moments on the towers, frozen in time at the bottom of the estuary.

Fatigue of Lugs

One further effect may then have come into play as the loose towers swayed a few inches side-to-side. Henry Law found wide variation in the state of the metalwork when he examined the wreckage in early 1880. The cast-iron parts showed a wide variation in the state of the metal, and the joints and connections varied widely too, by the presence or absence of defects, the roughness of the surface of the castings and so on. If some of the joints were doing their job and had not become loose, then it was those good joints in the wind cells which would have been forced to share a much greater proportion of the moment created by the swaying towers. Effectively, they would have to bear a greater load than had it been shared by other joints and connections of the loosened tie bars.

Everyone accepts that the coned bolt holes were the weakest link in the path of the load applied to the tie bars. It is here that crack growth might have started, near the outer corners where the stress was greatest, and perhaps the stress increased yet further by defects such as blow holes *(9.2)*. Each major oscillation produced by a fast heavy train travelling north would have stressed these faulty lugs, with a tiny crack growing at each passing. Cracks only grow in one direction, getting larger and larger until the rest of the material can no longer support that load, the crack grows suddenly, and the lugs part company. The lower lugs were probably the places where such fatigue cracks grew and, when this process started, the structural integrity of the towers was beyond recall. Since at least some of the towers had been seen by Bouch and Noble in mid-December 1879, the process had come close to criticality. Indeed, it is likely that all the tie bars were intact by the morning of the 29 December. Certainly no one spotted any dangling bars either from afar or close by, as far as is known.

The penultimate train, the local travelling north across the bridge an hour or two before the final express, did experience severe swaying, enough to create sparks from the wheels and disturb the crew in the guard's van at the rear. The driver did not notice anything amiss because the much heavier locomotive was only affected minimally. However, it is possible that some of the tie bars had reached criticality and had snapped as a result of the train passing overhead. No one would have noticed them in the dark and with the storm raging. When the following express train, with its much heavier engine, reached the high girders, the towers were strained to the very limit, and the tie bars fractured one by one in a chain reaction. Because the wave of oscillation encompassed the whole of the high section, all of the towers will have been affected, which goes some way in explaining why they all fell that night, not just those directly under the train.

Failure at the North or South?

The Inquiry could not decide whether the bridge failed from the north or the south. Rothery thought it more likely to have started collapsing at the north end, but Barlow and Yolland took the view that failure started at the south. The eyewitness evidence is equivocal, and it is difficult from the wreckage alone to determine the sequence of events. There are some objections to a northern failure, however. If it collapsed from the north, the driver will surely have seen the girders starting to fall ahead of him and reacted by shutting off the brakes or throttling down. The fact that he did not and was taken completely unawares, suggests that failure occurred behind him. Failure from the south seems more likely because of the extra load from the train itself, conservatively estimated by the Inquiry at 130 tons, and a significant proportion of the total load on the piers.

If the train also induced the oscillations at the start of the high girder section, then it started the collapse sequence when it entered the high girder section. Collapse of individual towers may actually have occurred relatively slowly, following the order of east-west tie bars first, then struts to produce two sub-towers, and then the final buckling of the sub-towers. Although John Cochrane said that the two sub-towers on pier No.5 sandwiched the girders (and so fell as separate units), the situation on the previous piers suggests a more complex fall. And collapse would have been subject to the strength of the flanges, those on piers No.1 and No.3 clearly being weaker at the tops of the tiers which survived on their bases.

10

Aftermath

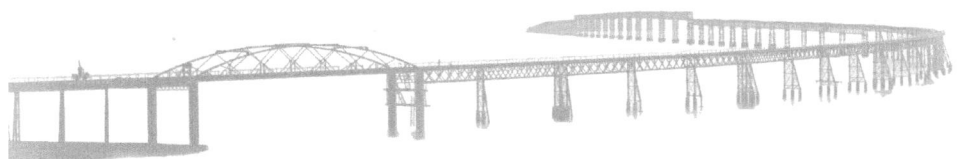

There is no doubt that the disaster marked a turning point in the way bridges were designed, built and managed. Most of the recommendations of the Inquiry were carried out by the government and, in the confusion of the change of administration from Disraeli to Gladstone, public anger relented a little. However, the event was not to be forgotten, like so many other major disasters. For a start, there was a visible reminder of that terrible night, in the form of the original piers left in the river (10.1).

Then there was the written record of the Inquiry, available to all through many libraries throughout the country, where the detailed record of the events before during and after are recorded in infinite detail. And there was, of course, the press, as well as Parliament to keep up the pressure on the government.

There was an immediate need for a new bridge across the Tay, both for passenger and goods traffic. There were two key issues to resolve: what to do with the old bridge and what design to choose for the new. Parliamentary approval would be needed, so a Select Committee was set up to look at the various options. In addition, the building of a new suspension bridge across the Forth had already been awarded to Bouch. Having been blamed personally for the accident, what was to be done about the Forth Bridge?

Another problem had been posed by the Inquiry: what pressures were developed by winds in Britain? Directly related to the issue was measurement of wind speed, the instrumentation needed and locations which would provide a national picture. A Royal Commission was set up in July 1880, with instructions to examine the problem.

Select Committee

The Select Committee was set up in the same month of 1880, just a few weeks after the Inquiry had reported to examine the problem of a new bridge for the Tay. It followed statements first by General Hutchinson and then a response by Joseph Chamberlain, president of the Board of Trade in the new Gladstone administration. Chamberlain defended the Board of Trade with some vigour. Hutchinson's statement repeated his earlier evidence before the Inquiry, essentially saying that he did not have the power to investigate the design in any detail, and that several of his original recommendations had not been fulfilled, especially regarding speed of trains across the bridge and the need to observe the structure in strong lateral winds. Chamberlain fully supported his position, and exculpated the government of responsibility for the accident. Both continued in their respective careers, unlike the hapless inspector of the Dee Bridge after the furore of 1847. A Bill was already before Parliament to rebuild the

(10.1) The piers of the old Tay Bridge alongside the new bridge built by the Barlows.

Tay Bridge, and was to be examined in detail by the Select Committee, chaired by Sir Massey Lopes.

They had several issues to discuss, including the position of any new bridge in relation to the old, the height of any new bridge and resolving the issue of navigation of high-masted ships up the river to Perth, and its construction to ensure its safety. They were to question many witnesses from the Inquiry, including John Leng, John Walker, Cochrane and Brunlees, Henry Law, Captain Scott and Henry Noble, as well as Colonel Yolland and W.H. Barlow. They had the report of the Inquiry before them to give them a basis for addressing the witnesses.

Walker, the general manager of the NBR, was the first to be questioned, and he gave a general picture of the way the bridge had transformed traffic across the estuary, stimulating growth of its jute industry. Carriage of coal from the Fife coal fields had grown from 400,000 tons when the bridge opened, to 500,000 at the fall. Its passenger services had grown from around twenty to ninety trains a day, over the same period. John Leng was the proprietor of the local paper, the *Dundee Advertiser*, as well as being a director of the Dundee, Perth and London Shipping Co., so knew much about the trade upriver. It was an original specification that the centre section was high enough to allow high masted ships to pass upriver in the navigation channel to Perth. But he had been in favour of a double line at lower height, even when the original proposal was discussed, and strongly supported a new bridge along the line of the old. Most traffic through to Perth were smacks and small schooners, many of which were towed upriver under the bridge by tugs. But traffic was light; sometimes a week would pass without any ships going upriver. Other witnesses, such as the local MP and the Town Clerk, supported a lowering of the new bridge to 77ft rather than the original 88ft in the specification. It would increase stability, especially if combined with a double line. Only a handful of very large schooners would exceed the height, and those could strike their topgallant masts easily.

Later on in the meetings, Perth traders disputed the figures, and mentioned two ships, the *Baltic* and *Yelva* each of around 200 tons, which had delivered goods to Perth. They had masts 105ft- and 95ft-high respectively, but had only visited Perth after the bridge had fallen in June 1880. Clearly, they had taken the opportunity of the demise of the structure to trade with the city. The objectors from Perth had forced Bouch to raise the pier heights to 88ft, and were still dissatisfied. They preferred the current situation with the bridge down. The enmity between the two towns was alive and kicking.

Henry Noble Reappears

Henry Noble was to appear as well, largely for any advice he could give about the river and its many sand banks, scour of the piers and so on. However, he was asked about the pier foundations and a proposal from Brunlees to build brick piers to replace the iron piers in the old bridge:

1301. I look upon you as perhaps knowing quite as much about it as Mr Brunlees? – You are quite right; but you see what a terrible bother I got in by taking too much upon myself, for just tightening a few bracings, so that I am really very careful. It was no more or less than making a thing rigid here and there, I am blamed for pulling part of the structure down; and I had rather not answer that question.

Noble was quite clearly very sensitive about the issue of his treatment of the joints, which was hardly surprising given the conclusions of the Court of Inquiry. He was still convinced that the train had crashed into the girders and caused the accident that night. The Committee were intrigued by his outburst, and explored the matter a little further. He had protested his ignorance of ironwork at the Inquiry, but had told Bouch about the four cracked columns, so:

1355. Where did you derive that experience which would enable you to superintend the iron portion of the bridge? – The experience which I derived was from seeing the ironwork, in a great measure, carried on during the first time they were doing it; the tightening of a few cotters is only a labourer's work at the best.

It was clear that he felt confused (and obviously hurt) by the criticism of his work on the joints and why he had not told Bouch about the matter, yet had told him about the cracked columns. But it turned out that he had inspected much of the erected ironwork after Macbeath left in 1877, and until the opening of the bridge in 1879. His duplicity in the whole affair was quite clear from his new testimony, but Bouch was still left to take the rap for the disaster.

Engineers' Advice

Henry Law, as the principal investigator for the Inquiry, gave evidence about the foundations and the weight they could bear safely. He had spent thirty-three days on the site of the disaster, and his partner and assistants were there for seventeen days and 130 days respectively, to examine the remains in great detail. In addressing the issue of how the bridge fell, he was also asked to look at the surviving structure, its stability and the potential for reconstruction. Although the structure was in reasonable condition with no tie bars broken, there was concern about the cracked columns found by Noble. Moreover, some of the joints in the tie bars had been packed with shims by Noble, just like those in the high girder section. Also, some of the joints between the girders were not always vertically above the centre of the piers which supported them. In some cases the centres deviated by 18in.

There was evidence of damage to some of the pier bases in the surviving stretch to the south, with disturbed masonry indicative of a strong disturbing force (presumably on the night of the disaster). The flanking columns gave little lateral stability to the piers. Like Noble, he was questioned in detail about the foundations of the bridge and the amount of scour after completion. There had been scour, which appeared to have been resisted by the deposition of large stones about the piers to stabilise them against river currents. His independent survey confirmed the reports of Noble concerning the problem. As for support from the strata upon which they had been built, he had seen no shift or settlement of the existing pier bases. He supported Brunlees in proposing to test all of the piers by weighing them down and observing any changes in their position. They should be tested to twice their existing capacity, up to 6 tons per square foot. New caissons could be sunk near the existing ones, although care would be needed not to disturb the latter. He was in favour of reconstructing the bridge using iron piers, but to an improved design, and to support a double rather than single line. This was a different position to that of Brunlees, who had recommended new brick piers rather then iron. If the existing surviving iron piers were to be reused, they would all need inspecting for the defects known to have been present in the high girder section. If the girders of the spans were to be reused they would need substantial modification to support a double line. Now he suggested use of a 'new' material, steel, which had in fact been available for some years although it apparently had not been approved by the BoT for use in bridges. Bessemer, the inventor of the eponymous converter as long ago as 1854, had been knighted by Queen Victoria at the same time as Bouch (1879). Although Bessemer had experienced problems in making steel, those problems had been overcome and there was now a thriving steel industry in Sheffield and elsewhere, especially as other methods for making it had been invented, such as the open hearth furnace of Siemens (1856). Here is his answer to a question about rebuilding the bridge:

2183. ...You suggested to the Committee yesterday that you were in favour of constructing an iron bridge as it was constructed by Sir Thomas Bouch, only strengthening it? – That was not my suggestion. I was asked what I thought would be the better plan of reconstructing that bridge, if it were constructed upon the present piers; and I said that certainly it must be done in iron, in wrought iron, or in milled steel.

This was a key issue to civil engineers because in Britain they had not exploited steel to anywhere near the extent as, for example, in the United States. Roebling and son were at that very moment building a suspension bridge between Brooklyn and Manhattan in New York, using steel wire for the main and subsidiary cables to support the roadway. The steel was twice the strength of existing iron wire, and was galvanised (coated with zinc) for corrosion protection. The Roeblings had a deserved reputation of being sticklers for only the best quality wire delivered to them by suppliers. When they discovered that some sub-standard wire had in fact been incorporated into their structure through fraud, they increased the size of the cables to allow for the lower strength material. The Brooklyn Bridge was opened to worldwide acclaim in May 1883, and stands there to this day, with iconic status.

Commissioners

As one of the three Commissioners on the Tay Inquiry, Yolland was called to give evidence. As Chief Inspector of Railways for the BoT, he naturally had a great deal to say about the role of government in approving structures and track. Initially, he had some words about the importance of guarding against toppling of carriages and wagons from the rails. They had in fact recommended substantial parapets be installed when wooden viaducts were being rebuilt in stone or brick. One such 4ft-high parapet had prevented a derailed train from falling over the edge of a viaduct at Walworth road station in London within the last six months. On the

Tay Bridge he opined that single lines are subject to special dangers, especially from collisions, and that a double track was now essential in the rebuilding. The existing iron fence on the surviving part of the bridge was far too insubstantial to protect against trains falling from the structure by whatever cause, although there was no basis for Bouch's allegations that the train derailing had caused the centre section to fall. He did say that there were very few cases known to him of carriages or wagons being overturned by wind pressure alone. The BoT's opinion on a new bridge was stated as follows by their counsel:

> Mr Michael…The view of the Board of Trade is this, that the line should be constructed, and that it should be reconstructed as nearly as possible on the present site; that it should be constructed of brick upon proper foundations, the whole of the foundations to be new; and that the line should be a double one.

The other Commissioner questioned, W.H. Barlow, was destined to have a pivotal role in the reconstruction. He also supported the creation of a double line, just as much for the increase in traffic expected as well as the increased stability. Doubling up on the existing structure was not feasible, owing to the sheer variability of the design of different piers, some with two, others four, and some even with elliptical rather than circular caissons *(10.1)*. He was not impressed by the proposal for all brick piers either – the designer should be allowed a free hand as to choice of materials. He recommended the testing of a selection of the existing piers and of new ones built beside the old. The new piers would need some form of protection from scour. As for the superstructure, he preferred wrought iron to brick, but with no cast iron whatsoever. The new bridge should be able to withstand a pressure of 50–56psf with a safety factor of four, that is a maximum of 200psf. He was sceptical of talk of wind pressures of 100psf measured in Britain.

Conclusions

The Committee duly reported its findings in August 1880. They thought that the bridge should be rebuilt at the present site, but with a lower elevation of 77ft. To mollify disgruntled traders of Perth, tugs for towing large ships upriver would be provided *gratis* by the NBR and they would guarantee to keep the navigable channel clear. However, they were not in favour of the proposals put to them, one of them being to reuse the existing piers linked physically to a new set parallel to the old, and supporting a new superstructure. There seemed to be an element of danger about using the old piers without testing them. They thought that some of the existing caissons had been sunk to an insufficient depth, and that scour had occurred, necessitating support from stones dropped close by. The Committee wanted a new bridge built on entirely new foundations, and tested to ensure their security. They wanted the junction at the south end of the bridge removed, and the lowering of the overall height of the highest section would lower the steep gradient on the approaches to Tay Bridge station.

The Committee had clearly been strongly influenced by the evidence from the recent Inquiry. The disaster was still very fresh in the public mind, the report had been withering in its criticism of the old bridge and the new government (and its supporters) were nervous about the proposals which had been advanced in the Bill.

Report on Wind Pressure

The Royal Commission appointed by Chamberlain reported back in May 1881, its members including Sir George Armstrong, the well-known arms manufacturer, and Sir John Hawkshaw. Armstrong had invented the rifled breech-loading howitzer, and that very year the government had asked for trials for potential use by the army. He would be among the first to introduce electric lighting at his spectacular country house at Cragside, Northumberland. Edison had invented the light bulb in 1879, with the local boy, Swan, claiming a similar priority date. Hawkshaw was an eminent civil engineer and helped finish Clifton Suspension Bridge with Barlow, to Brunel's original design. There were the by now familiar names of W.H. Barlow, G.G. Stokes and Colonel Yolland. They had been instructed to estimate the maximum pressures ever recorded in Britain, and so had to reconcile different kinds of results since at least two types of anemometer were then currently in operation, Osler's pressure instrument and Robinson's rotating cup machine (the latter device being familiar to us today owing to its standardisation and widespread use). They also summarised the results for the Continent and India. Apart from different instruments, they also had to allow for the precise location of the suggested stations because the wind could vary according to the local topography. The railways themselves could be an additional source of information on the problem because trains had been running regularly in many different locations, some highly exposed to winds, such as high embankments. When attempting to answer the question of the effects on large structures such as bridges, however, they needed to assess the effects of length and height of the structures, and thus the lateral extent of high winds recorded at particular locations. The report inevitably presented many tables of data and actual records from continuously recording instruments maintained by the Meteorological Office and other observers.

Their report summarised the results of thirteen stations from Aberdeen to Yarmouth over a period of around five years (1869–1875) using the rotating cup anemometer. Whether more recent records existed, but had not been digested, remains unknown. The maximum pressures they calculated varied enormously. The highest results came from Bidston in Liverpool, the station chosen to calibrate the formula between pressure and wind speed. Although pressure was proportional to the square of speed, the constant in the equation needed to be estimated experimentally. The maximum wind speed was 80mph, giving a pressure of 65.5psf. The highest pressure at Aberdeen over this period was 47.6psf, while that at Glasgow was 39.7psf. At Sandwick in Orkney, the greatest pressure was higher at 65.6psf, while the anemometer on top of Alnwick Castle gave a pressure of 46.2psf. Falmouth gave a maximum pressure of 53.3psf, but other southern stations gave much lower maxima. Kew, for example, could only produce a value of 27psf. Yarmouth on the other hand gave a result of 42.2psf. Continental stations also produced considerably lower maxima. Brussels produced a figure of 21.8psf, while Flushing in the Netherlands had a maximum of 26psf. Paris was even lower at 14.7psf, and Utrecht gave a value of 30psf. The maxima recorded by the pressure anemometer in India at just four stations was around 40psf.

However, the results are much higher than those presented by *(5.1)*, taken from a Met Office Manual from 1963. The Commission itself chose just one station for standardisation (Bidston), but admitted that the results recorded were out of line with all the other British stations. The maxima recorded were momentary, and not sustained for long periods. That there was some error in their results seems inescapable. In addition, Stokes and Armstrong wanted another clause added to the report, saying that they could not be sure of the lateral extent of the highest pressures. If highly localised, then it would be unfair to impose a high pressure restriction on very large structures such as bridges. It is an obvious point to make, because both types of anemometer used were small instruments, and there was no experimental evidence for the lateral or upward extent of wind gusts.

They also summarised the small number of accidents where railway carriages had been affected by storms, with five examples mentioned from Britain, from 1855 to 1874. Four of the five did not involve toppling at all, but trains being stopped by a headwind.

The Commission could not report much of relevance to the recent storm that had brought about the collapse of the bridge. However, there was a recording from Bidston for the storm which affected the Tay Bridge in 1879. The anemometer at Bidston had recorded a maximum wind pressure of 38psf, a value well below the theoretical pressure of over 60psf needed to knock the bridge over, but still higher than Baker's estimate. But then Bidston is a long way from Dundee, and may anyway have been producing anomalous results. There had been no anemometers at all in Dundee.

Conclusions of Report on Wind Pressure

So what to make of the results? The anomalously high maxima from Liverpool were attributed to the nature of the local environment, tending to concentrate the force of the wind. The Commission decided to choose a figure of 56psf as the maximum a girder bridge could experience, and designers should use that figure when planning a new structure. More detailed guidelines were provided by the Committee on how to interpret the effect of high wind pressures on railway structures. A safety factor of 2 should be assumed in all calculations.

We know that extremely high wind pressures are developed by hurricanes and typhoons, and even then meteorologists must have been aware of the great storm of 1703. Detailed by Daniel Defoe, the storm cut across southern England, demolishing hundreds of church steeples, barns and countless chimneys. The first Eddystone lighthouse was destroyed by the wind and sea and he estimated that 8,000 people lost their lives in the hurricane. But these are rare events in Britain, and a five-year set of records is hardly likely to have included such an event.

Nevertheless, there was no hurricane that fateful night in Dundee and while the wind was strong, it was not so strong to blow down the structure unassisted. It was well established by that time that the structure was in a perilous state owing to its many design defects, poor construction and negligent maintenance.

Some commentators, such as David Swinfen, have attributed the fall to '... an enormously powerful gust of wind'. The many defects in the structure have been quietly forgotten, and Bouch, after all these years, is posthumously vindicated. The evidence is said to be those witnesses who turned their backs at the very moment the bridge fell owing to the blast. It brings an element of metaphysics into the argument, when such a theory is quite unnecessary given the mountain of evidence to show that the bridge had deteriorated in the months before the disaster. David Swinfen also wonders at the mystery of the low strength of the lugs, when it is common engineering knowledge that a hole concentrates the stress by a factor of 3, almost the same factor by which the lugs were weaker than the solid. Others, such as Tom Martin and Malcolm Macleod, have recalculated the moments acting on the bridge using more sophisticated computer methods, which show that the weakest tier was the second up from the base. But the analysis assumes that all joints were equivalent, an assumption that is not borne out by the known facts brought before the Inquiry. The joints and connections were highly variable, partly thanks to Noble's efforts, but also to the negligence of the Wormit staff. Others have resuscitated Bouch's hypothesis of train derailment, a theory rejected by the Inquiry and by highly skilled experts at the time. According to Bill Dow, aerodynamic factors may have lifted the last carriages against the girders, so explaining the high position of the girder marks, without any supporting evidence from railway records or anywhere else, of such an effect.

Before the controversy over the new bridge had subsided, Bouch had retired to Moffat. He had become ill after returning from London in July, and he intended to recuperate there with the help of his wife. He died on 30 October 1880 at the relatively young age of fifty-eight.

New Tay Bridge

The contract for the new bridge was awarded to W.H. Barlow in July 1881, who had produced a unique design for the piers. Barlow had become enthusiastic about steel, following a visit to the USA in 1876.

Much of the design effort was put in by his son, Crawford Barlow. The twin rail line and its girders were supported by twin bases, consisting of ductile iron plates riveted together, and

Left: (10.2) An old pier seen through the arches of a pier from the new Tay Bridge. The valuable wrought-iron tie bars have been stripped away, presumably by scrap metal merchants.

Opposite: (10.3) The Forth Bridge, seen from the Queensferry side of the estuary.

supported by a steel frame internally. The structure is a monocoque form rather than a space frame like the old bridge, where the stresses are supported more by the skin than the frame. Stress concentrations are minimised by this form of construction. The new bridge parallels the line of the original bridge, displaced 60ft upstream to the west, the surviving piers acting as breakwaters for the new. William Arrol & Co. were the new contractors but did not actually start work until June 1882. The undamaged girders from the old bridge were reused in the new by cutting them down the centre and widening them for the double track. The bridge was inspected by General Hutchinson from 16–18 June 1887, using eight locomotives coupled together. Its structural integrity was approved fully, and it opened for traffic on 20 June 1887.

Forth Bridge

Bouch lost the Forth Bridge contract on which he had been so busy for so long, perhaps to the detriment of his supervision of the Tay Bridge, shortly after the Inquiry ended. Only a forlorn reminder of his work there remains, in the form of a pier crowned now by a lighthouse on Inchgarvie Island. The new contract was awarded to Sir John Fowler and his partner, Benjamin Baker. Allan Stewart was chief engineer, presumably employed for the mathematical skills he had shown at the Inquiry. Benjamin Baker had developed the concept of a cantilever bridge, involving few piers but massive superstructures which were extended outwards until they met, and the bridge created *(10.3)*.

Although the idea had been used before, this was by far the largest cantilever bridge anywhere in the world, and required a high level of innovation in construction methods to succeed. Rolled steel was used to create the structural units of the bridge, riveted together to make the final shapes. Riveted structures cannot be shaken free by vibrations. As at the new Tay Bridge, the contractor was again William Arrol & Co. But the project was not trouble free. Owing to the great working heights (among other factors) towards the end of the construction phase, fifty-six workers were killed (compared with forty at the old Tay Bridge). Attitudes to death and injury of workers were quite different then compared with the present.

The project started in 1873 and ended with its tests in 1890. The critics this time were not so much engineers but artists, like William Morris, who condemned it as '... the supremest specimen of all ugliness.' It was another facet of the ongoing battle between aesthetics and utilitarianism, a battle which continues to this day. No doubt Morris refused to travel across it when finished, just as Fowler had refused to cross the old Tay Bridge, but for very different reasons. It was inspected at regular quarterly intervals by none other than General Hutchinson under new BoT regulations. The reports make interesting reading for their overview of progress on building the bridge. The first report was issued by General Hutchinson on 12 June 1883. He described various preparatory work on the piers and their foundations on solid rock both on shore and Inchgarvie Island. Diagrams of the bridge had been provided by Fowler and Baker, which showed the strains on the proposed structure under worst loading conditions, that is, a 56psf wind blowing from any direction plus a rolling load of 3,500 tons on the track! The estimated maximum stress in the steel was computed at one quarter of its total strength of 30 tons per sq.in in tension. The inspections were to continue until completion of the bridge and its proof testing, all under the supervision of General Hutchinson. His final report (the twenty-eighth in the series), made on 24 February 1890, details the tests done. He used two trains, each made of two engines and tenders hauling forty-four trucks holding iron castings, weighing in total 901 tons. So the two trains weighed 1,802 tons. It caused a deflection of 7.65in at the ends of the cantilevers, and 1.58in at the central girders when placed to give the maximum load on the structure. Little vibration was found when the trains ran through at speed. The bridge had been liberally fitted with many different wind gauges and anemometers (some to Baker's own design), which had recorded a maximum pressure of about 34psf.

After being officially opened on 4 March 1890, the bridge became a great success, making the east coast route to Aberdeen faster and more comfortable. The bridge has become a national monument to engineering skill, successfully convincing the public that bridges could be safe under all possible adverse conditions. The bridge lives in the public imagination for other reasons: the painting effort needed to protect the structure against corrosion, and its allegedly excessive safety factor. The bridge actually comes out as more efficient than the Quebec cantilever bridge by virtue of its use of tubular beams rather than solid angled beams. But trains still have to slow down when crossing the Forth bridge.

Bridge Failures

Failures of bridges after the fall of the Tay Bridge have been more common than one might have expected, given the publicity after the disaster, and the lessons given, if not thoroughly learnt. They included appropriate bridge materials, rigorous testing before installation of finished components (not just the materials) and the importance of redundancy so that if one component fails, the whole structure is not compromised. Component design to maximise strength was a message which should have been taken to heart, but it was not for some time that engineers began to appreciate the problem of stress concentration. Monitoring component quality and effective management of large contracts were also vital lessons of the disaster.

Cast iron had been used very widely in many different types of structure, and sudden failures of bridges still occurred. A significant accident occurred at Norwood junction on 1 May 1891, the year after the Forth Bridge was opened. It happened when a London-bound express train from Brighton was moving at speed across the Portland Road Bridge, when part of the bridge collapsed beneath the weight of the train, causing it to derail *(10.4)*. The bridge dated from before 1852, but the cast-iron girders had not been installed until 1860.

The failure had occurred at the flanges of a cast-iron girder, according to the report by General Hutchinson. There was a large internal flaw in the form of an L-shaped hole around 10in long and several inches wide in the flange and running into the web. It was quite invisible to external inspection. The breaking strength of the girder was calculated at 71 tons, but had been reduced by the flaw to 53 tons, and should have had a strength (according to BoT rules) of around 83 tons. No one was killed or seriously injured by the fracture, but there were many similar bridges on this particular line. Sir John Fowler reported that there were eighty-one bridges of comparable construction, all of which he recommended be rebuilt using steel or wrought iron. All duly were. Just why so many cast-iron structures survived the purges of the late 1840s after the Dee disaster is curious. One problem with the ageing railway system was the progressive increase in locomotive weight and train speeds, imposing larger and larger loads on structures built for lighter and slower trains. We have seen a similar problem on road bridges in the 1990s, when EC rules increased the axle weights of large lorries, forcing closures and reconstruction of the weaker structures.

But many more bridges built essentially of horizontal cast-iron girders survive to the present day, giving Robert Stephenson the last laugh. There was a crisis in the Second World War, when civil engineers suddenly realised that many so-called 'over-bridges' might not be able to withstand tanks and other heavy armour trundling over them, on the way to the D-Day beaches and elsewhere. Over-bridges are the many small and seemingly innocuous bridges needed to carry roads over railways and canals. A survey was made at the time by the Building Research Establishment of the circa 4,000 such bridges made from cast-iron girders distantly similar to that used by Stephenson on the Dee. They were made with several girders laid parallel across the gap, and small brick arches built across the lower flanges. Most proved to be rather weak (hardly surprising, given what had happened at Chester), so new design rules were adopted to limit the loads which could be put upon them. Such bridges have advisory notices on their approaches, so are easy to recognise. How many survive today remains unknown.

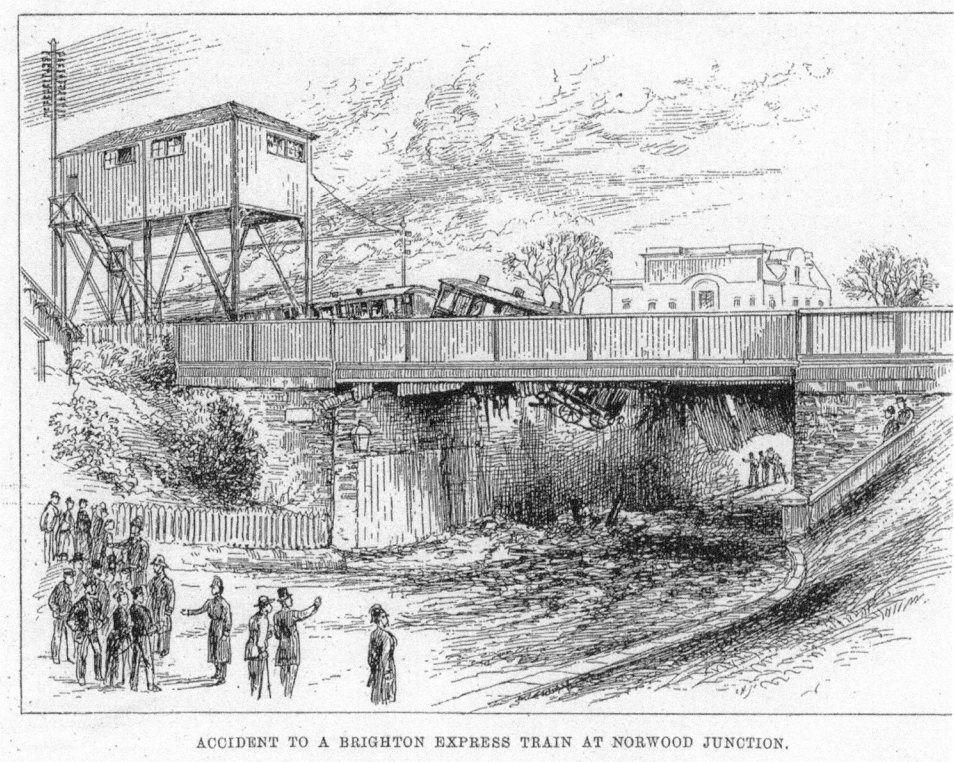

ACCIDENT TO A BRIGHTON EXPRESS TRAIN AT NORWOOD JUNCTION.

(10.4) The accident at Portland Road when a flange on a cast-iron girder failed suddenly.

A much older cast-iron bridge was discovered in 2004 on the rail approach to Paddington station, although it was arched in the manner of the famous Ironbridge at Coalbrookdale, rather than comprising straight girders. It was also fitted together like a wooden structure, and was designed by Brunel. It is being rebuilt for permanent display in Hyde Park nearby.

Engineers who admired the Forth Bridge attempted to apply the design to other bridging problems, most notoriously at Quebec in the crossing of the St Lawrence River. It failed not just once, but twice. But the failures occurred during, not after, construction, at the critical final phase when the girder link between the cantilevers was being hoisted into position. The first, more serious failure, occurred on 29 August 1907, just fifteen minutes before the end of a shift when the men would have left. Unfortunately, they were still there when a chord in an anchor arm buckled, and the structure collapsed into ruins, with the loss of eighty-five men. The structure had, like the old Tay Bridge, been under-designed. There had also been prior warnings from unusual movements in the structure, but work went ahead regardless. Another failure occurred in 1916 when it was being rebuilt, when the final section fell, carrying eleven men to their deaths. However, it was finally completed in 1917.

Tacoma Narrows

The problem of vibrations in bridges continues to bedevil designers. A major disaster had actually occurred a few years before the Tay fall, when a trussed girder bridge collapsed during a blizzard on 29 December 1876 at Ashtabula, Ohio. There were perhaps more than 100 victims who were killed by the fall into the 80ft-deep gorge below, or by the subsequent

(10.5) The retrofitted dampers on the new Millennium Bridge in London.

fire caused by overturning stoves. The bridge was over twenty years old at the time of its demise, and a reappraisal has suggested that fatigue of a cast-iron block used to hold tie bars and struts together may have been the cause of the failure. The disaster shocked America and it became known in the popular press as the 'Ashtabula Horror'.

However, a notorious failure occurred in 1940 of the new suspension bridge over the Tacoma Narrows in Washington state, USA. While extensive model tests on the design for the Golden Gate Bridge in San Francisco had helped eliminate the vibration problems, the builders of the Tacoma Bridge were not so lucky. Workers on the bridge had experienced excessive vibrations during its construction, but the bridge was completed anyway on 1 July 1940. It was a very long bridge with a clear single span of 2,800ft, and it fell dramatically just five months later in a 42mph lateral wind. The wind induced vertical oscillations in the roadway, which increased in size or amplitude until it fractured and fell into the river below, being filmed all the while, and is now part of every undergraduate engineering syllabus.

Fortunately, there had been ample warning of these dangerous vibrations, the bridge having gained the nickname 'Galloping Gertie' for its earlier oscillations. Investigation showed that the very shallow roadway suffered from so-called 'von Karman' vortices which were shed downwind of the road when lateral winds were blowing. Production of the vortices created vertical movement in the road, so that when a wind of just the right speed was blowing, it induced the structure to resonate at its natural frequency, with catastrophic results. There was only one fatality: a dog abandoned in a car left on the bridge. Such vortex shedding has caused a number of structural failures, especially for high steel chimneys and power station cooling towers in the years following Tacoma. The solutions have in most cases been easy to produce, a much deeper and aerodynamically designed roadway at Tacoma, fins welded to chimneys, and more careful placement of cooling towers. No doubt such failures could have been avoided altogether by model testing using a wind tunnel (a device used by both Eiffel and Baker in their bridge design work).

Contemporary with the Tacoma accident, a number of all-welded bridges in Belgium failed by brittle cracking during cold weather in March 1940 (a period known as the 'Phoney War'). They were similar to an earlier failure of a welded bridge at Hasselt in 1938, with brittle cracks growing from faulty welds and other stress concentrations. Loud sounds were heard by sentries guarding one of the bridges, so remedial action could be taken before a train entered the structure. These failures do not appear to have held up the German invasion however, which occurred a few months later. On the other hand, the failures did highlight the problems produced by welding, as opposed to riveting, structures together. Brittle cracks could grow unhindered by any mechanical joints, a problem encountered by some of the Liberty ships built in the USA a few years later for the war effort.

The dynamic behaviour of large structures can defeat the most ingenious of engineers and architects. A new footbridge was built in the late 1990s across the Thames in London, linking the city with Bankside power station, the new Tate Modern art gallery, not far from the Kirkaldy's test house in Southwark Street. It was effectively a very low profile suspension bridge, with the supporting arches almost level with the footway, so achieving what the architect termed a ' Blade of Light'. Unfortunately, when newly opened on 10 June 2000, it attracted thousands of sightseers who, when crossing, induced the bridge to oscillate sideways. The problem was solved by retrofitting (at great expense) giant pistons which damped out the vibrations *(10.5)*.

The problem was caused by many footfalls (at least 600 were needed) acting in unison, and the momentum transferred to the footway, which started to oscillate with increasing violence. The more it oscillated, the greater the footfall to maintain one's balance, giving an even greater impetus to the bridge (a condition known as positive feedback). So why had the problem not been anticipated? Extensive wind tunnel and computer modelling had been done for wind force, for example, but not for pedestrians using the bridge. Considering that the only function of a footbridge is to carry people, it is surprising that the problem was not foreseen. The dampers which were ultimately fitted are widely used to damp vibrations in skyscrapers, which are now so high and so large that wind-induced vibration must be controlled effectively.

The Problem of Fatigue

The problem of unwanted vibrations, which are not removed by damping them, can cause major problems with the integrity of a structure. There have been large structures (and many other products) which have failed catastrophically from vibrations or load cycling, perhaps the most famous being the fall of the Silver Bridge crossing the Ohio River between West Virginia and Ohio. It lasted for forty years before suddenly collapsing at 5.00 p.m. on 15 December 1967. It was crowded with rush hour traffic when witnesses later testified that they heard loud cracking noises just before it fell. It was a suspension bridge of two towers which supported massive chains from which similar chains dropped down to hold the roadway. Both towers collapsed completely after the chain failed, and it claimed forty-six victims *(10.6)*.

The collapse was famously recreated as an end piece in a film of 2001, *The Mothman Prophecies*, which then suggested (in the closing credits) that the cause of the failure was still unknown.

So what did initiate the collapse? After much effort in trawling the river, the parts of the chain were recovered, and a large brittle crack found in one of the eye-bar joints from which the roadway chains were slung. The presence of a brittle crack was unusual, since the material was a high-strength steel which was normally tough and ductile. In addition, the crack was found to be heavily corroded, and had started from a much smaller crack in a carburised layer near the surface of the hole in the eye-bar. It had been created during the forging of the component. The eye-bar had failed by fatigue aided by corrosion, a problem known as stress corrosion fatigue. The design was also faulty because failure of one part should not

(10.6) The memorial to the victims of the Silver Bridge collapse at Point Pleasant in West Virginia.

allow the whole structure to collapse, and the very few other bridges built to the same design were dismantled. So much for Hollywood fantasies! They and others continue to masquerade fantasy as fact, which is inexcusable for major tragedies which have known and identifiable causes, produced often after months of intensive research.

The Silver Bridge failure led directly to President Johnson ordering inspection of the many thousands of existing (often very old) bridges in the USA, and then a coherent maintenance programme. Despite the programme, however, catastrophic failures have continued, such as the Mianus River Bridge in Connecticut, one span of which failed suddenly on 27 June 1983, taking with it several cars and trucks on the bridge at the time. Three people were killed. It transpired that the span was held up by several steel pins, one of which had stress corrosion fatigued during the life of the bridge of eighteen years. It was not discovered during inspections because the crack was concealed behind a protective cap.

Fatigue affects all materials and has caused some of the worst disasters in recent times, especially in aircraft. Cracks always start at stress raisers in components, which may be holes, shoulders, corners or cracks, to name some common forms. It was well studied by a German engineer, Wöhler, who focused on railway axles and wheels from the 1850s onwards. Their sudden fracture caused numerous disasters (such as the Versailles tragedy) in the early railway age, and later. He built dedicated apparatus for testing axles under a bending load while being rotated at high speed, and evaluated the properties of different types of wrought iron, steels and so on. He established that there were safe levels of repeated loading, a concept known as the fatigue limit. He also showed how fatigue cracks always start at stress raisers such as sharp corners in the shoulder of a shaft, for example.

But his samples were typically subjected to millions of cycles (so-called high cycle fatigue), rather than just a few hundred or even less (low cycle fatigue). And it was this second type which proved deadly when the first jet passenger aircraft was being designed after the Second World War. Known as the Comet, it apparently heralded a new era of long-distance travel, but failures happened very quickly after its introduction to the public in the early 1950s.

They were all failures caused by fatigue cracks growing from old cracks at sharp corners in the fuselage, such as a port for a radio aerial or windows. Testing before the accidents had not revealed the problem, although better tests after the event confirmed the fatigue diagnosis. The problem was famously publicised by Nevil Shute in his novel *No Highway*. In August 1985, a fully laden Japanese Airlines Boeing 747 jumbo jet crashed killing 520 passengers. It was the single worst air disaster ever, and caused by a small fatigue crack from a bodged repair to the tail. The crack grew from a sharp corner near a rivet, until it reached a critical size and the tail broke off.

One of the worst rail disasters ever occurred at Eschede in Germany on 3 June 1998. The ICE train was travelling from Munich to Hamburg. A single wheel on the high-speed express train fractured and the train derailed at over 125mph when it met some points in its path. The rear carriages concertinered into a motorway bridge and 101 passengers died. The accident was traced to a fatigue crack inside the wheel, where a rubber core had been incorporated to improve damping, and so lower annoying vibrations for the passengers.

On the railways, privatisation in Britain led to the break up of a national system, to one of splintered responsibilities, especially for track maintenance and upkeep. The Hatfield disaster in October 2000 took the lives of four innocent passengers, and was caused by multiple crack growth from tiny defects in the rail surface when trains passed over (rolling contact fatigue). The stresses imposed by each wheel (with a contact area about the size of a 5 pence coin) caused them to grow to criticality. The problem was known about, but no action had been taken before the accident occurred, when the damaged steel rail broke into over 300 pieces, like brittle glass. The failure of the points at the later derailment at Potters Bar killed another eight people, but it appears that the points which caused the crash had not been inspected for many months. Final reports or actions (such as prosecutions) by the government on either accident are expected in 2005.

Outstanding Issues

There remain many outstanding issues from the Tay Bridge disaster which could help to clarify the causes. As far as is known, no cast-iron components have survived for present-day analysis. Several parts which have turned up have not been identified positively as coming from the original bridge, but no doubt some pipes may have survived intact as garden ornaments, for example. A very large fragment of the original girder from the high girder section survived as part of a house which was demolished in Dundee a few years ago, and now is exhibited in the Royal Scottish Museum in Edinburgh. The set of lugs and other tested or recovered parts kept by Kirkaldy disappeared during the Second World War, when his test house was bombed by the Luftwaffe. Material analysis and examination of lug fracture surfaces could help test the main theory concerning their weakness. Much still could remain at the bottom of the estuary, but is inaccessible.

The photographic evidence used by the Inquiry is larger than the current collections held at Dundee City Library and St Andrews University. Detailed pictures, for example, of the trace evidence on the girders used by Bouch to support his derailment theory, are referred to by the Inquiry, but cannot as yet be located. Similar comments apply to the many sketches made by witnesses, and other unique documents presented before the Inquiry. It seems strange that no close-up pictures were taken of the many lugs which had been collected by Henry Noble, apart from the original Valentine set taken *in situ*. Even sketches of the fractures would have been helpful, as was done with some of Wöhler's fatigue test samples, and published in a issue of 1867 of the journal *Engineering*.

There are other issues which, so far as can be seen from the transcript, were not raised. One of those was the so-called kink in the rails already discussed. But another key issue is this: just why was the express train allowed to enter the bridge from the south given the alleged ferocity of the storm? The signalmen knew about the problems the previous local train had experienced, so how could they let the second train through? Were there any NBR regulations to guide them in the matter? It seems that the question was raised neither at the Inquiry itself or the later Royal Commission on Wind, but why it was not remains a mystery.

In hindsight, it would have been wise to have catalogued the broken parts collected for the Inquiry, and detailed plans made of the evidence found on all of the piers. Fortunately, we do have the photographic archive preserved in Dundee, which has revealed so much about the state of the remains after the accident, and will no doubt continue to be a source of evidence for future investigations.

Present Remains

The present site of the disaster preserves many reminders of that terrible night. Most of the piers upon which the light and gimcrack towers were erected were kept as breakwaters for the new bridge, although some have succumbed to the fast currents in the estuary *(10.1)*. The Tay Bridge station is also well preserved, although some modernisation has changed the appearance at the entrance. The platforms are, however, much the same as they must have been that night *(10.7)*.

The tunnel which takes trains through to Aberdeen lies behind the picture, and was part of the original works constructed by Bouch as part of the overall project. The bridge he was then building at Montrose across the river Esk has long been demolished as part of the inevitable review of his engineering after the verdict of the Inquiry. It was modelled on the Tay Bridge, with cast-iron columns fitted with the notorious lugs. The local City Museum exhibits many pieces of memorabilia from the disaster, such as the final tickets collected from the doomed passengers. There are objects made from parts of the carriage-work and a model of the high girder section, probably from the original Inquiry. Kirkaldy's test house still exists in a museum at his original property in Southwark Street, London. The original tensile machine remains operational although there have been problems in renewing some of the seals for the

(10.7) The main platform at the Tay Bridge station.

(10.8) Kirkaldy's test house in Southwark Street, London.

(10.9) Meldon Viaduct on Dartmoor, now a footpath near a preserved steam line from Exeter.

(10.10) Bennerley Viaduct near Nottingham.

(10.11) Mumbles pier near Swansea in South Wales.

hydraulic-operating mechanism. It is hoped to undertake renovation to enable greater access to the general public, and so publicise more widely the importance of testing engineering components before they enter service *(10.8)*.

There are other surviving structures from the era which show that pipe bridges could work. Bouch's pipe bridge at Belah was demolished in the 1960s, as part of the Beeching cuts. The magnificent Crumlin Viaduct in South Wales was demolished at around the same time, although with some difficulty owing to its strength! Two pipe viaducts survive, however. One is the viaduct at Meldon on the edge of Dartmoor *(10.9)*. The other is the longer but less high Bennerley Viaduct near Nottingham *(10.10)*. Both were built earlier than the Tay Bridge but, like the Belah and Crumlin viaducts, were given a wide base to provide lateral stability. At the moment the viaduct survives like a prehistoric monument, with no function or use even as a footpath.

But the method of spaceframe support survives in another guise, as those ubiquitous piers in most of our coastal resorts. Many were built by the Victorians, but usually with wrought-iron columns or wrought-iron cores so as to have the inherent strength to resist the constant battering by waves *(10.11)*. The tie bars are now made from steel and usually attached clear of the columns.

Vertical spaceframes in steel have the capability of supporting fairground rides, such as roller coasters, among a variety of applications. Although the imposed loads are not especially onerous, they must have great integrity to provide complete security for the small trains which run upon them. The support tower of a tower crane must support the jib at the top, and all loads imposed on it, and their construction is testimony to the strength of the design using steel members.

In France many of Eiffel's early bridges survive intact and indeed well preserved, as scenic railways across spectacular gorges in the Massif Centrale. Like the Meldon and Belah viaducts, most were built for carrying minerals from mines and quarries. They remain as striking proof that pipe bridges could work, provided they were well designed, constructed and maintained.

Epilogue

The fall of the Tay Bridge shocked and horrified Britain, just as the Ashtabula horror had traumatised the United States three years earlier. It was the biggest railway accident ever in Britain, historic home of the technology. It ranked alongside another structural disaster which had occurred when a dam burst suddenly at Dale Dyke near Sheffield in 1864, and claimed 270 victims. The root causes of the Tay accident quickly became clear when the piles of wreckage were examined in detail. Whoever had designed this bridge had broken all the rules for building pipe bridges evolved around twenty years before. It seems as though the designer had rewritten the rules to cut corners, and so save time and money for the project. The basic problem lay in the survey for the foundations, which showed that the strata on which the piers would be built became less stable the further they extended the bridge into the estuary. To lower the load on the piers, they resorted to a pipe spaceframe using components made at a purpose-built foundry at Wormit at the south end of the bridge.

When those components were designed, they made the columns more complex than necessary by incorporating lugs into them for attaching the struts and tie bars, the essential stiffening elements in the final structure of the towers. It was well known that cast iron was a brittle material in tension, a fact long known and reinforced by the Dee Bridge accident in 1847 and the subsequent Royal Commission. Yet the new design used cast-iron lugs which would inevitably be tensioned to brace the towers. None of the pipe bridges built in the 1850s and 1860s used this feature, the attachments points being quite separate from the support columns. Those bridges used carefully machined parts to fit one another, not rough cast metal. Another significant change was to build the towers almost completely vertical, whereas the towers on previous viaducts had been given a generous lateral batter or rake, to protect them against lateral loads. The designer ignored known problems from vibrations of passing trains, such structures needing a high safety factor to be able to resist cyclical loads. By increasing the distance between the spans in the critical high girder section, the load on each of the piers here also increased since the girders supporting the track would need to be much more substantial than for shorter spans. The result was a set of top heavy metal towers with questionable bracing arrangements. The braces were not tested before use in the structure, and were much weaker than supposed. The bolt holes cast into most of the lugs were conical with a taper angle of around 10°, concentrating the load at the holes to unacceptable levels. To add insult to injury, the towers were not tied together at their tops with a single girder, but divided into two sub-girders, effectively dividing what should have been a single structure into two smaller towers weakly attached to one another.

The net effect of such a set of design flaws produced an inherently unsafe structure at the centre of the bridge, the high girder section. After being officially opened in June 1878, it was under repeated cyclical loads and vibrations from passing trains, especially those travelling north at speed. The structure began to deteriorate rapidly. By September 1878 the cottered joints in the tie bars were starting to loosen, and the rattling sound was stopped not by retensioning the joints, but by jamming them into their loosened state with shims of iron. It allowed lateral movement of the towers of a few inches, since there was play in all the bolted joints of the structure. By the summer of 1879, the movement at the top of the towers when trains passed over was sufficient to alarm workers on the bridge, and travellers on the trains. A lateral wave of low frequency could be seen in the high girder section when a train travelled north at excessive speed. It was possibly induced by a slight track abnormality at the start of the high girder section.

On the night of 28 December 1879, a storm was blowing down the Tay estuary, and a local train had experienced difficulty crossing the bridge into Dundee. The heavier express train which followed was allowed onto the structure, despite the increasing wind speed. As it entered the high girders, it induced lateral oscillations which sent all the towers into a critical condition. The critical bracing elements in the centre of each tower had probably already been broken by the previous train, and the express was riding on two smaller towers on each pier. They probably started to collapse behind the train as it proceeded deeper into the high girders, but all the towers were now unstable. They collapsed under the lateral loads from the oscillation wave, magnified by the westerly wind blowing against the train. Everyone on the train was doomed. If the centre section had not collapsed then, it would have done shortly after, so rotten was its state.

The Inquiry which followed identified the critical defects in the design and blamed the engineer, Sir Thomas Bouch, the NBR and the contractors, Hopkins Gilkes & Co. Matters had been worsened by poor construction practices and negligent maintenance. They might have added the many failures of communication, between Bouch and Noble, Bouch and foundry, Bouch and the painters, the painters and Noble, train passengers and the NBR, and the NBR and its train drivers. By their very size, the critical piers at the centre were difficult to access and not fitted with ladders for inspection via the railway line. Such a simple expedient might have given the warning as disaster loomed. The bridge was defective as built, and its failure was inevitable. The new bridge built to replace it supported a double track and was well braced using new materials such as steel. The new bridge over the river Forth was completed only in steel, to a new design using cantilevers. They were both inspected regularly and rigorously during construction and designed against very high winds, effectively of hurricane force. They both passed the rigorous final tests by the Board of Trade, and have served the public well for well over a century. Lessons were learnt and applied, although some cast-iron girders were still in place as late as 1891, when the Norwood Bridge failed. It led to wholesale replacement of similar structures.

In hindsight, the disaster at Dundee was foreseeable and preventable, if action had been taken in time to modify the design, structure and materials of construction. It was a project of worthy aims hindered by poor engineering, management and penny-pinching finances. The safety of users must always be at a premium and, if it is neglected, people will die unnecessarily. That simple message calls out loud and clear from the accident at Dundee, and is one that resounds with irony with every disaster since that terrible night on the Tay.

Glossary
Chronology
Dramatis Personae
Select Bibliography
Index

Glossary

batter:
(also rake angle)
the angle of inclination of the sides of a structure to the vertical.

beach mark:
a mark on a fracture surface where a fatigue crack has halted, allowing debris such as rust to accumulate and left behind as the crack grows again.

Beaufort Table:
summary of wind speeds and their effects on land or sea objects to help observers gauge the weather, originally developed for the Royal Navy.

beaumontage:
(also Beaumont's Egg)
mixture of resin and fillers used to fill holes in a smooth surface.

bending:
form of loading where material is distorted along an axis, as in a bent twig (contrast with compression and shear); the outer side is in tension and the inner side in compression.

blow hole (also void):
a spherical void in cast material caused by trapped gas.

bolt:
a connector consisting of a shaped head and shank with screwed thread to accept a nut for completion of a joint.

bridge:
any construction which connects two separate parts of land.

brittle fracture:
crack growth where bulk material is undeformed (contrast with ductile fracture).

cantilever:
bracket or beam projecting from wall or rigid support.

caisson:
cylinder sunk into the bed of a river to provide support for a pier.

cast iron:
one of the earliest forms of iron made in a blast furnace, and known as grey cast iron from the colour of the fracture surface; a very brittle material only suited for components in compression, possesses a high carbon content of about 4 per cent.

column:
vertical supporting structural element.

cold shut   see knit line.

compression: form of loading where material is pressed together, as in a table leg (also see tension and shear).

cotter (also cottar):   a wedge to be hammered into a slot in the parts to be joined, often a pair of cotters are used.

defect: a source of weakness in a component or bulk material, such as (in a casting) a blow hole, inclusion or knit line, which all act as a stress concentration.

ductile fracture: crack growth where bulk material is deformed.

ductility: the ability of a material to be drawn into a wire.

dynamics: branch of mechanics dealing with movement.

elastic behaviour: reversible response of a material to imposed load, stress being proportional to strain.

fatigue: intermittent crack growth caused by cyclical strain, which leaves beach marks or striations on the fracture surfaces.

fracture surfaces: the two surfaces formed when a crack grows.

fracture: crack formation and growth.

gib: a U-shaped component fitting into a slot in the parts to be joined, hence gib-and-cotter joint.

hairline crack: a fracture within a component often caused by fatigue, and difficult to observe since the component involved is usually stress-free when examined, and the crack has closed.

inclusion: defect in cast iron, usually by slag particles.

joint: the connection between different components.

knit line: (also cold shut)   line formed in a cast or moulded component, where molten material is forced around a hole, and fails to fuse correctly at the junction.

lug: projecting wing with bolt hole designed for attachment of tie bar ends.

modulus: measure of elastic response of a material, the slope of a stress/strain curve.

monocoque: structure where the imposed load is supported by a continuous shell (cf. spaceframe).

Glossary

parallax: forced error in a measurement caused by viewing at an angle, a problem of perspective.

Portland cement: a stiff brittle mortar of high strength invented in the early Victorian period.

rivet: a connector of wrought iron with head and shank, the free end of which is hammered flat to form the joint.

shear: form of loading where material is forced sideways, as in a stirred liquid (contrast with compression and tension).

shim: a piece of material, often a thin strip, used to wedge a loose joint tight.

spaceframe: structure where the imposed load is supported by framework (cf. monocoque).

span: that part of a bridge or viaduct which forms the connection to support a railway or roadway between abutments, towers or piers.

spigot: projecting rim on end of column designed to fit into tube of adjacent column, and so form a rigid joint.

statics: branch of mechanics dealing with the equilibrium of bodies at rest.

steel: a form of iron in which the carbon content has been reduced to around 0.4 per cent by treatment of cast iron in a Bessemer converter or open hearth furnace.

stiffness: the response of a material or component to an applied load; steel is generally very stiff compared with rubber, for example.

strain: a measure of the distortion of a material or component when stressed, such as the extension of a bar when tensioned, where it is expressed as the fraction (new length/original length).

strength: the ultimate load a material or component can withstand before fracture.

stress–strain test: a way of examining the properties of either materials or components by stretching in a tensometer; similarly, compressive, bending and shear tests etc.

stress: the load per unit area of a component.

stress concentration: (also stress raiser) point or zone in a component where the local stress is greater than the overall stress, such as a hole, void or sharp corner.

striation:	a mark left on a fatigue fracture surface showing where a crack has stopped.
strut:	lateral bracing element.
tension:	form of loading where material is forced apart, as in a stretched rubber band (contrast with compression and shear).
tensometer:	a machine for straining materials under controlled conditions.
tie bar:	bracing element, often diagonal.
tier:	an individual cell of a tower defined by horizontal struts at the top and bottom, and reinforced within by diagonal bracing bars.
tolerance:	permissible range of values during fit of parts.
torsion:	form of loading where material is twisted along an axis, as in a screw fastening (contrast with compression, tension and shear).
toughness:	the ability of a material to resist fracture.
tower:	a vertical structure for supporting the spans of a viaduct.
viaduct:	a bridge which allows for transport of wheeled vehicles or people by separate piers and spans.
wrought iron:	an early form of iron for engineering components where the carbon content is lowered by repeated hammering and forging; generally tough and ductile with an iron content in the region of around 0.4 per cent or less.
yield:	irreversible deformation of material when loaded, marking the end of elastic behaviour (q.v.).

Chronology

Early History of Engineered Iron

First cast-iron bridge built at Coalbrookdale	1779
First passenger service opened between Manchester and Liverpool	1830
First major disaster on railways, Versailles	1842
Construction of Dee Bridge by Stephenson at Chester	1846
Fall of Dee Bridge	May 1847
Royal Commission on Iron appointed	June 1847
Report of Royal Commission	1849
Crystal Palace built in six months (Great Exhibition)	1851
Crumlin Viaduct built in South Wales	1857
Belah Viaduct built in three months	1860
Eiffel viaducts built in France	1867-71

Tay Bridge Chronology before the Fall

First proposal by Bouch to build Tay Bridge	1854
Opening of Belah Bridge, Pennines	1861
Proposal to build Tay Bridge mooted at Thorntons, Dundee	1863
Prospectus published	1864
Bouch submits estimate of £237,000 for bridge	October 1869
Act to build Tay Bridge passed	July 1870

De Bergue given contract to build bridge	May 1871
Foundation stone laid	June 1871
De Bergue dies	April 1873
Survey of estuary bed fails to find bedrock in estuary	May 1873
Failure of pier No.54 caisson: six dead	August 1873
Contract passed to Hopkin Gilkes & Co., Middlesborough	1874
Electric arc lamps installed at Wormit	late 1876
Two girders blown from bridge in storm	February 1877
US President Grant visits bridge	September 1877
Director's train over bridge	September 1877
Inspection and tests on bridge by Hutchinson	February 1878
Official opening of bridge	May 1878
Tie bars heard to rattle by Noble	September/October 1878
Noble's first trip to purchase iron bar	October 1878
Noble's second trip to buy bar	November 1878
Noble's third trip to buy bar	December 1878
Bridge inspected by Pirie for painting estimate	May 1879
Queen Victoria crosses bridge	June 1879
Bridge painted by large crew	June to August 1879
Complaints made to stationmaster	December 1879
Bouch and Noble visit bridge	December 1879
High girders collapse in storm	28 December 1879

Tay Bridge Chronology after the Fall

First attempts to send boat to remains	28 December 1879
First diving attempts by Cox	29 December 1879
First victim recovered	29 December 1879
Court of Inquiry starts (eyewitnesses, painters, divers etc)	3 January 1880
Adjourns	6 January 1880
Returns to Dundee	26 February 1880
Adjourns at Dundee	3 March 1880
Resumes at Westminster	19 April 1880
Disraeli resigns after losing election, Gladstone new PM	23 April 1880
Kirkaldy's test results reported	7 May 1880
Report of Inquiry	30 June 1880
Select Committee Report	4 August 1880
Death of Sir Thomas Bouch	30 October 1880
Royal Commission on Wind Pressure (Railway Structures)	20 May 1881
Brooklyn Bridge opened	24 May 1883
New Tay Bridge opened	20 June 1887
Eiffel Tower finished	March 1889
Forth cantilever bridge opened	4 March 1890
Norwood Bridge collapse	1 May 1891

Dramatis Personae

Airy, Sir George — Astronomer Royal

Baker, Benjamin — expert to Inquiry

Balfour, J.B. — counsel for NBR

Barclay, Thomas — signalman at south box

Barlow, W.H. — civil engineer, Inquiry judge, builder of new Tay Bridge

Barlow, Crawford — son of W.H. Barlow, new Tay Bridge builder

Bidder — counsel for Sir Thomas Bouch

Bouch, Thomas — engineer to NBR, Tay Bridge

de Bergue, Charles — second contractor to Tay project

Beattie, Frank — chief draughtsman to project

Brunlees, James — expert to Inquiry

Camphuis, Gerard or Gerrit — assistant engineer, manager

Clark, Charles — weather witness

Cochrane, John — independent civil engineer, expert to Inquiry

Cruikshank, Ann — first victim to be recovered

Delpratt, William — draughtsman to project

Delpratt, Theodore — draughtsman to project

Dougall, Admiral — weather witness

Drummond, Dugald — NBR locomotive superintendent

dressers	Alexander Milne, Peter Tuite, John Gibb, John Tasker
erectors	William Oram, William Nixon, William Newcombe, Edward McGovern, George Macbeath
eyewitnesses of fall	James Lawson, George and William Clark, Alexander Maxwell, Willaim Roberston, Peter Barron
Fender, George	foreman machinist
Ferguson, Fergus	foreman foundryman
foundrymen	Richard Baird, James McGowan, Alexander Hampton, Fergus Ferguson, Hercules Strachan
Fowler, Sir John	eminent engineer, co-designer of Forth Bridge
Gilkes, Edgar	partner of Hopkins Gilkes & Co.
Greig, John	lighthouse keeper at Tayport
Grothe, Albert	contract manager
Hutchinson, Maj.-Gen	BoT inspector, approved bridge
Kirkaldy, David	testing engineer
Law, Henry	court expert to Inquiry
Leng, John	editor of the *Dundee Advertiser* and witness to travel across the bridge
Macbeath, George	foreman erector
McKelvie, William	Dundee cemetery superintendent
Mitchell, David	engine driver of the last train
Murray, George	permanent way inspector
Noble, Henry	inspector of bridge
Patterson, William	resident engineer to project
painters on bridge	David Dale, Peter Donegany, John Evans, John Gray, John Milne, John Nelson, David Pirie, Peter Robertson, Alexander Stewart, Wilson Winter, Edward Simpson
Robertson, William	provost of Dundee, eyewitness
Rothery, Hume	Commissioner of Wrecks, chairman of Inquiry

Scott, Captain	in charge of training ship *Mars*, moored below Tay Bridge
Simpson, Edward	foreman painter
Smith, James	stationmaster at Dundee
Somerville, Henry	signalman in north box
Stewart, Allan Duncan	Bouch's adviser, expert at Inquiry
Stewart, Alexander	carpenter who worked on bridge
Strachan, Hercules	foreman moulder at Wormit
Stokes, Sir George G.	Cambridge professor, expert in fluid dynamics
travellers on bridge	William Roberston, Thomas Baxter, George Hume, John Leng, Alexander Hutchison
Trayner, Mr	chief counsel to the Inquiry
Thornton, Thomas	Dundee solicitor of NBR
Valentine, William Dobson	court photographer
Walker, John	general manager to NBR
Watt, John	foreman railworker, in south signalbox, saw express on bridge
Wright, Charles	Captain of Tay ferry steamer
Yolland, Colonel	railway inspector, Inquiry judge

Select Bibliography

There is an extensive literature on the Tay Bridge disaster, both from the period and from Prebble's book onwards to the present. It is also the subject of some good websites, and is referred to by many more. Engineering/architectural websites which have proved invaluable during the course of my research include www.structurae.de, and www.archinform.net. There is a BBC website dedicated to the Tay disaster at www.open2.net, and another from Tom Martin at www.tts1.demon.co.uk/tay.html. A website is dedicated to the Crumlin Viaduct at www.welshcoalmining.co.uk. My papers about the Tay and Dee Bridge disasters can be downloaded from http://materials.open.ac.uk, and the site also presents some recent failure case studies.

The Dundee Central Library can be accessed at http://www.dundeecity.gov./library/main.htm, and it gives information about exhibitions, lectures on the disaster and the collections of photographs and documents.

The literature quoted below includes specialist literature, such as papers published in learned journals and engineering journals as well as specialised Victorian textbooks and modern reference works. Original copies of the Inquiry Report are held by the copyright libraries, such as The Bodleian Library, Oxford. However, a copy is available on microfiche in the Parliamentary Archive, and is held by most University and Public Libraries. Similar comments apply to the Lopes Select Committee Report of 1880, the earlier reports of the Dee disaster and most other serious railway accidents. Like all other contemporary material on the disaster, it is well out of copyright and so can be copied freely for research and scholarship.

The main archives of the disaster lie in the Scottish National Archive in Edinburgh, and includes witness precognitions (statements) among many other documents of direct relevance. The National Archive at Kew also has a small archive of documents, especially detailed plans of the pipe bridge at Belah. The Institution of Civil Engineering in London holds many plans and sections of the original Tay Bridge. The photographic archives are held at Dundee City Library (Inquiry set), and in the large Valentine collection at the University of St Andrews. The University of Dundee also holds some relevant material.

Adams, Charles Francis, *Notes on Railway Accidents*, G.P. Putnam's Sons (1879). Available on the web at http://catskillarchive.com
Andrews, Ewart S., *The Theory and Design of Structures: a Text Book*, (4th Ed), Chapman & Hall, London (1929).
Angus, H.T., *Cast Iron: Physical and Engineering Properties*, (2nd Ed), Butterworths (1976).
Anon, 'Dee Bridge Accident', *Chester Chronicle*, 4 June 1847, page 3, column 3; 10 June, 1847.

Baker, Benjamin, *Long Span Railway Bridges*, Baird, Philadelphia (1870).
Barlow, Crawford, *The New Tay Bridge*, E. and F.N. Spon, London (1889).
Beaumont, Robert, *The Railway King – A Biography of George Hudson*, Review Books (2002).
Becket, Paul, *Bridges – Great Buildings of the World*, Paul Hamlyn (1969).
Biddle, Gordon and O.S. Nock, *The Railway Heritage of Britain*, Michael Joseph, London (1983).
Billington, David, *The Tower and the Bridge*, Princeton University Press (1985).
Braithwaite, F., 'On the Fatigue and consequent Fracture of Metals' Proc. Instn Civ. Engs, Vol. XIII, 463–475 (1854).
Brayne, Martin, *The Greatest Storm, Britain's Night of Destruction 1703*, Sutton Publishing (2003).
Briggs, Asa, *Iron Bridge to Crystal Palace*, Thames and Hudson (1979).
Brown, David J., *Bridges: Three Thousand Years of Defying Nature*, Mitchell Beazley (1998).

Chettoe, C.S., Davey, N. and Mitchell, G.R., 'The Strength of Cast-Iron Girder Bridges', Inst. Civ. Eng., Vol. 22, pp 243–292 (1944).
Chiles, James R., *Inviting Disaster: Lessons from the Edge of Technology*, Harper Business (2002).
Cossens, Neil and Barrie Trinder, *The Iron Bridge, Symbol of the Industrial Revolution*, Moonraker press (1979).

Defoe, Daniel, *The Storm* (Edited by Richard Hamlyn), first published 1704, republished by Allen Lane (2003).
Den Hartog, *Mechanical Vibrations*, Dover Publications (1984).
Dow, W., 'Is this the real reason the Tay Bridge fell?', *Dundee Courier* 100th Anniversary Special (1979). Reply by John Thomas in subsequent edition of the paper dismisses Dow's theory of derailment.
Durie, Alastair J., *George Washington Wilson, Dundee and Angus*, AUL Publishing (1991).

Garfield, Simon, *The Last Journey of William Huskisson*, Faber and Faber (2002).
Grothe, Albert, *The Tay Bridge, Its History and Construction*, Jon Leng, Dundee (1878).

Hall, Stanley, *Railway Detectives*, Ian Allen (1990).
Harvie, David, Eiffel, *The Genius Who Reinvented Himself*, Sutton Publishing (2004).
Hawkshaw, J. (Chair) 'Report of the Committee appointed to consider the question of Wind Pressure on Railway Structures', HMSO (1881).
Hodgkinson, Eaton, *Experimental Researches on the Strength and Other properties of Cast Iron*, John Weale, London (1846).
Hopkins, H.J., *A Span of Bridges: An Illustrated History*, David & Charles (1970).
Humber, William, *A Practical Treatise of Cast and Wrought Iron Bridges*, E. and F.N. Spon (1857), reproduced by Archival Facsimiles Ltd (1987).

Hutchinson, Maj-Gen., Copy of 'Report to the Board of Trade of his inquiry into the circumstances which attended the accident that occurred on 1 May 1891 at Portland Road Bridge near Norwood Junction', HMSO 16 May 1891.

Hutchinson, Maj-Gen., 'First Report of Inspection by General Hutchinson R.E. and Maj. Marindin R.E., of the Works in Progress for the Construction of the Bridge over the River Forth', HMSO (June 1883), Parliamentary Papers Vol. LXI, 477 ff.
Hutchinson, Maj-Gen, 'Twenty-Eighth and Final Quarterly Report of Inspection by General Hutchinson R.E. and Maj. Marindin R.E., of the Bridge over the River Forth', HMSO (February 1890).

Illustrated London News, 12 June 1847, page 380; 10 Jan, 1880 *et seq.*, 7 May 1891.
Inglis, C.E., *A Mathematical Treatise on Vibrations in Railway Bridges*, Cambridge University Press (1934).

Jones, D.R.H., *Engineering Materials: Materials Failure Analysis*, Pergamon Press (1993), Chapters 27 and 28.

Koerte, Arnold, *Firth of Forth, Firth of Tay: Two Railway Bridges of an Era*, Birkhauser Verlag (1992).
Kirkaldy, W.G., *Illustrations of David Kirkaldy's System of Mechanical Testing*, Sampson Low, London (1891).

Leapman, Michael, *The World for a Shilling: How the Great Exhibition of 1851 shaped a Nation*, Headline Book Publishing (2001).
Levy, Matthys and Mario Salvadori, *Why Buildings Fall Down: How Structures Fail*, W.W. Norton & Co. (1992).
Lewis, Peter Rhys, Ken Reynolds and Colin Gagg, *Forensic Materials Engineering: Case Studies*, CRC Press (2003).
Lewis, P.R. and Colin Gagg, 'Aesthetics versus Function: the Dee Bridge disaster 1847', Interdisciplinary Science Reviews, 29, Vol. 45 (2004).
Lewis, P.R. and Ken Reynolds, 'Forensic Engineering: a reappraisal of the Tay Bridge Disaster', Interdisciplinary Science Reviews, Vol. 27, 287 (2002).
Lewis, P.R., Walker, P.M.B., Braithwaite, N.J., Reynolds, K. and Weidmann, G.W., *Chambers Materials Science and Technology Dictionary*, Chambers (1993).
Lopes, Sir Massey, 'Report of the Select Committee on the North British Railway (Tay Bridge) Bill, together with Proceedings of the Committee and Minutes of evidence, House of Commons', 4 August 1880.

Martin, Tom and Macleod, I., 'The Tay Bridge Disaster: a reappraisal based on modern analysis methods' Proc. Instn Civ. Engs (Civil Engineering), Vol. 108, 77–83 (1995); Developments in Structural Engineering, Forth Rail Bridge Centenary Conference, Spon, London (1990).
Maynard, Henry, *Handbook of the Crumlin Viaduct*, J.M. Wilson (1862).
McKean, John, *Lost Masterpieces: Joseph Paxton, Crystal Palace*, Phaidon Press (1999).

Nock, O.S., *Scottish Railways*, Thomas Nelson & Sons Ltd (1950).

Petroski, Henry, *Engineers of Dreams*, Vintage Books, New York, (1996).
Pilkey, Walter D., *Peterson's Stress Concentration Factors* (2nd Ed), John Wiley & Sons Inc (1997).

Prebble, John, *The High Girders*, Penguin (1956).

Rankine, W.J.M., 'On the Causes of the Unexpected Breakage of the journals of Railway Axles', Proc. Instn Civ. Engs, Vol. 2, 105-8 (1842).
Rapley, John, *The Britannia & Other Tubular Bridges*, Tempus (2003).
'Report of the Joint Committee concerning the Ashtabula Bridge Disaster', Hopkins & Myers, State Printers, Columbus, Ohio (1876).
Rolt, L.T.C. *Red for Danger: The Classic History of Railway Disasters* (1st Ed, 1955; republished by Sutton, 1998).
Rothery, H.C., Barlow, W.H. and Yolland, Col., 'Tay Bridge disaster: Report of the Court of Inquiry and Report of Mr Rothery upon the Circumstances attending the Fall of the Tay Bridge on the 28 December 1879', published by George Edward Eyre and William Spottiswoode for HMSO, June 1880. Parliamentary Papers Vol. XXXIX, 1 ff (1880).

Schneider, Ascanio and Armin Mase, *Railway Accidents of Great Britain and Europe: Their Cause and Consequences (translated from the German by E.L. Dellow)*, David & Charles (1970).
Schutz, Walter, A History of Fatigue, Engineering Fracture Mechanics, Vol. 54 (2), 263–300 (1996).
Shipley, J.S., 'Tay Rail Bridge Centenary – Some Notes on its Construction 1882–87', Proc. Instn Civ. Engs, Part 1, 86 (Dec), 1089-1109 (1989).
Simmons, Captain and Mr Walker, 'Report to the Commissioners of Railways on the Fatal Accident on the 24th day of May, 1847, by the falling of the Bridge over the River Dee, on the Chester and Holyhead Railway; together with any of the Minutes of the Commissioners thereupon', published by the House of Commons, 30 June 1847; Parliamentary Papers Vol. LXIV, 287 ff (1847).
Simmons, Jack, *The Railways of Britain* (2nd Ed), Macmillan/St Martin's Press (1968).
Simmons, Jack and Biddle, Gordon (Eds), *The Oxford Companion to British Railway History*, Oxford University Press (2003).
Smith, R.A. (Ed), 'Fatigue Crack Growth: 30 years of progress' in Proceedings of a conference on fatigue crack growth, Cambridge, UK, 20 September, Pergamon (1986).
Smith, R.A., 'The Versailles Railway Accident of 1842 and the First Research into Metal Fatigue', Fatigue 90, EMAS Conf Proc, Vol IV, 2033-2041 (1990).
Swinfen, David, *The Fall of the Tay Bridge*, Mercat (1994).

Thomas, John, *The Tay Bridge Disaster*, David & Charles (1972).
Thomas, John, *The North British Railway*, Volumes One and Two, David & Charles (1975).
Timoshenko, Stephen P., *History of Strength of Materials*, McGraw-Hill (1953).
Tredgold, Thomas, *Practical Essay on The Strength of Cast Iron and Other Metals*, (with notes by Eaton Hodgkinson), John Weale, London (1842).

Vogwell, J, and Minguez, J.M., 'Failure in Lug Joints and Plates with Holes', Engineering Failure Analysis, Vol. 2 (2), 129-135 (1995).

Webster, N.W., *Joseph Locke: Railway Revolutionary*, George Allen & Unwin Ltd (1970).
Wulpi, Donald J., *Understanding How Components Fail*, American Society for Metals (1985).

Young, Warren, *Roark's Formulas for Stress and Strain* (6th Ed), McGraw-Hill Inc (1989).

Index

Aerospace disasters
  Comet 15, 162
  Hindenburg 7
  Japanese airlines 163

Bridge failures
  Ashtabula horror 159, 169
  Belgian bridges 161
  Dee Bridge 15ff, 39, 47, 69, 89, 100, 111, 149, 158
  Mianus River 162
  Portland Road 158
  Quebec failures 158, 159
  Silver Bridge 161
  Tacoma Narrows 159

Bridges
  Barrakur 25
  Belah 30ff, 103, 116-7, 129-31, 167
  Bouble 25, 167
  Britannia 15, 20
  Brooklyn Bridge 112, 152
  Cannon Street 114
  Charing Cross 114
  Clifton Suspension 154
  Coalbrookdale 19, 20, 21, 159, 177
  Conway 20
  Crumlin Viaduct 22, 30, 34, 103, 167
  Dee (see Bridge failures)
  Deepdale Viaduct 30, 116
  Ebro 25
  Eiffel viaducts 25, 167
  elevated viaduct 112
  Forth Bridge 11, 13, 40, 43, 46, 115, 126, 129, 156ff, 170
  Golden Gate 46, 160
  Hay 132
  Maidenhead 13
  Millennium footbridge 143, 161

  New Tay Bridge 13, 155ff
  over-bridges 158
  Paddington 20, 159
  pipe bridges 25ff, 167
  Saltash 27
  Staithes Viaduct 112
  Tagus 25
  Tees 25
  Tiber 25
  Velletri 25
  Westminster 114

Board of Trade
  approval 11, 25, 39
  Beaufort table 69
  counsel 69
  criticism of 132
  defence of 149
  Forth Bridge 156ff
  Hutchinson 39, 46, 53, 56, 89, 118, 121ff, 123, 128, 130, 132, 143, 149, 156ff, 158, 187
  legislation 130
  inspection 39
  proof testing 25, 39
  Rail Inspectorate 16-17, 39, 130
  Simmons 17ff, 188

Buildings
  Crystal Palace 21ff
  skyscraper 161
  Statue of Liberty 26
  Tower of Pisa 140

Cast iron
  casting box 103
  core 76, 79, 86, 103
  girders 13, 14, 15ff
  moulding 36, 76ff, 86ff, 129

products 34
sand 34-36, 76
steam engine beams 14
trussed 17, 20ff
Wormit foundry 31-2, 37, 43, 46, 75ff,
    126-7, 155

Commissioners
Barlow 13, 21, 69, 117, 123, 131-2, 148,
    150, 153, 155, 188
Rothery 69, 123ff, 140, 148, 188
Yolland 50, 69, 117, 123, 131-2, 148, 150,
    188

Defects
batter 103, 169, 173
beaumontage 77, 86-7, 103, 126, 173
blow holes 18, 77-9, 83, 84-6, 87, 103, 126,
    128, 135, 148, 173
burning-in 37, 76-79, 82, 86-7
cold shuts
construction 103ff
cracks 14, 16-18, 20-21, 37, 46, 56, 59, 77,
    79-81, 83, 86-7, 100-101, 103, 120, 131,
    135, 138-9, 140, 145, 148, 151, 158,
    161-2
design 102ff
inclusions 103, 174
L-shaped girders 40, 115, 129
lateral stability 30, 33, 40, 102-4, 129-130,
    132, 140-1, 152
lugs, 34-36, 76ff, 101-2, 134ff
scabbing 77
slag 83, 103
stress raisers 135, 162, 175
surface roughness 147
wall thickness 76, 83

Engineers
Arrol 156-7
Baker 13, 107, 112ff, 126, 154, 156ff
Barlow (see Commissioners)
Bazalgette 31
Bessemer 43, 152
Bouch 11, 25, 29ff, 36, 39-40, 45, 54-6, 81,
    89, 107-8, 111, 114, 116ff, 123ff, 148, 149,
    151-2, 155-6, 163, 167
Braithwaite 14, 186
Brunel 13, 27, 115, 154, 159
Brunlees 150-1
Cochrane 107, 114ff, 148, 150
Eiffel 25, 31, 32, 143, 160, 167
Fairbairn 20-21
Fowler 13, 40, 156ff

Gooch 18
Kennard 22, 25
Locke 17, 18, 188
Paxton 21
Rankine 14
Roebling 152
Smeaton 71
Stephenson 13, 15ff, 100, 111, 115, 158
Telford, 13
Vignoles, 18
Wöhler, 163

Fatigue
beach marks 135
crack growth 133ff, 147
fatigue limit 20
hairline cracks 77, 82, 87
initiation 135
problem in cast iron 14, 20, 135
rolling contact 163
stress concentration 147
stress corrosion 161-2
studies 161ff
wheel tapping 59

Films
Brief Encounter 13
The French Connection 112
The Mothman Prophecies 161
Nightmail 13
The Signalman 13
The Thirty-nine Steps 13

Inquiry
composition 69
Dundee 69ff
questions for Henry Law 90
victims 75

Joints
chattering 43ff, 119-20, 127, 140-3
cotter 36, 38
defects 45-6, 104, 121, 143, 147-8, 151,
    170
fitment 81ff, 95-6
flange 35, 76, 139
gib 36, 38
shims 45ff, 143, 151
strength 101
tie bar 81ff, 121, 143, 170

Maintenance
foundations 25, 32ff, 44ff, 84, 115, 117-8,
    123-4, 127ff, 140, 151ff

microscope 86
Noble 31, 38, 43ff, 49, 51, 54, 56, 80, 90, 96, 104, 108, 118ff, 124, 127, 131-2, 143-4, 151ff
painting 16, 26, 40, 46ff, 75, 77, 80, 82, 86, 131, 143-4, 146, 158
spiral staircase 24-26, 143

Marine accidents
Liberty ships 161
Titanic 133

Periodicals
Engineering magazine 85
Illustrated London News, 15, 60-1
The Times 132

Photography
Daguerrotype 90
dry plate 90
Fox-Talbot 90
underwater 70
Valentines 70, 90
wet plate 90
Wilson 90, 113

Politics
Afghanistan 11, 132
Chamberlain 149, 153
Disraeli 11, 89
Gladstone 11, 89, 149
Irish Problem 132
Isandhlwana 11
Queen Victoria 11, 43, 55, 145, 152
Rorke's Drift 11
Zulu war 11

Properties of Materials
brittle 18-19, 20, 34, 100ff, 124, 136, 138, 161ff
density 46
ductile 136, 155, 161, 174
stiffness 82, 130, 143, 169, 175
strength 17-19, 34, 77, 80, 82ff, 91, 100ff, 117ff, 128, 132, 136, 152, 155, 157ff, 175

Railways
Caledonian 27ff, 41
Drummond 38, 68, 107, 111-2, 126
Edinburgh & Northern 29
ferry 27, 29, 43, 52-3, 57, 59, 65, 74
Gannat 25
guard rail 17, 44, 58-9, 120
locomotive 14-5, 25, 38-9, 43, 54, 59, 68, 107-8, 111-2, 120-1, 126, 146, 148, 156, 158
NBR 27ff, 40, 43, 54, 69-70, 81, 83, 90, 107-8, 119, 123, 130, 146, 150, 153, 164
Tay Bridge station 38, 40, 55, 60, 91, 113, 128, 153, 164
Westinghouse brakes 60, 112

Railway Accidents
Abbots Ripton 11
Clayton tunnel 13
Dee Bridge (see Bridge Failures)
Eschede 9, 163
Hatfield 9, 15, 163
Huskisson fatality 14, 186
Norwood Junction (see Portland road)
Oxford 11, 59, 69
Portland road 158-9
Potters Bar 142, 163
Staplehurst 13
Versailles 14
Weedon 142

Royal Commission
effect of wind on railway structures 153ff
iron in railway structures 19ff, 89, 116

Scientists
Airy 21, 115ff, 117
Beaufort 71ff
Edison 154
Fitzroy 70
Inglis 143
Stokes 116ff
Swan 154

Select Committee
New Tay Bridge 149ff

Steel
Bessemer converter 43, 152
Brooklyn Bridge 152
Board of Trade approval 152
composition 175
Forth Bridge 157
high-strength 161-2
Siemens open-hearth 152
strength 34
use in bridges 152, 155, 157, 158, 161, 167

Structures
centre of gravity 104, 118, 140-1
dynamics 21-22, 89, 108, 161

equilibrium 104, 116
moments 104, 140
monocoque 156
oscillation 38, 49, 51ff, 83, 86, 108, 122, 132, 146, 148, 160-1, 170
spaceframe 36, 167
stability 30, 33, 84, 103, 108, 114, 117, 121, 128, 130, 138, 150-2, 153, 167
static 18, 68, 104, 108, 124, 126, 175
trussed girders 25, 159
top-heavy piers 34, 40, 140, 169
toppling 11, 44, 96, 104, 109, 111, 120, 126, 140, 152, 154
vibrations 18, 47ff, 82ff, 104, 121-2, 138, 140-3, 157, 159-163, 169
von Karman vortice 160

Testing
cast iron 99ff, 118
hammer test 37, 45, 77, 82-3, 127
Kirkaldy 89, 98ff, 108, 118-9, 123, 127, 131, 136, 163
lugs 100ff, 136
proof test 25, 39, 156-7
samples 100ff
tensometer 99ff
test house 98ff, 123, 136, 161

Theories
Barlow/Yolland 131
Benjamin Baker 112-4
Bouch 120
Cochrane 114-5
Dow 146, 155
Henry Law 89ff
Lewis and Reynolds 169-70
Martin and Macleod 155
Pole/Stewart 107-111
Rothery 128
Swinfen 155

Wind Pressure
anemometer 74, 116, 154-5
Beaufort tables 71-2, 126,
Benjamin Baker 112-4
Captain Scott 73, 126, 150
Daniel Defoe 155, 186
hurricane 75, 146, 155, 170
relation to speed 71-2, 116

Witnesses
carpenter 50
cemetery 74
dressers 86ff
erectors 80ff
eye-witnesses 16, 62ff
foundrymen 75ff
lighthouse 74
machinists 79ff
managers 82ff
meteorologists 70ff
painters 16, 46ff
passengers 19, 51ff, 58-9
sailors 73-5
signalmen 60-2
stationmaster 54-5
ticket collector 60, 75

Wrought Iron
axles 14, 59, 162
bolts 49, 84, 96, 112
girders 21, 25, 112,
high girders 32ff, 37-8, 67, 100, 109-10, 151-2
hoops 37, 46, 120
ladder 25-6
lugs 82
properties 46, 100, 162, 176
rails 17
rivetted plate 20, 155
strength 34, 100ff, 118, 124, 136, 151-2
salvage 156
tie bars 22, 26, 30, 36-7, 96, 124, 125, 136
truss 17ff
tube 27
value 114, 156

If you are interested in purchasing
other books published by The History Press, or in case you have
difficulty finding any of our books in your local bookshop,
you can also place orders directly through our website

www.thehistorypress.co.uk